THE *NEW* RETIRE-MENTALITY

PLANNING YOUR LIFE AND LIVING YOUR DREAMS... AT ANY AGE *YOU* WANT

Second Edition

Mitch Anthony

KAPLAN PUBLISHING

President, Kaplan Publishing: Roy Lipner
Vice President and Publisher: Maureen McMahon
Senior Managing Editor: Jack Kiburz
Typesetting: the dotted i
Cover Design: Scott Rattray, Rattray Design

The New Retirementality™ is a registered trademark of Mitch Anthony.

© 2001 by Dearborn Financial Publishing, Inc.
© 2006 by Mitch Anthony

Published by Kaplan Publishing,
a division of Kaplan, Inc.

Printed in the United States of America

06 07 08 10 9 8 7 6 5 4 3 2 1

Library of Congress Cataloging-in-Publication Data

Anthony, Mitch.
    The new retirementality : planning your life and living your dreams— at any age you want / Mitch Anthony.— 2nd ed.
        p.   cm.
    Includes bibliographical references and index.
    ISBN-13: 978-1-4195-3724-0
    ISBN-10: 1-4195-3724-5
    1. Retirement—United States. 2. Older people—United States—Finance, Personal. I. Title: New retire-mentality. II. Title.
HQ1064.U5A69 2006
646.7′9—dc22

                                                                        2005036038

Dedication

This book is dedicated to my mother,
Bettie Anthony Huntley,
who has never been afraid to
blaze her own trails and to follow her dreams.
A generous portion of her spirit
guides my life as well.

Contents

Preface

When I wrote the first edition of *The New Retirementality* in 2000, we lived in a different world than we live in today. Not only have many realities changed, but our level of awareness on many money/life issues has evolved as well. In 2000, my thoughts and theories about the anachronistic nature of traditional retirement were quite novel, yet they seemed to strike a chord of recognition and resonance with many people. These were people who either had retired to personally experience what I was describing or had made firsthand observations about the mirage of leisure/life retirement.

My goal in writing the book was to get the attention of the baby boomer crowd, who were nearing 55 years of age at the time and needed to re-examine the traditional retirement proposition carefully. It seems that I was a little early to the dance. Boomers were embracing the ideas but were delaying their personal preparations. Now that the front-edge boomers are entering their 60s and retirement is pounding on the door, many are ready to tackle the question, "What do I want to do with *my* life?" This is what *The New Retirementality* is all about.

What was viewed as avant garde thinking six years ago has become almost universally accepted today. Such is the case with some of the myths surrounding retirement:

- Age 65 is no longer the marker for "old."
- Retirement no longer means "not working."
- A life of total ease is one step from a life of disease.
- You do not have to wait until you are 62 to live the life you want.

These traditional assumptions have begun to topple, and a new awareness has emerged that is impacting every aspect of our society. We have all seen, heard, and read enough to recognize these ideals are applicable to us today; the evidence surrounds us. Studies have been conducted to prove that these issues are real and that there are huge implications in store for our society, our businesses, our careers, and, most important, our personal well-being. In the past several years, many books have examined the sociological and demographic story (a good read would be *The*

Power Years by Ken Dychtwald) as well as a few others that have addressed the spiritual and philosophical underpinnings of this irreversible paradigm shift in our world (see *Claiming Your Place at the Fire* by Richard Leider).

A Pensive New World

I believe that the confluence of four events in the past few years has forever affected our decision-making processes regarding money and life. What the Great Depression was as a money/life reference point to our grandparents, these cumulative events are to us. These four events are:

1. 9/11
2. The "dot-bomb" technology crash and bear market of 2001–2002
3. Reports of widespread corruption in financial markets
4. Recurring natural disasters

The horror of 9/11 brought home the transitory, quickly vaporizing opportunities that life offers. We don't know what will happen next and how much time we have left. Security that once seemed impregnable is but an ephemeral memory. The devastation of the Southeast Asian tsunamis and recent hurricanes also have accentuated our sense of vulnerability and reminded us of the transitory nature of our accumulations and belongings. We've been reminded that our children don't grow up twice, and that time with family and friends is more important than climbing somebody else's ladder to burnout. Our priorities shifted internally even if our outward realities did not. The events of 9/11 left an indelible mark on our psyches— and we all recognize we must live the best we can, while we can.

The dot-bomb bust and subsequent market slide taught most of us a hard lesson about speculation and its relationship to "gravity." The markets are indeed rational, after all. As Warren Buffett (who declined to participate in the "laughing gas" madness of 1999–2000) so adroitly stated: "A rising tide lifts all the boats, it's not until the tide goes out that we find out who's swimming naked."

Raise your hand with me if you were caught swimming naked in the Nasdaq pond. Worse is the plight of many of our mothers and fathers who don't have another 20 years to make up for their losses. It hurts to see them financially wounded (and none of us wanted to see our parents swimming naked).

I have heard it said that the three worst crises of the 20th century were WWI, WWII, and WWW. For many this is a bitter truth. Some were financially devastated; many others were wounded to varying degrees. All of us learned firsthand that anything that goes up can come down, and it can fall faster than it rises. And damage is done when gravity takes over. We will be more careful in the future. Add to this the awareness that comes from watching major airlines and other businesses declare bankruptcy and subsequently break retirement promises made for 40 years—and we have a doubly doubtful view of who we can count on for future financial returns.

We have witnessed a seemingly never-ending parade of corporate shame with CEOs throwing penny candy to their employees while robbing the corporate tills. This parade began with Anderson Consulting and proceeded to Enron, Adelphia, World-Com, and the multiple, complicit Wall-Street firms whose ads had always told us they had our best interests at heart. Viewing this spectacle effectively eroded our level of trust in corporations, financial reporting, and investment recommendations. These conflicts of interest created a number of emotional conflicts for us regarding our hard-fought spoils of employment: Who can we really trust? Are they recommending this investment for my account or for theirs? What if all the books are cooked and this company is not what it says it is? Our financial journey was difficult enough as it was—now we learn we need an armored truck to survive it.

Our Means and Our Meaning

Taken together, these events have left an indelible mark in our brains and souls: Our life is not a dress rehearsal; we have some living to do while we are able. We must accomplish our life agenda within the bounds of reasonable returns on our investments. Finding partners to help us may take more work and scrutiny than we thought. We need to consider what we want to be when we grow up. These are the current realities in the new retirement—and to successfully navigate these waters will take nothing less than a New Retirementality.

I was convinced in the year 2000, and I am exponentially convinced today, that we need a breakthrough approach to retirement planning that goes beyond the numbers and helps us plan the rest of our lives. Beyond just planning what we want to do, we must also plan how we are going to pay for what we want to do. It is about finding and funding our lives. This book is a unique hybrid of the philosophical and fiscal examinations necessary to fully liberate our lives into a state of balance and meaning that we so desperately desire, yet often prevent by our own choices.

I view money as a means to meaning. If managed properly, money can be employed as a utility, like a sail on a ship, to move us around the adventurous seas of exploration and the calm harbors of family togetherness. Misuse this utility and you'll find your best intentions shipwrecked, tasting the bitter salt of failed dreams.

I wrote this book for a very simple reason. I want to see people live their best life NOW! That would be a life of balance. That would be a life filled with purpose. That would be a life that includes the joy of meaningful work.

This second edition of *The New Retirementality* addresses these issues and the new realities, and offers ideas, tools, and processes for "doing the math" of shaping a fulfilling life.

A great privilege comes with the release of this second edition of *The New Retirementality*. As the author, I already have seen the fruits of these ideas in the lives of others. I have crossed this continent for the past five years telling this story, and, every time, somebody walks up to me afterward, eyes wide open with a fresh epiphany. What I usually hear is something like, "I made up my mind while you were talking that I'm going to do what I want with my life. I don't want to settle for retiring the way 'they' tell me I ought to retire."

I have also received scores of letters from readers who shared how the message in this book changed their lives or the lives of their spouses who were trapped in a carousel of boredom or menial and meaningless pursuit. Some wrote to thank me for affirming what they always suspected. Others offered gratitude that I "gave them permission" to live life on their own terms, in spite of cultural expectations and norms.

If you ever plan on retiring, make sure you retire *on purpose*. I suspect that you have many years ahead of you and that you have much to give and to live. I hope your life will be imbued with the New Retirementality, which is a belief that cannot be stated any better than the words penned by George Elliot: "It's never too late to be what you might have been."

If you find this book helpful in planning the rest of your life, I hope that you will pass it on.

Mitch Anthony

Acknowledgments

This book has an audience primarily because of the belief and encouragement provided by Kaplan Publishing Publisher Cynthia Zigmund.

The bulk of financial advice shared in this book was contributed by Bruce Bruinsma of The Life-Stage Companies. Bruce has the unusual gift of being not only a smart financial advisor but a wise financial philosopher as well.

Whatever degree of refinement the reader finds in this text is due to the ever watchful and always caring eye of my wife and first-line editor, Debbie.

For her incisive eye and diligent archeology, I wish to thank my researcher, Megan Stubbendeck, for a job well done.

I wish to acknowledge the many authors quoted in this book whose ideas may have seemed to find the bleeding edge instead of the cutting edge because they were ahead of their time. Their ideas about retirement life and changes are the seeds that have the power to ultimately enrich many frustrated souls.

PART | ONE

Out with the Old

What Retire Meant

The End of Retirement as We Know It

> The U.S. standard gauge railroad track is four feet, eight and one-half inches wide. Why such an odd measure? Because that was the width in England and the United States when railroads were built by British expatriates.
>
> Where did the English get that measure? The first rail lines were built by the same people who built the tramways that preceded railroads; and they built the trams with the same jigs and tools used for building wagons. The wagons were built to what is now the standard gauge railroad track so their wheels would fit the ruts of England's ancient long-distance roads.
>
> The ruts had been made by the war chariots brought to England by the occupying imperial Roman army. And the chariots were four feet, eight and one-half inches wide to accommodate the rear ends of two horses. You're not alone if you struggle with change.

Retiring Old Ideas about Retirement

Face it—retirement is not a great idea, especially at age 62. In fact, retirement as we know it today is a relic from a time and a world that have long since passed. In the context of our modern age, conventional ideas about retirement are not only inappropriate but they are counterproductive. The concept of retirement was a shortsighted political machination and social manipulation, which is no longer relevant and is hopelessly out of touch with our times.

We are subjected daily to messages that pummel our brains with warnings that we should save more if we hope to leap off the economic cliff known as age 62. And many of us have been convinced that we want to jump off that cliff earlier—if possible, much earlier. The new retirement resembles a bell curve rather than a cliff. Rather than jumping off, we will gradually slow down. Do we really want to quit working? Sadly, because so many people are working in jobs, industries, and offices they hate, they have convinced themselves that the answer is the end of their working days (retirement). But the fact remains that they wouldn't be obsessed with the idea of quitting if they were doing what they wanted with their life in the first place.

Many people think that the answer is to quit working altogether, because they don't like the working circumstances they find themselves stuck in. This is akin to getting a frontal lobotomy simply because of a headache. Many others want to quit what they are doing now to be able to do something else; they need or want a change but are convinced that they need a mountain of money to make the switch. So they decide to postpone their dreams, assuming that when they do finally acquire the required substance, they will still have the desire and drive necessary to follow their dreams. People in these circumstances—and there are many—should stop to contemplate the psychologically sobering fact that as they drive themselves in a career they despise, they are running on tires with a slow leak. The ride often gets rougher and tougher until they find their aspirations in the ditch and little energy left to begin a new journey.

The same could be said for those who have a lukewarm approach to their work. Such a tepid approach results in a lack of growth, a lack of incentive and mental application, and compromised energy levels. When this lukewarm approach becomes our status quo, we are well on our way to a life and career of underachievement.

The Artificial Finish Line

"Once we become adults, we often lose track of life's simple pleasures and of our own personal goals. We take a wrong turn or two,

then spend a good part of our lives doing things we'd rather not—
while not doing many things we'd enjoy. While we may obsess about
how unhappy we are, we don't focus clearly on what we can do to
change the situation: on how we can invest our time, energy and,
yes, our money to consciously create the life we want."
—Marc Eisenson, author, Invest in Yourself: Six Secrets to a Rich Life

Doing work we despise or being in circumstances we deplore depletes our spirit. The reason so many find themselves in such scenarios is because they have been sold on an idea about retirement that is flawed to the core: *the idea that we should do what we do not enjoy to accumulate the money we need to someday do what we want.* This hope of doing what we want is why the concept of traditional retirement is alluring to so many. Many individuals are not in the race they want to run in. They see getting to the age of 62 with a mountain of money as the only way to get in that race. The problem is compounded when we realize that we have been convinced to run toward an artificial finish line in a race that was never meant to end. This artificial finish line is age 62, or whatever age you believe you should retire. The race is the employment of our skills and ideas as long as we still enjoy using them. If we truly love what we do, although we may slow down our pace or change the event we run in, we never truly quit the race.

And why have so many people given their life to work they don't enjoy? The reason is simply because they need the money. Why do they need the money? So they can have enough to retire at age 62 and do what they want. Great! We sacrifice 40 prime productive years so we can have a speculative, free reign for the autumn and/or winter years.

Although you may not have heard much about it, those who do get to the magic age of 62 and drop out of the race are not always altogether happy with their decision. They often do it, however, because they felt as though they had to. Disillusionment rates are sky-high for retirees. According to one survey, 41 percent say retirement was the most difficult adjustment of their life and most still struggle with the monotony, boredom, lack of purpose, and lack of intellectual stimulation that traditional retirement offers. There is a good reason these retirees are not happy—*retirement is an unnatural idea.* The concept runs contrary to the preservation of the human spirit. Most people don't really want retirement as we know it. What they want is freedom to pursue their own goals and interests. They want to call their own shots. They want to do what they want, when they want, and where they want. They want change from the rut that their life of employment has become. We have been told that the right amount of money alone can buy that emancipation.

And that is why we are so vulnerable to the messages that tell us we need $2 million to set ourselves free. But this simply is not true. This book is full of examples of people who are living the life they want—*today*—and not all have a million dollars in assets or investments. Because of twisted ideas about retirement, we have put the money cart ahead of the "life" horse. We say we are saving money so that we can someday have a life, but in the process we are delaying having a life so that we can scrounge up enough money. Too many people wait far too long.

With some financial creativity and a new mind-set regarding retirement, you can both find and fund the life you really want—if not now, it is entirely possible within the next five years. Achieving emancipation from your working life will involve negotiating your lifestyle, philosophy, and fiscal habits, and finding a way to put first things first. First, decide the path you must take to do the work you love, and, second, put together a plan to pay for that privilege. We must adopt a much more resourceful approach if we hope to make the transition into a life of doing what we love. Chapter 9 offers some of the more resourceful approaches people are using in order to pursue their passions and dreams.

Illusions, Delusions, and Hype

A financial advisor told me the following:

> If you were to ask me, "Who are the most distraught clients you see?" I think my answer would surprise you. They are not the couples in their 50s who are discouraged to find out they will not be able to retire when they thought. They are not the clients whose portfolios have had less than spectacular returns and must extend their plans for early retirement. They are the retirees with the great portfolios who are bored out of their minds. These individuals feel like they have been removed from the mainstream of life, are watching from the sidelines, and are not allowed to get back in. As one guy put it, "Retirement is a spectator sport. I don't want to sit here and watch the world go by. I liked being in the game!"

Yet strangely enough, millions are in a mad rush to get to the place where this despondent man lives—on the sidelines. Many of us, however, have already seen enough of our parents' and forerunners' retirement scenarios to know that this is not the life for us. We have figured out that our life will be one of challenge, relevance, stimulation, and occupational adventure. We are not interested in finishing this race!

Once people get the money they need, they are able to better understand what the money is all about—liberty to do what they want when they want. What is the point of using that kind of liberty to do nothing but play golf? It's hard to convince someone who doesn't have the money that it really is not about the money. It's about doing what you love, doing what you want. It's about balancing work and relationships.

This point became especially clear to me recently when a friend asked me if I had plans to retire early. I thought about it for a moment, and then it dawned on me, *I like what I do!* I write, I speak, I consult with companies and organizations on how to build more meaningful relationships. Why would I quit doing that? If I did quit, I think I would begin to self-destruct. This realization was important because it helped me to realize that I no longer had to be concerned with having any specific amount of money at any age. There will always be something for me to do and I will always enjoy doing it. You don't make plans to retire from your passion in life.

Does this idea cause me to spend away my future and disregard the value of my investment savings? To the contrary! *Because I value freedom so much, I exercise the necessary financial discipline to maintain it.* I know that I am just one foolish purchase or investment away from reattaching the chains of miserable employment to my life. There is wisdom in balance. Just because I love what I do does not negate the need to plan for financial freedom. Life can present us with vicissitudes that can radically alter our course: disability, a death in the family, divorce, and so on. We must plan ahead financially because we change our minds over time. What invigorates me today may bore me a decade from today. Investment savings are necessary to purchase the freedom to change course when we want.

Two types of people should forget their plans for complete retirement at age 62 or earlier—those who *can't* afford to retire at 62 and those who *can* afford to retire at 62. Age 62 is an artificial finish line. A modern measure of success seems to be how many years you can retire ahead of age 62. Is accelerating your pace into boredom and despondency really such a good idea? On the other hand, a modern measure of failure has been to measure how many years beyond 62 you had to wait so you could retire. The further past 62 you had to wait to retire, the greater failure you were in the context of retirement. Those measures are about to change. If the coming generation of 50-year-old-plus citizens has anything to say about it, those perceptions will be turned entirely on their head. Those who have to work will not be the losers, because they are still in the game and they will find that work keeps them vital, involved, and healthier. Those who will be able to drop out entirely will choose not to because they don't want to enter a slow track of intellectual atrophy, boredom, and monotonous leisure.

We are still in the early stages of a New Retirementality—a modern perspective of what retirement really means. People are still haunted by the old rules and media hype that bemoan their lack of preparedness to reach the artificial goal line. You just can't seem to get away from the news stories and the advertisements that beat this sorry old retirement horse to death.

Old Messages and New Realities

For many, these messages inspire urgency and thrift; for many others, they inspire only fear, self-loathing, and hopelessness. Such messages as "You won't have enough" or "If you would have bought this fund 30 years ago, it would be worth x million dollars today" create a sense of dread and failure in those listeners who were buying more dime bags than mutual funds with their disposable income 30 years ago.

For the millions of Americans who don't own a fat nest egg (median financial assets are $51,000, according to a 2004 study by John Gist), these messages stir feelings of hopelessness because they are convinced that they will arrive at the age 62 economic leap with no safety net or precious metals parachute based on their current income and level of savings. They know they will never be able to amass the small fortune that "retirement experts" tell them they must hoard to have anything but a beggar's sunset in their life. The modern retirement portrait, as painted by the financial services industry, is truly a double-headed dragon, because the vision that has been promoted for the last 50 years is not only an illusion but is also unrealistic.

The illusion has been that of sipping tropical drinks on a Caribbean beach and setting tee times for the rest of your waking life. "All this is yours" once you retire, and the earlier you retire the better. Possibly you've met some people who swallowed this illusion and are living with the hangover of boredom and purposelessness in their life. I have met many such people, and the look in their eyes inspired me to write this book. Many who bought the story of retiring from the race find themselves bored with not being in the race. Many have found that this boredom has led them to self-destructive patterns of behavior. Many have accelerated their aging process as the chains of disenfranchised habits grew heavier and weighed on their health. It all adds up to one inescapable conclusion: *retirement is an unnatural condition! Even if you can afford to retire, the worst thing you can do is withdraw completely from the race.*

When you ask retirees how they're doing, they often reply, "I'm keeping busy." This is an acknowledgment of the activity void that retirement has brought. They are truly happy when they are busy doing what they love. If they are not busy, they are most likely not very happy.

The image of retirement that we have been sold has simply been untrue. According to an American Demographics poll, 41 percent of retirees report that retirement was a difficult adjustment. Only 12 percent of newlyweds polled felt marriage was a difficult adjustment, and only 23 percent felt that parenting was a difficult adjustment. The reason the adjustment to retirement is so difficult to so many is simple: retirement as it has been defined for us was never meant to be. Retirement is an illusion because those who can afford the illusion are disillusioned by it and those who cannot afford the illusion are haunted by it.

Which brings us to the dragon's other head; many people cannot afford to retire in the manner that has been promoted by the retirement savings industry. It is simply unrealistic for many to find a way to put away enough money every month to have a million dollars waiting to serve them at age 62, or at any other age for that matter. True, many people could save more as well as exercise more financial discipline. But why should the one-third of our population that is doing its best with what it has walk around feeling bad about today because it cannot reach a tomorrow that somebody else has defined for it? A 2004 Roper Starch investor's survey states that about one-third of boomers are unsatisfied with the amount of money they are putting away today for retirement. Too many of these people are worried needlessly. They have been given the various ominous headlines for their future: "Social Security will not exist; your homes will be devalued; you don't have sufficient savings and inflation will eat up what little you do have."

Two problems are apparent with these pervasive and frequently reported scare tactics. First, they can be easily disputed and disproven. Second, these arguments are founded on a fabricated and now crumbling philosophical foundation—that is, we *should* retire at age 62 or even earlier if possible. Most of us will not completely retire at 62 or at any other age for that matter. We, as a generation, are not interested in artificial finish lines.

The New Retirementality Challenge

Is the goal to be invested and well, or well and invested?
Think about it: Should I review my own thoughts about retirement?
Research it: What am I saving? Where am I saving?
Decide and take action:

- Talk to my spouse or significant other about retirement.
- Collect and organize my financial information.

CHAPTER 2

The End of Social Insecurity and Other Retirement Fears

The financial foundation for people beyond the age of 65 will be Social Security in spite of all reports to the contrary. There is a clear disconnection between the expectations of people toward Social Security and the financial reality of later years. We, as a generation, have been taught *not* to expect Social Security to be around. Consequently, a majority of people say they are not counting on Social Security in their retirement planning. In reality, however, Social Security is a major part of the foundation for most retirees' fiscal houses and will continue to be for many years to come.

The Demise of Social Security: Fact or Fiction?

Let's take a closer look at the fearful future for Social Security being projected by the doomsayers and the logical underpinnings that this horror story's plot is built on. As you inspect these rationales, you will see that much of it is hype, myth, or unbridled pessimism. Closer inspection shows that all of the prophesied circumstances that may or may not be in our future are manageable.

One of the favorite portents of "the gray sky is falling" crowd is that "Social Insecurity" will lead to "AARP-Ageddon"! According to this old warning, the Social Security system will be insolvent by the time you need it. Its bankruptcy was originally scheduled for the year 2013 and then moved to 2020; and early in 2000 the insolvency date was moved all the way to the year 2037. The latest projections by the congressional budget office (2005) put the date of insolvency out to the year 2052. This postponement was no small frustration for the prophets of doom. The year 2013 was the foundational fact for doomsday messages about our bleak future. The Social Security system would be insolvent by 2013, and millions would be without support. "Everyone is headed toward eventual retirement and we have nothing to look forward to," we were told. These messages of "Social Insecurity" seem to be losing their punch. A poll of boomer views on retirement (Roper Starch, 2004/2005) revealed that 51 percent of the respondents felt confident that Social Security would be around when they retired (compared with 36 percent in 1998). Only 15 percent expected to rely on it for "most or all" of their retirement income. Less than half of the respondents said they were counting on Social Security as a source of retirement income. But the majority (63 percent) stated they felt "they had put money into the Social Security system and expect to get it back." I'm inclined to believe that if the baby boomers want something, they will find a way to get it! This is not a generation of people who are easily dissuaded when they decide they want something. Maybe this is part of the reason that the DOA date for Social Security keeps getting moved out.

Ironically, this fearmongering may have paid an unexpected dividend. Because of the belief that Social Security will not be around long enough for people to collect, many began to take control of their financial destiny and garnered sizable financial assets. Individuals who didn't plan on receiving Social Security payments as part of their retirement income will be pleasantly surprised to find they will have more income than they had expected.

The doomsday plot thickens as the financial pressure on the "baby bust" generation to support 75 million retired baby boomers is supposed to lead to generational warfare in the streets (picture here a geriatric with a walker equipped with laser shields). According to the warnings, the burden on the "baby bust" generation to support Social Security payments for the boomers will hit the breaking point, and a gray dawn will emerge as these two generations battle it out in political and social arenas. Will the retired boomers become victimized by their descendants? Is this truly what we can expect?

Promising Signs

Only a fool would utter the words *baby boomer* and *victim* in the same breath. The baby boomers have never been victims and simply will not tolerate being victims in retirement. To the contrary, as they have always done, they will break the existing rules and make their own rules about their future. Let's not forget which generation got the vote at 18, told the nation when to end a war, delayed marriage and child-rearing, and spurred the greatest economy in history. Such a generation will not be trumped by a generation of 40 million fewer people. There is strength in numbers—and the numbers are on the side of the boomers. Consider these facts:

- Today's 50-plus crowd controls 80 percent of the money in our savings and loan institutions and 66¢ of every dollar in the stock market. It owns 60 percent of all annuities, 50 percent of IRAs and Keoghs, and 40 percent of all mutual funds. In total, it controls over $7 trillion in wealth, or 70 percent. Money is power.
- By the time the last boomers turn 55 (2020), they will own $20 trillion in assets, or $461,000 per household on average.
- By far the most powerful political lobby in our nation is the American Association of Retired Persons (AARP) with over 36 million members and growing. AARP has more members than the AFL-CIO, national PTA, Boy Scouts of America, the NRA, the NAACP, and the League of Women Voters combined! And guess who goes to the polls more than any other group? By a wide margin, it is the 55–85 age group that casts the most ballots with voter participation peaking in the 65–74 age group. There is power in numbers.
- According to the Census Bureau, the total U.S. population under the age of 18 reached 73.4 million (larger than the peak of the baby boom). In the next decade, this group will go to work and pay Social Security.

Considering these numbers and the fact that baby boomers began turning 50 in 1996, you can safely assume that Social Security is on their radar and the chances of it going bust are highly unlikely. It's not going to happen on the boomers' watch! Although modern scribes are fond of telling us how bleak a place our world will be when the baby boomers reach retirement en masse starting in 2011—when the first boomers reach 65 years of age—the simple truth is that steps are already under way that will secure the Social Security system until the last boomer drops. To feel more optimistic about the future of Social Security, one needs only to consider the following:

- The earnings limit has been lifted for retirees.
- Discussions of privatizing at least part of the Social Security fund are ongoing.

Early in the year 2000 the U.S. Senate voted 100–0 to repeal the much reviled earnings limit for seniors aged 64 to 69 following a 422–0 vote in the House of Representatives. Before this law was repealed, retirees had to forfeit one of every three dollars earned above $17,000 a year. Congress, at the time, estimated that the earnings limit was causing over 800,000 seniors to lose an average of $8,154 in benefits annually. The unanimous repeal vote, which is a rare event in a normally bipartisan system, reflects how little sense it makes in today's world to penalize a retiree for working. Senator Daniel Moynihan commented, "Is there anyone who can remember when a substantive piece of legislation affecting millions of Americans and dealing with the Social Security Act would pass 100–0? I can't." This is one early signal of things to come. The incentive of abolishing an earnings limit will put more seniors to work, resulting in more productivity, more money in government coffers, and less economic stress for retirees.

Talk of privatization of at least some of the Social Security assets has been prominent, and despite politicizing and polarizing of the issue, it may someday be a reality. Robert J. Froehlich, author of the 1997 investment tome *The Three Bears Are Dead,* claims that the demographic imperative—namely, there will not be enough adults of working age to support all the retiring baby boomers—will force at least the partial privatization of the Social Security system. Proposals to begin allocating substantial portions of the Social Security payroll tax to self-directed personal savings accounts are proliferating now. The model for retirement fund privatization already exists and has proven it can work. Chilean pensions today are 50 to 100 percent higher than they were prior to privatization. Workers and retirees control their own pensions, which are managed by a private administration company. Employee contributions are a mandatory 10 percent, but people may contribute more if they wish. As of 2005, 95 percent of Chileans had joined the system. The mandatory contribution has also been a great success in Australia, where workforce coverage has increased from 40 percent to 90 percent. Contributions to the Australian Superannuation funds grew from $40 billion in 1985 to over $569 billion by 2004.

The long and short of it is that all the talk about the end of Social Security for our future is overcooked. If the fearmongers have gotten under your skin, put that concern behind you! The end of Social Security as we know it is near, but a new and improved Social Security system is in our future. One factor that rarely gets mentioned yet needs to be factored into the future health of Social Security is the number of people who plan on continuing some form of part-time or full-time work, even in retirement. By virtue of our own approach to work in later years, we will be continuing to contribute to the system.

Another suggestion that may get notice in the future is to offer a tax incentive to those well-off retirees who are eligible for benefits but don't need the income. This is an idea well worth considering, as it can relieve enormous and unnecessary pressure on the Social Security system.

Seniors' Refrain: "We Want to Work"

A study by the AARP conducted by Roper Starch Worldwide showed that over 80 percent of us plan on working through the retirement years (I presume they will cease calling them retirement years once we work through them). One-third of the respondents believed they would be working because they would have to for needed income. The majority (67 percent), however, said they would continue working because they *wanted* to work. Another study conducted by Gallup and Paine Webber—*Retirement Revisited*—revealed more of why we want to continue working. This study reveals details of what investors want to do after they retire. Eighty-five percent said they wanted to continue work in some form. Respondents' answers fell into the following five categories:

1. I want to work as long as I can—doing what I do now (15 percent).
2. I want to become an entrepreneur (26 percent).
3. I want to find a new job (34 percent).

4. I want to find some balance between work and life (10 percent).
5. I want the "traditional" retirement (15 percent).

We will visit this issue in more depth in Chapter 6. For now, suffice it to say that we have looked traditional retirement in the eye and have rejected it outright—that is, all but about 15 percent of us. People have often referred to retirement as "getting out of the race." The fact is that we no longer want out of the race. We simply want to run at our own pace. We want to make the decision whether we run, jog, or walk. We want to be able to sit out once in a while and reenter the race at our own choosing. And, most important, we want to run on the track of our choosing. This is the modern vision of retirement. It has become clear to most of us that we don't want "our father's retirement"; the only thing that needs to be retired are old ideas about retirement.

You're Going to Get Options After All

You're going to have plenty of options facing you in your working future and not necessarily the stock options you may be thinking of. The options I speak of are not those that you purchased at $1 and are now worth $200 but rather the options that will give you the same thing: *freedom to design the work life you want.* Your company isn't going to send you an e-mail telling you this, but it needs you more than you may think. The costs and frustrations of trying to replace you in our current marketplace are providing companies with the necessary motivation to do whatever it takes to keep you onboard.

Not only do the majority of us want to work to varying degrees, but the workplace is going to need us as we mature and are tempted to leave. A major demographic shift is beginning that will continue to frustrate corporations. As boomers begin to retire, not enough younger workers will be coming up to replace them, especially in management positions for those between 35 and 50. This phenomenon is becoming known as the "brain drain" and will provide plenty of flexible opportunities in the future for all of us. (See Figure 2.1.) Already, it's allowing a select group of bright corporate stars to restructure their jobs almost any way they choose, including downshifting from full-time to part-time and to consulting, mentoring, and working at the office of their choosing. The age-related brain drain has already begun and is being felt by companies that are stressed with a tight labor crunch.

FIGURE 2.1 | The Brain Drain

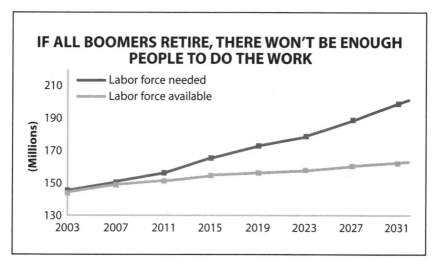

Source: Employment Policy Foundation analysis and projections of Census/BLS and BEA data.

Many companies watch in frustration as experience walks out the door. Many workers who are nearing retirement have benefited from their investments and so have the freedom to leave, thus exacerbating the already acute shortage of smart management. According to human resources consultant William C. Byham: "There's a knowledge problem in organizations and all the history is walking out the door."

A friend of mine, a former retiree, told me the following story:

My company pretty much involuntarily retired me. I don't mean they fired me, but they gave me an "early out" incentive, which felt like being fired with a $125,000 kick in the rear. I was given the choice to take the $125,000 incentive or stay on and risk a layoff with no incentive later.

Here I was in my late 40s with plenty of ideas and ambition— and unemployed. I didn't enjoy my early retirement nearly as much as my friends thought I would. I'm just not the type who wants to freelance alone all the time. Anyway, after a few years the firm that had "eased" me out found themselves in need of my expertise. It seems times had changed and so had their attitude. I now work as a consultant, work hours to my liking, and can still

do some freelancing when and where I want. I feel much more secure this way than with an umbilical cord connected to one company that can cut it at any time.

You too may have more options than you think in this current marketplace. Finding the working life you want is no longer just a matter
of saving enough money so you can leave. There are many ways to negotiate such a transition. The working life you dream of may be just a
couple of years—or a couple of decisions—away. One thing is for certain, though; the workplace of tomorrow needs you more than it may
want to let on. It's your turn to start learning how to play hard to get.
Companies can no longer afford the expense of the revenue drain when
experience and know-how walk out the door. According to the demographics of the next 15 years, the brain drain trend promises to continue.

Is the Financial Clock Ticking?

For some reason, some members of the financial services industry
have been very slow to comprehend the philosophical shift about retirement. Some in the industry are still promoting old ideas that don't
resonate with the spirit of the modern generation. Ironically, many in
the financial services industry wring their hands in frustration at the
baby boomers' lack of responsiveness to save for retirement. It has been
both stated and implied that this generation is morally flawed, lacks
discipline, is shortsighted, and is financially spoiled and misguided. It
is just now beginning to occur to those issuing pleas for retirement savings that they may have been promoting the wrong picture, and it explains why no one is paying much attention. Still, many of the
messages continue:
  "You need enough to be able to quit working at age 62."
  "You must save for the day when you can kiss work good-bye."
  "If you don't save this much for this long, you won't have what you
need and you won't be able to retire."
  The emotional undercurrent of these messages seem to translate to
fear and shame for many that hear them. I have interviewed hundreds
of people who say they feel like losers because it seems, from what they
hear, that everybody but them is the millionaire next door. They read

about people with gratuitous stock options and fat accounts. Following a television news story about a wealthy day trader is an ad telling them that had they bought *X* fund instead of that car, they would have had it made "in the shade." What the financial services industry needs to do to start resonating with the spirit of the modern public is to begin re-defining the term *retirement* and help people write an idiosyncratic def-inition of the term for their own life. And that definition needs to be realistic! Not everybody will have $1.5 million in investable assets ready to support them at the contrived retirement age of 62. There is no reason that these individuals should not be able to sit down with a plan-ner, advisor, or the like and come up with a plan to help them buy what they really want; and what they really want is liberty—the freedom to do what they love for as long as they love it. Because of all the public-ity centered on the nouveau millionaire in America, the fact that some-how gets lost on the public is that 50 percent of the boomers have just over $40,000 in net worth! Do these people need help? Absolutely, but not the kind of help that starts with "you don't and won't have enough."

The bottom line is that most of us want work in our lives! Some of us want to work because we want to matter, to play an active role in the society we live in. Some of us want to work because it keeps us men-tally sharp and involved with life. Some of us want to work because honest labor has a purifying and edifying quality. We don't need to hear any more about the pot of gold that must be full by the age of 62. It would be nice to have a plan in place that fits our own life vision and desires—a vision that marries making money with doing what we love and inspires in us more hope than dread. It has become obvious that the old messages about retirement planning no longer apply nor should they. The fact that many of us will find work we love and will never want to quit bodes well for our financial future.

Our greatest fear and insecurity for our later years should not be about the Social Security system or about being broke but rather about being broken without purpose and meaningful engagement.

Social Security will be there. If you save with discipline, your money will grow and be there to help you. If you find work you love, you will always be earning. In this scenario you may not necessarily be rich or completely retired, but you will be happy.

The New Retirementality Challenge

What do I think about Social Security?

Think about it: How much will I count on Social Security? What am I afraid of concerning my financial future?

Research it: Where is my money now? Is it invested? Is it just resting? Review the latest Social Security statement (or order a new one from the Social Security Administration).

Decide and take action:

- Take action to learn about my money and where it is.
- Include my spouse or significant other in the learning process.
- List my money fears.
- Decide how to go about attacking those fears (*Hint:* knowledge drives out fear).

CHAPTER 3

A Short History of Retirement

Retirement, as we understand it today, did not exist in preindustrial America. In those days, older members of society weren't sent to the sidelines. They actually held a more prominent place as a resource for their insight, knowledge of skills and crafts, and lessons gained from experience. It was the industrialization era that accelerated the conditions that gave us the traditional version of retirement. Industrialization ushered in a profound redefinition of work. Mass production became the popular mode of work, and workers began to be viewed as parts in the system, subject to wear and replaceable.

With the advent of industrialization came a population shift from the country to the cities. This brought about a significant lifestyle adjustment as people went from self-sufficiency to dependency. Work became a means to an end—an income to live on—as opposed to a way of life. In his book *The Sociology of Retirement,* Robert C. Atchley made an insightful comparison between a craftsman and a worker. A craftsman controls the process and the product, which makes his work both satisfying and integral to his identity. An industrial worker is responsible for one little part of the process. Consequently, the work offers little reward. Atchley also noted that the words *job* and *occupation* soon began to replace the terms *craft* and *vocation* in the American laborer's lexicon. We can trace the eventual degradation of the American work ethic to this point in history, which comes as no surprise as you expect people to become lethargic about work that offers no emotional reward.

As other nations were embracing industrialization, the world became a competitive commercial environment. America was intent on proving itself to be a world leader, and progress was the mantra of the industrialists. As a result, they began looking for ways to sweep away anything that stood in the path of progress. A major obstacle to progress, some decided, were people of maturity. Because of advances in safety and health care, people were living longer and the workforce was aging. Mature people were beginning to be viewed as a threat to progress. It was assumed that older people would not acclimate easily to changing procedures, and changes were needed for industry to become an efficient, well-oiled machine. The seeds of ageism were beginning to be sown. Those seeds of prejudice were then watered by a widely reported speech by Dr. William Osler, one of the nation's most prominent physicians, given in 1905 at Johns Hopkins University. Osler's thesis was that any man over 40 years was useless to society.

"Take the sum of human achievement in action, in science, in art, in literature," Osler said. "Subtract the work of men above 40, and while we would miss great treasures, even priceless treasures, we would practically be where we are today." In short, Osler was postulating that any person over 40 was dispensable to the cause of progress. Osler went on to say that people over 60 were "entirely useless" and a drain on society because of their inelastic minds. Osler's articulation helped to embolden a growing intellectual trend and opportunistically served to answer the growing societal problem of unemployment. It seemed obvious, these intellectuals asserted, to replace the old with the new. All that was left was to come up with a way to get rid of the old. Mandatory retirement was one answer.

Another emerging force in this drama was the labor union, which was struggling to survive and fighting for the right to strike. Labor unions quickly embraced the idea of retirement because forcing out the older workers gave them the opportunity to deliver the jobs and job security they were promising their membership. Business leaders, labor leaders, and social engineers were all singing the retirement chorus. Older workers didn't have a chance—and soon wouldn't have a choice.

There was, however, one massive obstacle standing in the way of this strategy. What would these new retirees live on? In the late 1800s, Chancellor Otto von Bismarck had come up with a disability insurance program in the German Empire for all disabled workers 70 and older. This was instituted by von Bismarck, in part to undermine demands for democracy and to reaffirm workers' commitment to the government. Around that same time, American Express created the first private pension in America. In 1900 the Pattern Makers League of North America became the first union to offer pensions to its members. Up until that time, pensions were typically available to veterans and some civil servants such as policemen and firefighters (and, in some states, teachers).

It was not until 1910 that the pension movement gained steam. That year the Taft administration started promoting pensions as a major piece of its platform on industrial efficiency. From 1910 to 1920, more than 200 new pension plans were formed. A change in the corporate tax law that made pension plans more tax advantageous resulted in the doubling of new plans in 1920. Overall, the penetration rate for pensions was quite slow, with only 15 percent of American workers covered by a plan by 1932. The watershed moment came in 1933, in the deepest, darkest depths of the Great Depression. Social conditions had reached an explosive point because of the unemployment of one-fourth of the labor force. Franklin D. Roosevelt (FDR) and the New Dealers were in a precarious and potentially disastrous situation with masses of angry young men demonstrating in the streets. Roosevelt had already seen where these situations could lead by the examples set in Germany and Italy. It was exactly these conditions that gave rise to both Hitler and Mussolini. The New Dealers' plan to get young people working again was to offer a public pension so the older men would retire.

Combine this reality with the fact that a movement was afoot with the elderly to demand pensions from those over 60. People wanted the federal government to get involved. At that time, 28 states had pension programs—which made little difference in the lives of the recipients because the programs were sparsely funded because of the Great Depression. Many corporate pensions were defaulting as well. As a result, 50 percent of the elderly were living in poverty.

The New Dealers needed to test their plan before implementing it on a national scale. Would the older workers like the idea? Senator Robert F. Wagner introduced a bill in 1934 that established a pension for retir-

ing railroad workers. Wagner compelled 50,000 workers to consider retiring immediately. The bill passed. Wagner played a major role in 1935
in persuading FDR to introduce the Social Security Act, the statute that
would forever change our views of work and retirement. However,
Roosevelt had to settle two major issues that would echo through the
generations. How would Social Security be paid for and at what age
would workers become eligible? This Social Security program would
not work if it failed to provide instant benefits for those who were currently at the retirement age. Rather than taxing these people for their
own retirement, the politicians came up with the idea of taxing those
who were still working on behalf of retirees. Tax the younger generation to pay for the retiring generation. When the Social Security Act
was implemented, there was a small enough number of employees so
that no one would have to pay much for the plan.

Now the biggest question had to be answered: At what age can one
receive Social Security? Precedents existed at the time in Germany,
Great Britain, and France with ages pegged to the ages of 60, 65, and
70. Citing a biblical reference to "threescore and ten years," Bismarck's
original retirement marker was set at 70, allowing the workers enough
time to pick out a gravestone if they should be lucky enough to live
much longer. Germany lowered the age to 65—18 years later—because
very few people lived to 70 to collect the benefits. And what was the
average life expectancy at that time? All of 46 years!

The retirement plans designed by Bismarck and others had obviously not been intended to give a worker any time for enjoyment—not
with a life expectancy of 46 and a retirement age of 65. It helps to move
to our modern age to understand Bismarck's original intent. The age of
retirement was 19 years beyond the average life expectancy. In those
days a person who was 65 was indeed old—much older than today's
65-year-old.

When FDR and the New Dealers settled on the age of 65 in 1935,
the average life expectancy in America was 63 years. Bear in mind, however, that life expectancy statistics can be misleading because factors
such as infant mortality are calculated into them. In fact, the average
number of years lived in retirement today is just four years more than
in 1935. The obvious conclusion one could make is that retirement was
never intended to remove people with strong productivity potential out
of the workplace. Our view is skewed on this issue, however, as a result

of the difference in the constitution of a 65-year-old today and that of a 65-year-old in 1935. Because the retirement markers were set later than the average life expectancy, many people didn't live long enough to collect Social Security benefits. FDR eventually moved to have the age of retirement set to age 62.

The benefits that a retiree did receive were just enough to support a meager lifestyle, providing bare sustenance. It was this generation of retirees that evoked the images of widows wearing full winter gear for lack of heat in decrepit one-room apartments in the winter and eating cat food to survive. It would take another 20 years before the social net and workplace manipulation known as retirement would become a part of the American way of life.

The retirement lifestyle got a major boost during the Second World War when workers' wages were frozen. Because wages were nonnegotiable, union leaders began bargaining for pensions where they didn't exist and for bigger employer contributions where they did exist. These contributions were tax deductible, and future pension obligations weren't reflected in a company's balance sheet. Second World War conditions caused pension coverages to flourish across most industries. The timing could not have been better for the Social Security system, which was being roundly criticized for allowing retirees to live in poverty. Opportunistic politicians in the following decades began to push for broadened coverages to include husbands of working women, farmers, the self-employed, members of the armed forces, and so on. Coverage itself was expanded to include health and disability insurance, welfare for the disabled, and, as an answer to the senior poverty issue, annual cost-of-living adjustments to keep up with inflation.

With all these changes, retirement began to shed its destitute and forsaken image. Combining Social Security payments with pension checks allowed people to live out a respectable, if modest, retirement—but it still typically lasted only a year or two at best. It was during this period of retirement's image transition that financial services companies stepped up their efforts. They began to market retirement as *an individual's rightful reward for his or her years of labor and loyal service.* People began buying more retirement investment products and looked forward to an era of reward that would be timed on their new gold watch.

William Greabner, in his *History of Retirement,* shares an interesting anecdote regarding a shift in the financial services sector's marketing of retirement. The story is told that in 1952, H. G. Kenagy of Mutual Life Insurance advised business leaders on the National Industrial Conference Board about the best way to sell retirement to their employees. The tack he suggested was distributing stories by these business leaders via company newsletters and the like about happily retired people fishing or playing golf and sipping martinis. Sell the blissful retirement life and don't forget to mention how to get to nirvana by investing in both the company plan and other financial vehicles. This was not a difficult story to sell to a workforce that now had jobs instead of vocations. As one 82-year-old nonretiree put it, "They that lack a vocation are always longing for a vacation." Retirement had now become the permanent vacation—without the kids! This retirement pitch from 1952 has hardly changed over 50 years later. Although some firms in the retirement products industry are catching on to the philosophical shift regarding what people really want out of their longer lives, many companies in the industry lag woefully behind with antiquated images of fishing pond, beachside, and golf course heaven.

People began to retire in unprecedented numbers because (1) they felt they had to and (2) the unexpected appreciation in home prices made comfortable retirement a real possibility. The implied message to workers: "You don't have a choice. Once you hit 62, you're out the door." No employers were begging them to stay around for a while or maybe to just cut back their hours. It was universally accepted that you were no longer welcome in the working world at retirement age.

Retirement certainly would not have been received with such willingness and resignation had it not been for the fortuitous gains this generation of retirees made in real estate. A couple who bought a home in the early 1950s and sold it in the early 1980s was sitting on a tenfold appreciation in the value of their home. If they bought the house for $12,500, they sold it for $120,000 to $150,000. A modern version of this trend has taken place in California with retirees cashing out massive real estate gains and moving eastward to Utah and Nevada. By cashing in on the sizable profit from selling their home and combining it with their Social Security payments and pension checks, retirees looked forward to easy living. In addition to all this, they had Medicare and Medicaid. The lives of these people, at least ascetically, began to resemble the couples' pictures on the retirement brochures—golf courses, martinis, and . . . headaches. Headaches? Yes, headaches. Call it the retirement hangover. Retirement for many became buyer's remorse for the rest of their life.

The Day After

"I used to go down to the café where all the retired folks gathered to drink coffee, loiter, tell stories, and play cards. I noticed that after about two weeks you had heard all the stories, and they were going into reruns. I also noticed that now that the retirees had nothing to do to keep themselves fit, they had plenty of time to find things wrong with their health. I decided that I didn't want to be bored to sickness and eventually death, and there was no way I could endure all those reruns, so I gave up any fantasy I ever had about fully retiring."
—Kenny, 74-year-old active rancher

The retirement hangover kicks in at different times for different people and not at all for others. The ones who most enjoy retirement often seem to be the people who were so burned out by what they did in the working world that the thought of going back causes instant contentment.

Many of us have witnessed our parents' struggle with the emotional realities of retirement. The hangover can start within a week or two. It begins when the retiree starts asking, "Is this all I've got to do for the rest of my days?" They have literally grown "ill at ease." It seems that everyone has a story about someone who took retirement and immediately began to disintegrate and was buried within a year or two. Removing these individuals from meaningful work literally took the life right out of them.

Until recently, retirees from some of our major corporations could expect to receive no more than 20 to 24 pension checks. Remember the statistic I presented in Chapter 1 from the American Demographics poll showing that 41 percent of retirees said retirement was a difficult adjustment compared with 12 percent of the newly married, who saw marriage as a difficult adjustment. The difficulty of the adjustment is that we are asking people to do something that is unnatural and is founded on some very dangerous assumptions.

We are not asking retirees to simply make an adjustment to a retired lifestyle; we are asking them to make "age-justments"—to turn off who they are and the activities that drive their pulse—simply because they have reached the age of 62. The true adjustments of age should be related to our health, our mobility, and our mental acuity. These physical changes happen when they happen. Nature catches up. The outward man decays and we adjust.

Retirement historically has imposed a counterfeit "age-justment" that tells people once they reach a certain age they are no longer in the race. We are just now coming to grips with the false promises of a false god in our society: retirement. It is a lifestyle promise that is built largely on myths. These myths or false assumptions regarding retirement are in slow decline in the hearts and minds of the ascending generations and in many of those who have already eaten the fruit of traditional retirement. One irrefutable fact that is surfacing is that retirement will no longer be what its originators intended it to be. Times have changed—and so should our thinking about traditional retirement as a life choice.

CHAPTER 4

The Great "Retiremyths"

This chapter introduces and deconstructs the myths that have led to both dissatisfied retirements and the anxiety-ridden pursuit of a retirement dream. When you've finished reading, I hope you will have a more realistic picture of what you want from your money and your life. You will be able to go to sleep at night knowing you no longer have to worry about being able to jump off an economic ledge at age 62, and you will be able to wake each morning with a continuing sense of purpose for each upcoming day. Here are the myths that have ruled the concept of retirement up to the present:

- Age 65 is old.
- Being retired means you're not working.
- You have to be 62 to do what you really want to do.
- Retirement is an economic event exclusively.
- A life of ease is the ultimate retirement goal.
- I can do this by myself.

Sixty-Five Is Old

Old ain't what it used to be! Remember when the age for retirement was set; a majority of people didn't even live until retirement age. Now we live 20 to 30 years past the retirement age. The age of 65 in this day and age has little resemblance to the age of 65 in, say, 1970. Most people are not old at 65 today. They may or may not have slowed down. Thirty years ago you didn't see many men in their 70s jumping out of airplanes or flying in outer space as our generation has seen with people like George Bush and John Glenn. The behavior of these men may well serve as portents of the active lifestyles in seniors of the future. We will see more and more of the aging role models in years to come.

It is ironic that our society, rather than adjusting to this longevity trend, continues to promote a retirement age that was established over 100 years ago. Even more ironic is that many, with wealth supplied by a robust and resilient economy, have convinced themselves to take up early retirement. Many of these people have failed to comprehend that if they retire at 55, for example, they will spend as many years in their retirement as they did in their entire working career. This is great if you have some invigorating and challenging pursuits before you in those 30 years. If you don't, history shows that you'll never see those 30 extra years.

How old will you be when you really become old? It seems that the answer to that question is as individual as the person answering it. We know that the marker for old is no longer 65. Some recent surveys show that most seniors now feel that the marker for old is somewhere between 75 and 80. Expect that number to keep moving up with the baby boom generation. Three-fourths of Americans feel that "old" is defined by a decline in mental or physical abilities, while less than half feel it is defined by age (HSBC 2005). In Chapter 7, I will guide you in figuring out how old you *truly* are in mind and body, and introduce you to people who are defying the so-called limitations of age. These individuals have not bought into the idea that they need to move aside for the next generation—or anyone else for that matter. They will leave the race when they are good and ready!

Retirement Means Not Working

The retirement of the future will no longer be a "cold turkey" abstinence from labor. The retirement of the future will be defined by one person—you! You will decide how much you want to work, where you want to work, and when you want to work. The growing trends in workplace flexibility motivated by a tight labor market spell only freedom for you and your future. People will design a retirement they can live with. This will mean working part-time for some and entering and exiting the job market as they wish for others. The old model for retirement resembled a cliff-jumping-off point (that's why we needed a parachute). The new model represents a bell curve with a gradual decline or phasing of work life. The two extremes of the old retirement model—all work or no work—is simply a relic of the past. In this book we explore the manifold possibilities for you and your work at any age.

You Have to Be 62 to Do What You Want to Do

Millions of people are sacrificing the present in hopes of following their heart at 62, or whatever other age they retire. Many people who want to pursue a passion or a new focus see this as their only hope. We have discovered many other options that people have exercised to free their life from the drudgery of draining and stressful toils to the avocational pursuits they had previously entertained only in their daydreams. There are many creative approaches available that you may have not yet considered—approaches that integrate your assets and your income with your passions and your life.

Is your life about making money or is your money about making a life? A theme that is strongly promoted in our society is that we should always choose the path with the biggest bucks. Consequently, many people put their soul's work on the back burner while they travel a career path paved with the biggest bucks. Why? So they can someday have enough money to do what they really want. This flawed philosophy of putting first things second in our career and life is the reason why so many today are so motivated to retire, that is, so they can do what they want. They have chosen to use their life to make money rather than to use money to make a life. By using some innovative approaches to financial life planning, you can make the transition into what you want with your life sooner than you may think.

This book provides a portrait of those who discovered what it takes to do what they want with their life—sooner instead of later. Many of these people have found work that feels like play. They are doing the thing that comes naturally and are getting paid to do it! With proper planning and prioritization, you can liberate yourself into a fulfilling pursuit of your uncharted passions within five years or less. All you have to decide is . . . what you want to be when you grow up.

Retirement Is an Economic Event

This implication has been the biggest mistake of the retirement savings industry. The idea that retirement is simply an economic cliff for which we must have a parachute ready at age 62 has been the primary motivational message the industry has offered for the last 40 years. The problem is that *many people are preparing a golden nest egg that will be placed in a dying tree.* The nest egg is their retirement savings and the dying tree is their retirement life. Retirement is a life event, not an economic event. We must stop treating retirement as an exclusive economic event. We need to develop a more holistic approach that integrates an individual's aspirations, life stage, familial responsibilities, health issues, and concerns about money. People want to explore the connection between their money, their soul, and their life as a whole. There are many wise advisors in the retirement planning industry that have realized the importance of a life planning approach versus the monotonous money-crunching, myopic retirement planning.

> *"Instead of absorbing an obsolete view of retirement, we should consider . . . a flexible life plan that provides for your financial, vocational, physical, emotional, and spiritual needs. Unless you look at your future holistically, merely saving up a pile of money will be a meaningless act."*
> —John F. Wasik, author, The Late-Start Investor

In the wheel of life, money is but one spoke. It is not the wheel and it is not the hub. People today want to talk to those advisors who recognize the need to look at the stage of life where they are and the stage of life they are approaching, and then explore the money issues that are relevant at these stages.

A Life of Ease Is the Ultimate Retirement Goal

A life of total ease is one step from a life of disease. The reason so many retirees are ill at ease is because without the contrast and paradox of meaningful labor, leisure loses its meaning. First you become bored and then you become boring. Fishing and golfing are great fun, but they make poor full-time occupations for a period of 25 years for most.

There are far too many "grumpy old men" roaming the retirement landscape. They are grumpy because they are bored. This book debunks the myth of fulfilling full-time leisure as pictured in the retirement brochures. Many of us find meaning and purpose in our work and a needed catharsis in our leisure. It's difficult to enjoy the one without the other. It is a necessary paradox in our lives. This is the reason that over one-third of male retirees go back to some form of work within one year of retirement, and over two-thirds of them take full-time jobs. They would die if they didn't. There *is* a way to a balanced approach to retirement planning that can provide both fun and fulfillment.

You're Going to Spend Most of Your Retirement Income on Doctors and Pills

This universal assumption about retirement is going to be turned on its head by evidence that if you plan a healthier and engaging retirement, you will spend much less on doctors and pills. Bored retirees form bad habits. Purposeless retirees are sick retirees. Unchallenged retirees have no motivation to exercise their body, mind, or spirit. In Chapter 7, I present gerontological evidence regarding the physical well-being, mental acuity, and health care expenditures for challenged versus unchallenged retirees. The proper attitude and approach to our later years will result in healthier economics as well.

I Can Do This by Myself

The proliferation of the self-directed 401(k) and the advent of online trading have led many people to believe that they don't need any help in planning their financial future. This is akin to saying, "Because I can buy my own vitamins and pills, I don't need a doctor." Are you buying the right vitamins and pills for your situation? When is the last time you had a checkup? Or would you rather not have one and believe you're not at risk? When it comes to dealing with the health of our wealth, many people fall into easy denial. The self-care phenomenon in health care is a good thing as long as we do not begin believing that we know all that we need to know. Just as there is a time and a place for a health expert, there is a time and a place in our life for a wealth expert, advisor, or money coach as well.

> *"I'm 37 years old. I've got my MBA and I've been working in the re-tirement services arena for 15 years, and I'm still not sure about all the issues I need to be thinking about for a guy my age with two chil-dren. It gives me a great level of comfort to be able to talk to some-one who can make me aware of all the issues that will affect my money and my future. I'm just too busy and lack the specific knowl-edge to do it on my own."*
>
> *—Michael Houston, retirement specialist*

When I heard these words from a professional in the financial arena, it struck me how easy it is to dupe ourselves into believing we can run this race without any coaching. Such a delusion is especially pronounced in a bull market where the rising tide lifts all ships. The bear market of the 1990s has illuminated for many the inherent weakness and insecurity in the do-it-yourself approach. The fact is that many of us lack either the specific knowledge, the planning expertise, and/or the discipline to do this on our own. When we hire someone to help us sort out what we want out of our life and our money, we are not just paying for advice, we are also getting direction and a needed degree of financial discipline and accountability. If you are not yet at the place you want to be or don't have a clue when you'll be there, you must face one inescapable fact: if you were really capable of doing this on your own, you would have done so by now!

Does the fact that you can buy your own airline tickets exclude the need to consult with a travel consultant? I'm a frequent traveler and know about the many unpleasant surprises that can be waiting when you arrive in strange and exotic places. I want to talk to someone who has been there—someone who can guide me to make the right and safe choices about where I go, where I stay, and how I get there. The key for you is to find the right money coach, one who understands you and your unique dreams and situation, one you can trust and will support and direct you in this journey.

A New Definition

> *"Retirement is changing. Many individuals are retiring from their career professions only to take on new work. These changes point to*

*the need for reshaping our ideas and institutions associated with re-
tirement and developing new perspectives on the nature of work."*
          —Dr. Phyllis Moen, Director, Bronfenbrenner Life Course Center

*"We need to change the term 'retirement' because it sounds like
dying. We have to substitute something that offers new possibilities
at whatever stage in one's life a change happens."*
                                    —Dr. Ruth Westheimer, sex therapist

I think Dr. Ruth was right. We need a sexier term for retirement. It
doesn't fit anymore. Retirement has been built on myths. The concept of
retirement is going through a slow but seismic redefinition; for most of
us, it is no longer about dropping entirely out of the race. It is a chance
to refire, rehire, rewire—anything but retire. It is our opportunity to capitalize on everything we have learned about work and about life. A failure is a person who has blundered and not been able to cash in on the
experience. We need to begin to call retirement and retirement savings
what they really are: a second chance and emancipation money. Many
of you are simply looking forward to launching a brand-new you. Many
of you want to try something out of the ordinary. Many of you want to
play around with ideas you have had for years. Many of you want to
hunker down with loved ones and simplify your life for the time being.

The reason no one else can define retirement for you is because it is
about *your* life and *your* dreams. My goal is for you to take yourself
through one simple mental exercise. Ask yourself this one question,
"What if there were no finish line?" How would it change the way you
live today and plan for tomorrow if you stopped running toward the artificial goal of retiring at age 62, or any other age for that matter? Remove this contrived finish line from your mind and your life, and it will
liberate both your mind and life. Disentangle yourself from retirement
myths and deal with life's realities. Once the finish line is removed, we
are left to ponder our present realities and future hopes. We will stop
sacrificing the present to pursue an illusion of bliss in the sweet by-and-
by. We will begin to focus on doing work *today* that capitalizes on our
gifts and gives expression to our deepest-felt avocational desires. We
will begin our quest to find work that feels like play.

Once the finish line is removed we take away the ever-present fiscal
pressure to arrive at a certain age with so much money. When this pres-

sure is removed, we can begin to make choices that are not based solely on money and that sacrifice of our soul, but on doing work that brings us a sense of purpose and satisfaction. A strange phenomenon that is hard to explain is how money seems to find its way to those who follow their hearts and pursue their interests with passion. Something else comes your way when you follow your heart—contentment—and that's a precious commodity that no amount of money can buy.

The New Retirementality Is ...

- Asking yourself, What is it about retirement that has been drawing or repelling me?
- Asking yourself, What am I most looking forward to?
- Asking yourself, What am I most concerned about?

End of the Work/Retire Ultimatum

A tight labor market is a motivating factor for many senior employers to stay in their current jobs, at least on a part-time basis. The baby boomer generation was followed by a birth dearth that is going to place an even higher premium on senior working skills for the next 20 years. For corporate America, labor shortages may become a fact of life. By the year 2020 there will be several million fewer people aged 35 to 54 than we have today. The law of supply and demand may be moving to the side of the experienced worker for many years to come. What this spells for the individuals looking forward to working retirement years is the ability to write their own ticket in terms of job flexibility and responsibilities. Your workplace will need your experience, and it will grow increasingly willing to let you work on your terms.

As stated earlier, two things must change to give us more options regarding our working lives; those things are how we think and the way our corporations think. Having read this far, I hope you are convinced that some form of work will always be an integral, even if reduced, part of your life. Our corporations are beginning to see that they will need to change their attitude and culture toward an aging workforce if they hope to compete in the next decades. Companies that do not begin to respond to the new age working realities are in for a rude wake-up call.

The models of hiring, developing, and retiring employees that have worked in the past will backfire if used in the next decade or two. Two simple facts point to this looming employer crisis. First, the baby boom generation, the largest segment of the workforce, is aging fast. Second, the shortage of young talent is growing more acute with each passing day. These significant demographic trends will have very profound implications for how companies manage their people. These trends will force companies to:

- Rethink how they attract and retain people.
- Change how they motivate and reward their help.
- Work out how an aging workforce will affect innovation and productivity.

The companies that begin to address these demographic realities and begin catering to the valuable, but aging, employee will thrive in the coming years as they attract the best talent available. Employers are just beginning to feel the first tremors of a talent shortage that will reach "workquake" proportions within the next 15–20 years.

The Talent Shortage

According to a study of the growth of the U.S. workforce in the years 2000–2010 by the U.S. Bureau of Labor Statistics, the number of workers 65+ is growing at 30 percent, while the number of workers 35–44 is *declining* at 10 percent! Those workers approaching traditional retirement ages who are now 55–64 are growing at 52 percent. This is a clear trend that will become more pronounced as boomers continue to reexamine their views of retirement and as corporations continue to face the dearth of experienced labor. Something will change, because if traditional trends continue, there will be a shortage of over 35 million workers by the year 2030.

The obvious good news for you is that there just won't be enough young talent available to fill your shoes should you be inclined to leave the workforce in the next 20 to 30 years. Employers are going to have to make changes to keep you around for a longer period of time. Until recently, companies could afford to let older workers walk out the door because there were plenty of baby boomers available to take their place.

Now, with the beginning of the boomer aging trend, companies have nowhere to turn but to the current worker.

The Cost Companies Will Pay

The cost of ignoring the impact of the aging worker on the corporate culture will be broad and pervasive. This issue will affect attraction and retention, productivity, innovation, competitiveness, and the nature of the corporate culture itself if not met head on by corporate leaders very soon. The companies that possess foresight have already begun to prepare the way for the graying workforce.

Attraction and Retention of Top Talent

Attracting and keeping the top talent is already a major issue for companies that are fervently competing for the skills of available younger workers. As the resource pool of younger workers begins to decline, employers will begin to look to the ranks of more mature people aged 45 and older to fill the void. All the existing paradigms about work, reward, advancement, motivation, and personal growth will have to change to attract the much needed 45-year-old and older employee. The carrots that attract and retain a 24-year-old may not necessarily trip the trigger of a 48-year-old.

If companies want to attract the gray-haired crowd in the future, they will have to deal with some prevalent ageist biases today. Business today is characterized as high performance and innovative; and these two descriptors conjure up images of youth—the college-age guys who develop a great new software idea in their garage or the Young Turks who turn a corporation around. Are high productivity and innovation the exclusive mindscape of the young? The Watson Wyatt study "Managing the Workplace of the Future" states:

> The acceptance of the psychological link between innovation and youth is so strong that many employers will need to develop ways to create innovative cultures that are age irrelevant. . . . They will need to create cultures that engage people and motivate performance regardless of age. In the same way that companies have invested in the renewal of their operations over the past decade, they will now have to invest in the renewal of their human capital.

Productivity and Competitiveness

The changing demographics are bound to affect an organization's ability to produce and compete in the marketplace. What will happen to a company's productivity if all of its experience and intellectual capital continue to take the "retirement" exit ramp with no one to fill the voids? How long will it take this company to replace and retrain to the level of the departing talent? Technological advancements can help in dealing with some of the human capital loss issues, but there is no technology available to fill the void of personal knowledge and experience. At first glance the popular high-performance work culture of today seems at odds with a predominantly older workforce. Companies may have to overcome the idea that high performance means youth. Then again, maybe they won't have to convince baby boomers of that idea at all. I would expect the boomers to contradict the paradigms of youth-related innovation, productivity, and competitiveness, just as they've crashed through every other paradigm in their revolutionary life span.

The Brain Drain

"There's a knowledge problem in organizations. All the history is going out the door."
—William C. Byham, president and chief executive of human resources, Development Dimensions International

We are in the early stages of a human capital drought that companies need to address to have any hope of retaining valuable talent past their intended retirement age. This impending demographic drought has already been recognized by the more sagacious companies in our culture, who are already making the necessary changes needed to retain valuable experience and knowledge before it walks out the door. It is a coming corporate crisis that was characterized by *BusinessWeek* magazine as a "brain drain."

Niels, a retired sales executive, received a call from his paper company one year into retirement. They missed him—and the results in his territory showed it. It was difficult for a fresh, young sales executive to achieve the level of rapport Niels had engendered over the years. So, he came back on a part-time basis and quickly turned the missing results into business for his firm. Eight years later, he's still at it! As a sidebar, Niels told me that he was glad to get reengaged both for the intellectual stimulation as well as the social aspects of the work. A year into his retirement he'd already noticed that he wasn't quite as articulate, couldn't read as fast, and even missed having deadlines. This is the sort of motivation that corporations dream of.

Older executives, who were given generous pensions, are getting set to leave the workplace en masse just as many of their companies are facing management crunches. Some sectors will be especially hard hit as more than 40 percent of the U.S. labor force reaches the traditional retirement age by the end of this decade. Close to half of the nation's electric utilities workers will be eligible to retire in the next five years, according to Michael Ashworth, a researcher at Carnegie Mellon University. Half of the U.S. government's civilian workforce will be eligible for retirement in the same period.

Add to this the warning from the National Association of Manufacturers that the manufacturing workforce will decline by 40 percent in the next ten years. With estimates of the skilled workforce being undersupplied by five million workers between 2010 and 2012, I expect that a lot of people (like Niels) will be receiving calls to consider coming back to help.

For example, Southern Co., an Atlanta-based utility, created a "retiree reservists pool" to deal with short-term projects and emergencies. Lincoln National Corp., a financial services firm in Philadelphia, put together a task force to create flexible work arrangments for older employees and is asking mature managers to mentor trainees.

IBM's 300,000+ employees are being asked to detail their experience in a directory called "the blue pages" so the company can locate key knowledge "before it walks out the door," according to Eric Lesser, an associate partner in IBM's business consulting unit. (Kelly Greene, "Bye-Bye to Boomers?" *Wall Street Journal,* 20 September 2005)

Firms like Deloitte Consulting are responding by allowing some of their valuable partners, who have less fiscal incentive to stay, to literally design their dream job. Deloitte is allowing these individuals to restructure their jobs almost any way they want. Some are shifting from working full-time to part-time, and others are moving from consulting to mentoring up-and-comers in the organization. Douglas MacCracken,

Deloitte's managing director for the Americas, said, "We looked at the demographic risk of losing significant partners; the firm was vulnerable. We're dealing with it." Deloitte has been early in its recognition and response to a problem that all organizations are about to face head-on: the age-related brain drain. This scenario is exacerbated by the fact that boomers are now passing 50 years of age, and many of them have windfalls from history's greatest bull market. Add to this picture the fact that most companies are already feeling the crunch of a shortage of competent managers.

Some companies, including Monsanto, Chevron, and Prudential Insurance, are now tailoring contracts for senior employees to work part-time and on a consulting basis. The wisdom and experience of their senior employees has been utilized to temporarily fill critical skill gaps, to travel the world as corporate diplomats, and to transfer their lifetime of learning to younger colleagues. It is hoped that this shift in attitude toward maturity and age as a source for wisdom and experience will spill out into all industries—and into our society as a whole. The time has come to bury ageist biases that have relegated older individuals to spectator status in our society.

Frederick Hudson, 70, a corporate coach and author, is on a mission to eliminate the word *retirement* from American minds. Hudson urges businesses to give up their ageism. "If people can perform effectively and want to keep on, why not encourage them to stay on. It's cheaper than recruiting and training."

> *"If companies continue to require that working for them is an all-or-nothing proposition, they will find people reaching 55 and going to work for competitors who are offering flexible employment opportunities."*
> —Dennis R. Coleman, principal, PricewaterhouseCoopers

Flextime, part-time, the virtual office, telecommuting, innovative consulting arrangements, and phased retirements are all signs that old ideas about employment have turned to ashes. Although the majority of companies do not yet practice all these fluid and flexible employment principles, their adoption rate is on the rise. Companies have no choice but to become more flexible or risk the exodus of top talent to companies that are. This is especially true of those employees who possess the greatest asset of all: *experience.* This fact portends more self-designed employment for all of us as we reach ages and life stages where we want to slow down, change course, change settings, or experiment with new challenges.

Does your company offer a phased retirement program? If they do not, then they are either not paying attention or they are hampered by government regulations. Sixty-five percent of companies surveyed by the Employment Policy Foundation said they would offer phased-in retirement but say government regulations keep them from doing so. For instance, workers covered by a defined-benefit pension plan currently cannot participate in a phased retirement program without eroding the amount of their eventual pension payment. The answer is to make workers eligible at earlier ages. The IRS recommends eligibility for phased retirement at 59½, whereas the AARP supports offering it at 62. Look for the rules to change in the near future.

Corporations need to pay closer attention. According to a 2003 study by the Society of Human Resource Managers, 35 percent of companies are just becoming aware of the issue, 23 percent are beginning to examine their policies, 4 percent have proposed specific changes, and only 3 percent have defined a plan. Thirty-five percent said they "don't know." Their wakeup call will come when their best aging talent goes elsewhere to work. (2005 Watson-Wyatt survey of 600 employers)

What kind of phased retirement programs can companies offer? Everything from part-time work to "retirees" to consulting agreements to job-sharing and extended leaves of absence. The key word here is *flexibility.* Give experienced talent the opportunity for some freedom and balance in their lives, and they will give companies their best in the time they choose to work.

And why will they bring their "A" game to work in later years? Because they want the work. Yes, many individuals need the money and want the benefits, but they are equally driven by the need to remain mentally and physically active and productive and useful.

The bottom line is this: according to an AARP public opinions study on attitudes toward phased retirement, nearly 80 percent said that the availability of such a plan would encourage them to work past their expected retirement age.

Companies can no longer afford to dictate and ignore this issue. Two factors work against the company that resists change. One, we live in a knowledge-based economy, and, two, the baby bust generation (1965–1980) cannot supply the necessary workers. According to Develop Dimensions International, between now and 2010, the number of managerial jobs will increase by 21 percent, while the number of people between 35 and 50 will fall by 5 percent. In 1979 the average age in the workforce was 34.9; today the average age is over 40. So the trend toward a more mature workplace is already fixed. Because we saw so much downsizing in the last two decades, many businesses have not yet seen the demographic writing on the wall and consequently will find themselves shorthanded if they are not doing everything in their power to retain and cater to their most experienced people.

> *"I don't want to play golf all the time for God's sake."*
> *—Jesse B. Krider, part-time global advisor, 63*

Chevron Corporation is an example of a company that is trying to be more flexible with its senior stars, and the company is reaping benefits to its bottom line in the process. Rather than imposing the retirement ultimatum on Jesse Krider, Chevron asked him to switch from a full-time operations executive to a part-time trainer of young executives. This option gave Krider the fresh challenge he wanted. He says, "If I had not gone into teaching and mentoring and helping others, there's a good chance I would have retired earlier." Chevron's flexibility has worked to benefit workers and the workplace.

Alexander Aird is codeveloper of the Senior Leaders Program that is working to help Deloitte hang on to their aging talent. Deloitte's own retirement program created a problem that the Senior Leaders Program is trying to repair. The talents it is trying to keep are often nearing 62 years, which is Deloitte's retirement age. The senior leaders are offering new and exciting jobs that include variety and flexibility. Many are encouraged to split their time between mentoring and staying in contact with top clients. The need for this type of program serves to illustrate just how foolish and archaic mandatory retirement ages are, no matter where they are set. Remember that when the age of 62 was set in 1935, people had a life expectancy of 63. Today's retirees live to an average of 83 years. Mentoring is one of the better examples of the immeasurable contribution senior stars can bring to the competitive workplace. What is the point of relegating all the wisdom and experience to the grandstand to watch? Many retired individuals are growing more miserable each passing day by sitting on a lifetime of knowledge that no one seems interested in anymore. Dr. Richard Johnson, author of the Retirement Preparedness Survey, says that if you are not preparing to become a mentor, you are preparing to become a curmudgeon.

What business does not have problems to solve that could not be addressed in part by the skills and savvy of a largely ignored population of 65 plus? And the idea that more mature workers are afraid of technology is fading as well. Surveys now show that those over 55 who are tech savvy spend as much time online as any other group. ThirdAge .com is a Web site that is aimed at boomers and even older users; it pulls over 1 million visits per month and has signed on over 10,000 people for courses in online technology. About a third of the people who work for ThirdAge are over 50 and tech savvy—exploding the myth that the new world of technology is the exclusive domain of pimple-faced revolutionaries.

> *"I wasn't ready to wrap my arms around my money and die."*
> —*Howard L. Agee, formerly retired retiree, 74*

Working for a "Playcheck"

For some folks in the retirement age group, the prospect of being able to work on something of significance is reward enough, especially after spending a considerable amount of time watching the clock and the world go around in traditional retirement. One company that has offered retirement age workers an opportunity to collect a "playcheck" (where the chief reward desired is the satisfaction of doing good work) is the Prudential Insurance Company of America, which offers people a couple of ways to get involved. Prudential offers both a temp service staffed by retirees and has launched Retirees Offering Community Service, a group of volunteers who meet monthly to organize such projects as food distribution and reading fairs.

We do not all work simply for a paycheck. There is so much more to defining the rewards of work than in strictly monetary terms. Currently, a vast army of experienced and eager individuals over 65 in this nation want to put their skills, their wisdom, and their hearts to work as well as their hands. All the companies and individuals we have mentioned thus far who are working past the traditional retirement boundaries are doing it, in part at least, to collect a playcheck. They derive a sense of satisfaction from the work, a sense of familial fraternization from the workplace, and a sense of personal identity from what they accomplish. It is soft-pedaling to simply call the ultimatum of retirement unnatural, for in some cases it is cruel. When the ultimatum of retirement removes an individual from the identity, satisfaction, and fellowship that brings a sense of purpose simply on the basis of age, that is indeed cruel.

Clearly the time has come for all companies to read the demographics, accept the fact that retirement should not be an either-or proposition, and begin offering its workforce the more natural and flexible *phased retirement*. The either-or approach to work and retirement does not work well for most retirees, and considering the demographics of the next 20 to 30 years, it will not work well for the corporation.

A Smoother Transition

"I used to roll around at night trying to figure out what I was going to do with all my time. Yes, I had been working for over 40 years, but I honestly liked many aspects of the work and especially some of the long-term client relationships I had formed. Friends would say, 'You've paid your dues, take some time for yourself.' The problem in taking all this time for myself was what to do with myself. I'm a hack golfer. I don't fish. I don't carve wood. I like action. I like chasing the deal. It bothered me that my company didn't have any middle ground for someone like me. I honestly wasn't up to the 50-hour weeks anymore, but a couple or three days a week would have suited me just fine. I approached the company about it, but they said it wasn't a part of their policy. Eight months after I retired I get a phone call from my old boss saying that the guy they hired to replace me had made a shambles of the territory. He did less work in a month than I used to do in a week and the clients didn't much like him. My ex-employer also told me that the company was introducing a new 'phased retirement' program and asked me if I would like to be one of the first to try it out. I about jumped right through the phone. I now work 10 to 12 days a month and I work hard when I

> *work. I'm productive, I'm back in contact with people I truly missed,*
> *and, let me tell you, the extra money doesn't hurt either. Why it took*
> *so long for somebody to come up with this is beyond me!"*
> —Marlin, "nonretired retiree," 66

We have witnessed many well-known executives staying productive because of their love for the game. Some examples are Kirk Kerkorian and Sumner Redstone wheeling and dealing in their 80s and Warren Buffett and Rupert Murdoch well into their 70s. Lee Iacocca, who re-appeared in ads at age 80, admits that he "flunked retirement."

Frederick Hudson, who believes age is a poor reason to put anyone on the shelf, thinks a better option than retirement is just "shifting gears

FIGURE 5.1 | Bell Curve or a Cliff?

The Retirement Cliff

The Gradual Retirement

The In & Out Retirement

every now and then—and not stopping doing anything." Stopping is where the danger starts. Hudson urges people 55 and older: "Look within yourself to find meaningful work and then make it happen!" There is no need for a work/retirement ultimatum in our corporations or in your life.

The New Retirementality Challenge

Do I have a plan for the future, or just a future with no plan?

Think about it: Do I have an ultimatum to retire? What might be my options? Can I see myself working for fun and reward rather than for just a paycheck?

Research it: What are the retirement policies of my current employer? What will be my resources, money, and skills at age 55, 65, 75? What are my options and future alternatives for work as I see it now?

Decide and take action:

- I will plan the balance of my life with transitions in mind.
- I (we) will begin to explore what life transitions may mean for me (us).

PART TWO

A New Way of Thinking

CHAPTER | 6

Work May Always
Be a Part
of Your Life

"How dull it is to pause, to make an end, to rust unburnished, not to shine in use! As though to breathe were life."

—*Alfred, Lord Tennyson*

Keeping Our Shine

When Tennyson wrote *Ulysses*, he took up the story of Ulysses where Homer left off. He is now an older man who finds that the home and the love he longed for while sojourning are not enough for contentment in these years. A life of idleness became a burden. Tennyson's story is a shining articulation of what can happen in traditional retirement. Retirement today puts people on society's back burner and tells them they should be happy to be there—but many are not. Many of those in retirement want to "shine in use." Tennyson's conclusion in poetry was also reached by Freud in science—that is, love and work are essentials in human life.

To many, *work* is a dirty word they want cleansed from their lives. At the outset of a new discussion around work, allow me to offer my own definition of what I mean when I use the word *work*—*a meaningful and productive engagement, paid or unpaid.* The focus is on doing something you find meaningful and that society finds productive. For such activities, we can collect either a material or an emotional pay-check—or both. Whether it be for pay or volunteer, we all need to know we can be useful.

As many baby boomers begin to enter their late 50s and 60s and re-alize they may be able to retire, they will have to grapple with the deci-sion of whether they will be happy doing little work or doing no work. An informal survey conducted by Businessweek Online found that a high percentage of people are concerned that their skills won't be used to the fullest as they near and pass retirement. Following are some of their answers to the poll:

1. Do you agree that over-55 workers constitute a talent pool that too many companies leave untapped?
   - Very much—64%
   - Somewhat—27%
2. Are you concerned that your skills won't be used to their fullest as you approach retirement and after retirement?
   - Very much—27%
   - Somewhat—38%
   - Slightly—13%
3. If your current employer offered you the opportunity to continue working on a less than full-time basis as you approach retirement or afterward, would you be interested?
   - Very much—48%
   - Somewhat—30%
   - Slightly—8%
4. If a new employer offered you the same opportunity, would you be interested?
   - Very much—47%
   - Somewhat—30%
5. Are you concerned that without some kind of employment, your postretirement years would be lacking?
   - Very much—23%
   - Somewhat—29%
   - Slightly—21%

Bear in mind when looking at these numbers that they refer to peo-ple who are looking *ahead* to retirement. As we'll see later in this chap-ter, the illusion of a blissful workless retirement diminishes the closer one gets to actual retirement and all but evaporates once one actually tastes a few months of retirement life. Generally speaking, we are not a species that is engineered to be happy doing nothing.

Imagine your average day in retirement. You get out of bed at 10 AM, wander around the house in your pajamas drinking a cup of coffee. You then turn on *Power Lunch* on TV, grab a book, and go to the club for lunch and your 2:00 PM tee-time. You come home after the round of golf for an evening of viewing sitcoms on television. How does this day sound to you? The people who feel imprisoned by their job impulsively say, "Yeah! That would work for me!" But the reality check is in contemplating this routine for the next 10,950 days of your life. If you were to retire at age 55, you've got another 30 years of your life to invest! The reality check is also asking what you're going to do on the days that it rains. I can't count the number of people I have met who reached this early retirement scenario by obsessing over investing their financial assets and gave little or no thought to how they would invest their chief asset—their life and energy. I have also met far too many retirees with little else to do than fret and obsess over their investments every waking day.

What is missing in this scenario? Let's add one more activity to this portrait and see what a difference it makes. You get out of bed at 7:00 AM and wander around the house in your pajamas drinking your coffee and contemplating your consulting work for the morning, which includes a conference call with a client at 11:00 AM. After that your working day is over and you head out to the club. If it rains, you have hobby or charitable activities to occupy your afternoon. Could you endure a routine like this for the next 10,950 days of your life? By adding engaging work and activities to this portrait, we make it a much more inviting and desirable picture.

To eradicate work from our life is to deny a meaningful aspect of our life. It is a denial of our very soul. Our soul finds pleasure in meaningful labor and productivity. Booker T. Washington in *Up from Slavery* wrote: "Hard work should not be avoided but sought out because it is hard work that makes the soul honest." This he wrote when observing the impact on the quality of life that worklessness wrought in the life of slaves who rejected work as evil. The bitter taste of slavery in their psyche caused many of them to avoid all work. Washington tried to show them that this view of work had led them into a new degradation of their own choosing. Is there an analogy here for those who have felt that workless retirement was the just solution for the years they spent "slaving" for a corporation they grew to despise? Is the workless state really a mirage that appears most enticing to the bitter and the burned out?

> *"I had achieved my American dream when I retired early at age 55. I was the envy of my peers. I had worked hard and invested well. I had been motivated by visions of fairway days and beachfront nights in Florida. I would never answer to anyone again. It didn't take long before I began getting this eerie feeling on the first tee that I was too young and valuable to be wasting all my life energy on leisure. But I just kept pushing those thoughts back. 'This is your reward,' I told myself, 'you've got what everyone else wants.' I was beginning to get bored and was spending more and more time at the 19th hole. I was forming bad habits. My wife couldn't wait to see me go out the door each day. My true reality check came one day when I ran into an old colleague who was five years older than me and who was still working. He looked great. I was now 62 but I looked like I was 70. He didn't say anything but the look in his eyes when he first saw me gave it away. A life of nothing but leisure had led to my accelerated decline. No one had ever mentioned anything about this side of the early retirement story."*
>
> —*Evan, retiree, 62*

The Significance of Work

We are, I believe, coming to grips with the significance that work brings into our life. Rather than viewing retirement as a cold turkey exit from the working world or a jump from the cliff of employment, we are beginning to view it as a transition or a segue. The transition ramp may be a gradual decline of hours spent on the job. It may be ramping up into free agency or another career. Why do so many retirees come back to work soon after they retire? Obviously they miss the significant aspects that work brings into their life.

Why do almost 80 percent of us say we want to continue working in some way, shape, or form? Because we realize that for all that we give to our work, work gives something back to us. When we strip away the

FIGURE 6.1 | Important Reasons for Working

Reasons	Percentage
To keep you mentally active	67%
To keep you physically active	57%
To keep you connected to others	48%
To keep health insurance and other benefits	45%
To help you make money	37%

Source: The Merrill Lynch New Retirement Survey, 2005.

annoying personalities and the frustrating tasks that our current job offers, we realize that work can provide great intangible rewards to our mind and spirit; camaraderie; shared victories and disappointments; identity; the adrenaline rush of the chase; building something out of nothing; moving from a concept to a reality; the realization that our efforts have influenced or helped people and the world we live in; relationships; and a sense of accomplishment. These benefits should not be underrated when assessing the place of work in our life.

Our nation's evolving attitude toward work was revealed in a 2005 HSBC study entitled "The Future of Retirement in a World of Rising Life Expectancies." In this study, 93 percent of Americans state that they should be able to go on working at any age if they are still capable; 64 percent feel that retirement is a chance to write a whole new chapter in their lives (versus 23 percent who see retirement as a relaxation period); and 46 percent indicate a desire to move back and forth between work and leisure. Add to this the fact that 35 percent of the respondents in a Merrill Lynch/Dychtwald study stated unequivocally that they would *never* retire.

By an overwhelming majority, retirees have decided that the best reason to keep involved is because of the vitality, energy, and perspicacity that work arouses. They have recognized the enjoyment that work brings even if part of their motive is the need for money. The realization comes to the majority of retirees sooner or later that the choice to retire entirely from productive engagements is not a good one.

End of the Ultimatum

We live in a society that still largely presents retirement as an ultimatum. Either you work or you retire. This ultimatum is foolish, counterintuitive, and counterproductive for the good of society. The recent changes in Social Security removing working limits from retirees is a flare signaling that we are no longer willing to be controlled by such ultimatums regarding work. Authors Stephen Pollan and Mark Levine said it well when they wrote that we are "no longer forced into patterns born in the industrial age." We can "forge patterns for the information age, an age in which work is more closely attuned to life. As their most powerful weapon, Boomers can call on common sense. The marketing of retirement has produced a society that's ill at ease and full of contradictions." They conclude with a statement that reveals the utter irony of retirement as an ultimatum: "Think about it. Isn't there something wrong when we kvetch that people with limited skills collect welfare rather than work—but ask our most valuable contributors to spend their days on a golf course?"

Yes, there is something wrong with this picture. In this chapter, you will be taken on a tour revealing how our generation feels about the place of work in our life and how and why we want to continue working. We saw in the previous chapter the force that our collective voice is exerting on corporate America to desert the ultimatum, the either-or approach to working and retirement. A few years from now, retirement as a cold turkey choice will no longer exist except in the most backward of corporate locales. Soon, mature employees will determine how long and how much they will work. This idea of phased retirement is just now gaining a foothold, and your voice will help to firmly entrench the idea as a permanent fixture in the work/retirement landscape.

First, we as individuals will reshape our ideas about work and retirement and then we individuals will reshape our institutions. Once our ideas become grounded in the realities of the age we live in, the institutions will have no choice but to follow. It is just a matter of time before the New Retirementality that will govern the next few decades rises from below the surface to shape the policies and programs of our corporations, our government, and the retirement savings industry as well. As we have already seen in Chapter 2, this New Retirementality led to the disappearance of work limitations on Social Security recipients. In Chapter 5, you saw how this mentality is causing a restructuring of corporate retirement programs into a more flexible and self-defined model. This new model of retirement will be significantly accelerated as employees begin to assert their expectations and demands for "working retirement."

New Retirement Realities

The Gallup organization and PaineWebber have conducted an on-going series of interviews with American investors from which they produce the *Index of Investor Optimism.* A report entitled *Retirement Revisited* provides an in-depth look at investors' changing perspectives toward retirement. This report was based on interviews conducted with 986 investors—all of whom are nonretired. Fifty-seven percent of those interviewed had investable assets of $10,000 to $100,000. The other 43 percent had investable assets of more than $100,000. The composite picture these people show of the retirement they desire is a far cry from the cold turkey exodus from the working world that retirees of the past have taken.

What do people want to do in retirement? The study reveals that the vast majority expect to continue with work to some degree. It doesn't seem to be work itself that people want to escape from but quite possibly the people they work for. This study reveals that the majority would like to try their hand at being their own boss. I suspect that this desire for autonomy has as much to do with the frustration of working for the inept, the control freak, and the duplicitous as much as it has to do with self-sufficiency. That aside, this study reveals four basic but distinct motivations for retirement:

1. Work as long as I can in the job I'm in (15 percent)—*"I'm going to die with my boots on."* The people in this group do not want to stop the work they are currently in. They enjoy the people they work with as well as the work they do. The only thing that will stop this group from working is waking up one day to face their inability to do the job—or not waking up at all! These individuals have found their niche and have no illusions about leaving.

2. Seek a new job or become an entrepreneur (60 percent)—*"It's time to do my own thing."* The people in this group see retirement as a chance to start their own business and follow their own dreams. First, there are those who would like to start a full-fledged business but want the security of retirement to take on such a venture.

Second, there are those who would like to turn their hobby or passion into an income-producing venture.

3. Seek work-life balance (10 percent)—*"There's more to life than making money."* The people in this group recognize the need for balance in their life. Many have been speeding along on a career carousel and feel that a preoccupation with work has caused much of life to go past them in a blur. They want to continue working but at a reduced or saner pace. They want to balance their work with the considerations of family, leisure, and general peace of mind. Many in this group want to find a way to work part-time or as a consultant. The marks of this motivation are a more relaxed pace and a trend toward simplification.

4. Enjoy a "traditional" retirement (15 percent)—*"Give me my passport, I'm outta here!"* This is the group that has had enough of work and just desires to spend the rest of their life enjoying the fruit of their labors. Their plans include travel, leisure, and sitting around contemplating how much they enjoy not having to go to work anymore. Some of the individuals in this group enjoyed their work throughout their career but simply feel that they have had enough of work and desire to travel and do what they want— with no deadlines or agendas. Others in this group so hated the work that they did and the toll of stress and hardship it exacted that they now have a strong enough aversion to work to keep them from ever going back. This group might also include some who are just inherently lazy and probably spent much of their "working" career dodging work anyway.

Some interesting patterns emerge from a closer look. For example, much can be learned about the philosophical shifts of maturity from the gradual increase in the Segment 1 response: *Work as long as I can.* The percentage of people saying they want to continue in their current job as long as they can rises dramatically with each age group, peaking with the 50- to 64-year-old. The most dramatic jump in this response is with women between the ages of 35 and 49 and between 50 and 64, with a leap from 12 percent to 22 percent—that is a gain of 83 percent! (See Figure 6.2.) The Merrill Lynch study confirms the Gallup opinions with some new twists—one being that 42 percent of respondents indi-

FIGURE 6.2 | Workforce Mobility

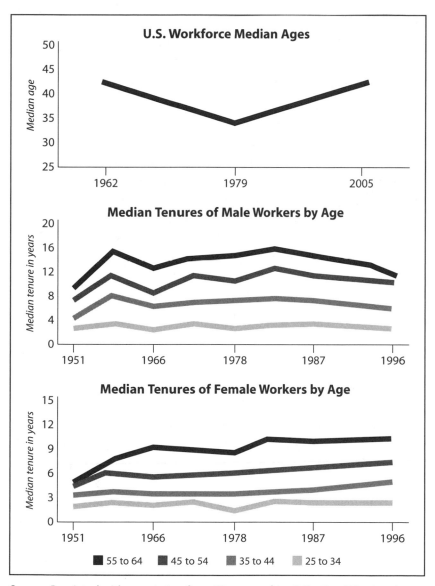

Source: Reprinted with permission from "Demographics & Destiny: Winning the War for Talent," copyright Watson Wyatt Worldwide, 1999.

cate a desire to "cycle between work and leisure." Only 17 percent in the study said they never wanted to work for money again. There are two conclusions we could draw from this trend in age-based thinking:

1. The more you mature, the more you appreciate the value of work in your life.
2. The increasing desire to work as you age will allay some of your fiscal fears and pressures of retirement.

Let's examine these conclusions more closely.

You appreciate the value of work in your life more as you mature.
My barber, Dave, who recently turned 50, informed me that listening to the postretirement stories in his chair convinced him to make some changes in his retirement goals. He has now decided, health providing, to keep cutting hair at least a couple of days a week, until he is in his 80s. He has also decided to not deny himself some of the pleasures of travel and leisure that he was putting off until his "retirement" years. "Why should I wait until I'm less mobile to do all the things I want to do? Why not do them while I can fully enjoy them? Plus, I enjoy this work and the contacts it provides. Why should I leave it altogether?"

My barber has recognized that the compartmentalization of work and leisure into "working" years and "retirement" years is not a healthy thing. Just as it is important to always have time for leisure, it is equally important to always have some time for work.

It is possibly a condition of youth to undervalue the ameliorating aspects of meaningful labor. It is unlikely that the young worker who sits and dreams of retiring at 35 has seriously contemplated the realities of 50 years of worklessness. There is no doubt that the closer today's workers get to retirement, the less thrilled they are with the thought of a workless life. The desirability of their career seems to grow in attraction as people age. This parallel between age and the desire to stay in one's current job might also be an indication that by the time people reach a certain age, they have settled in careers they are quite comfortable with. We might ask, for example, if you haven't found the work you like by the time you are 45 to 50 years old, are you ever going to find it? If a person hasn't found work he or she likes by the age of 50, the law of averages is against that person making such a move after 50 for financial security reasons.

Research shows that as the workforce ages, it becomes less mobile. (See Figure 6.2.) This is as true of baby boomers as it is of any other generation. When people reach a certain age (45 and older), they look for a much more secure working situation. The average job tenure for a 45-year-old male or female worker is typically twice that of a 35-year-old worker (6 to 8 years versus 3 to 4 years). The average tenure for a 55-year-old is three times that of the 35-year-old (12 years). As the boomers age, their job tenures also rise dramatically. Another reason baby boomers will change jobs much less as they age and will begin to look for more paternalistic cultures is to feel more of a sense of safety in their mature years. Because many baby boomers have insufficient savings when they reach 45 or beyond, they will be looking more to employers for retirement security.

A majority of people have already made a number of career shifts by the time they reach these later working years and have an increased level of comfort in the jobs they find themselves in. When you look at the age at which people are expecting to retire based on their current age, the same pattern of mature workers desiring continued work emerges—at least for males. Thirty-two percent of males aged 50 to 64 expect to work past age 66 into their 70s, compared with only 15 percent of males aged 35 to 49. About one-third of the respondents who expected to keep working stated the reason was finances compared with two-thirds who stated that it was a matter of choice. It could be said that it is an illusion of youth to desire a "workless" life.

> *"I started noticing that my mother was growing progressively more uptight the closer she moved to her retirement date, which was coming in the summer. She was turning 65 and had told us about her plans to increase her gardening and her social life and maybe even to travel and see some family members she had lost touch with. But whenever we brought up the approaching date, she grew short and dismissive in her tone. So finally I asked, 'Mom, are you not excited about retiring anymore?'*
>
> *"'No,' she said, 'from a distance it looks like the greatest thing in the world. But as the final sands of work are falling, I realize how much I love this job. I enjoy the friendship of the people I work with and all the clients I've gotten to know through the years. They are all like an extended family to me. It almost feels like it did when all of*

you kids left home, except this time it's me that's leaving. We talk at work about how we'll keep in touch and all that but I know it will never be the same.'

"I asked my mom if she had talked to the owner about staying on in a part-time role. She said she hadn't because she thought it would be inconvenient for him because the job required full-time attention. I told her to go ahead and have the conversation, and that she might be surprised at his response. She called me back a couple of days later full of excitement. Her boss was absolutely thrilled to have her stay on for any amount of hours she was comfortable with. He said he trusted her and would be much more comfortable knowing that she was still around to keep an eye on things and to interact with his clients."

—Laura, 37

Once we find work we really enjoy, the payoff becomes more than the paycheck. Why walk away from a meaningful payoff if you don't need to? As people age, they must be careful to not confuse the desire to cut back on working hours with the choice to retire altogether. Many reading this book may have parents who are living according to the old paradigm of the work or retirement ultimatum. They may be grudgingly accepting a situation they are not going to be happy with, like Laura's mother. In such cases the children may need to play the role of explaining the options that today's corporate climate might offer to the parent. For the person who really wants to continue working, there is a way to make it work.

The Societal Payoff

The increasing desire to work as you age will allay some of your fiscal fears and pressures of retirement. It is this simple desire to keep working that will redeem not only the solvency of our Social Security system but our personal retirement scenarios as well. It is ironic to note that the work ethic of the baby boomers may be the saving grace of the Social Security system that boomers have so little confidence in. According to a Harris Interactive survey, only 50 percent of the baby boomers believe that Social Security will deliver every dollar it has promised compared with the 79 percent in the preceding generation who have faith in Social Security. Whether baby boomers end up working past traditional retirement age because they need to or because they want to, their continuing to work will add life expectancy to Social Security coffers.

As traditional retirement continues to go out of style, the U.S. economy will benefit in many ways:

- The U.S. government will realize an enormous tax windfall, assuming taxation rates continue as they are.
- Much more money will be added to Social Security and Medicare, thereby postponing or eliminating the risk of insolvency.
- By working through retirement years, boomers will delay the jettisoning of their financial assets. The fact that they are working will give them more time to add to their 401(k) and IRA assets.
- We can safely speculate that retaining the talent and abilities of this experienced group in the workplace will end up fueling economic growth.

> *"I remember reading all those retirement tables that said I had to have enough money to get 80 percent of my current income to be able to enjoy my retirement years. It used to make me so depressed to read those tables and calculate my shortfall. I think it's ironic how things have actually worked out. I decided to take Social Security at age 62. My employer agreed to put me on a part-time consulting contract. My mortgage is now paid, my children are grown up, and my general expenses are lower. I don't even need to take distributions from my retirement funds, and they are still growing. The financially miserable retirement hell I once envisioned has never materialized and it's more like retirement heaven. I have the money I need and I have an interesting balance of things to do to occupy my mind and time."*
>
> *—Tom T., nonretired worker, 66*

Many of you will continue working because you want to. Some of you will continue working because you need to; even if this is the case, you will one day realize that it was not a bad thing. Freud observed that love and work were essential to finding meaning and happiness in life. Understanding how these two forces work together can lead to lasting happiness. Lasting love requires work. Lasting work requires that we love what we do.

The New Retirementality Is . . .	• Seeking retirement with meaningful work as a part of it.
	• Knowing that work can play a significant role in your life at any age.
	• Finding work that you enjoy and that keeps you sharp and involved.

The New Retirementality Challenge

Is my financial information easily available or is it scattered in the drawers and files of neglect?

Think about it: Am I willing to do the work to put my financial information in order? Am I really challenged and invigorated by work?

Research it: What monies do I have now?

Company pension plans: How much? Where?

Personal tax-deferred savings: IRA? Roth IRA? Variable annuities? Life insurance with cash value?

Other long-term savings accounts: Real estate? Stock or business ownership? Other assets?

Decide and take action:

• What more (or less) can I (or should I) do?
• Are we in agreement on the necessity of developing a plan for our future?

CHAPTER 7

"You're Only Old When You Think You Are"

Mapmakers in medieval times faced a real problem. They were given the job of charting the continent but were not exactly well traveled themselves. So when they came to a border they had not crossed, they drew fire-breathing dragons toward their own country's boundaries. These maps, when viewed by the common masses, caused people to believe that if they crossed the border, they would be consumed by these infernal beasts. Needless to say, travel agents were having a tough go of it.

Being fully enlightened today, we know there are no dragons to fear. Yet the great majority of the masses never cross the restricting borders they face.

Many people, when challenged to try new things, to go to new places, or to try doing things in a different way, simply refuse. When asked, "Why?" they simply respond, "I don't know—I just don't want to."

We can all try new ventures, we can all stretch our abilities, we can all give more than we do. Each of us has the ability to test our endurance a bit further. Without taking risks, we settle into a quicksand called "complacency." You can make the decision to cross a new border—unless, of course, you believe in dragons.

"I think that anytime you say that after 65 is the time to retire, it's crazy. Some people are old and tired at 55, and some people are wild men at 72."

—J. Peter Grace, senior executive

"I think the notion of retiring makes people old."

—Penelope Russianoff, psychotherapist

How old is old? What exactly do we mean when we say someone is old? Are we referring to the person's years on the planet or the person's state of being? Or both? By old, do we mean that a person is in a state of decline? Is there a predictable age when this decline commences for all people? Is "old" a manmade border? And do the dragons of decline exist mostly in our mind? Henry Ford said that when a person stops learning, he is old, whether he is 29 or 65. As you will discover in the pages ahead, there isn't much we can do about aging, but there is an awful lot we can do about growing old. We hold "old" at bay by focusing on successful aging.

As demonstrated in Chapter 1, the cornerstone of traditional retirement is the premise that a person is old at 65. When retirement was invented, many could expect to live a few months to a couple of years past their retirement age. It was safer to say that, at that time, 65 was old. Today, however, if you retire as a 65-year-old, you can expect to live another 20 years. Where does your marker for old fall? 70? 80? 90?

We, as a generation, are a people obsessed with youthfulness and longevity. Most of us have no interest in becoming old. Although some choose only superficial fixes to delay the ascetic signs of aging, most of us are interested in the internal and lifestyle fixes that will delay the process of aging and becoming old. According to a Roper/AARP study, "Boomers Envision Retirement II," 63 percent of boomers feel younger than their actual age, up from 47 percent in 1998. Those who feel younger attribute the difference to a general attitude of feeling younger (41 percent), having good health (26 percent), and staying in good shape (19 percent). In this chapter, we will discover just how the definition of old is changing and exactly what we can do to keep aging at bay. We can all become the fortunate recipients of the insights gained from modern studies on aging and longevity. As it turns out, one of the greatest enablers of the aging process is the old, worn-out concept of *retirement.*

If not put to use, the fruit extracted from the vine will simply rot. For many, the date of retirement is the date of extraction. We will explore the beneficial findings about successful aging and hear the stories of those who live and breathe these truths in their later years.

Thriving, Not Just Surviving

I have personally always found a great deal of inspiration from active, vital people in their later years of life. I enjoy studying not only their habits but their personalities and attitudes as well. I think a holistic view of successful aging is necessary because there are always exceptions to the lists of aging do's and don'ts. I have met individuals who eat hearty portions of eggs and bacon every morning, smoke all day, drink whiskey at night, and are living vibrant, productive lives in their 90s. Although I realize they are violating all the recommended physical habits, there is something in their overall approach to life that has helped them survive and thrive as long as they have. Some would argue that it is simply a matter of good genes—but good genes can help us only to survive, not thrive.

In studying how people thrive late into life, I have read numerous biographies of people whose life and careers outlasted their peers. While reading these biographies and autobiographies, I have searched for the intangibles that these people had in common. These biographies have included people like Winston Churchill, Dr. Albert Schweitzer, Linus Pauling, Norman Vincent Peale, and some modern examples like Peter Drucker, Studs Terkel, and many more of lesser notoriety but longer lives. The common thread through all these stories is that they outlasted their peers not only in longevity but in usefulness and purposeful living as well. One of my favorite and most illustrative biographies was an old book on the life of Satchel Paige.

Satchel Paige was arguably the best pitcher to ever play professional baseball. It is estimated that he won over 800 games in his unparalleled career. Because of racial boundaries, he didn't get the opportunity to display his talents outside the Negro leagues until the color barrier was broken by Jackie Robinson. When Satchel Paige did get his chance to pitch in the major leagues, he was elected the American League Rookie of the Year at the age of 43! Think about this. A very short list of men have possessed the endurance to pitch at age 43. Satchel Paige was the

Rookie of the Year at that age! He pitched in the majors until he was in his early 50s and continued to pitch professionally until he was 63 years old. Satchel Paige understood a few things about longevity.

Because of preconceptions about age and ability, Satchel Paige always tried to keep his age a mystery. Whenever he was queried about his age, he would provide a memorable quip like, "How old would you be if you didn't know how old you were?" Or "I never look back on Father Time . . . he might be gaining on me."

Hardening of the Attitudes

Paige's biography reveals some good habit patterns not only physically but attitudinally as well. Because of stomach problems early in his life, Paige stopped eating fried foods and ate boiled chicken and broccoli as a regular part of his diet. Obviously, he worked out every day. What most impressed me, however, were his mental habits. He displayed certain personality traits that I have also noted in a high percentage of the long-lasting crowd. There were a certain pugnacity and stubbornness that led to his not giving in to social norms and expectations. It is an attitude that says, "No one but me will define what my life will be." Such attitudes seem to be carried by those with a strong independent streak who, at times, seem as though they have something to prove. That "something" they have to prove seems to be that age shows up in the mind long before it shows up in the body.

Enduring Attitudes

Other characteristics apparent from biographies of the "enduring" are their ready wit and lively sense of humor—especially regarding themselves. That those exhibiting longevity seem to share a self-deprecating approach to life tells me that such an approach is crucial to reducing stress. The connection between stress and illness is well established. The connection between one's attitude and stress level is obvious. Satchel Paige and others I have read about seemed to possess not only a lively sense of humor but other survivor attitudes toward life's stressors. Most were forward-looking and concerned about the future as well as the present. Most refused to succumb to society's limiting views of age-related behavior and activity. They were people who truly believed they could control their own destiny.

In a speech entitled "Don't Ever Grow Old," I share insights into the lives of Paige, Schweitzer, Pauling, and others, and then ask the audience to answer the question, "How old would *you* be if you didn't know how old you were?" Most people can immediately give an age—and that age is often 15 to 20 years less than the one on their driver's license.

Author Dr. Michael F. Roizen has written a *New York Times* bestseller entitled *Real Age* that enlarges on this idea of locating each individual's "real age," which is the true reflection of one's physical and mental state. Roizen and his associates, after poring over 25,000 medical studies, came to the conclusion that age is much more than a chronological marker. Dr. Roizen presents physical, mental, and lifestyle criteria by which each individual can gauge his or her own aging process. In fact, Roizen and his associates came up with over 100 different health behaviors, ranging from diet to stress control, that enable you to assess your real age. More than a chronological marker, age is really the rate at which your internal guardians of health—cardiovascular and immune systems—decline. There is much we can do to slow that decline.

Roizen's book includes a real age test that you can take to see how old you really are. This test covers a broad range of health factors, including habits and conditions (smoking, sex, diet, exercise, driving, drinking, prescription drugs, exposure to dangerous activities), nutritional intake, weight, health history, family genes, stress, social connections, and relaxation practices. After this assessment, Roizen challenges readers to develop an Age Reduction Program. He provides evidence that such a program helps you live and feel up to 26 years younger; many physical, mental, and spiritual practices can add years to our lives.

A MacArthur Foundation study on aging described how one ages successfully. It used the term *a sense of mastery* to describe how individuals must believe in their ability to influence events and control their outcomes to be positive and productive in their later years. They found that during a period of less than three years, those who increased their sense of mastery also increased their productivity. The opposite also held true—those whose sense of personal mastery decreased saw a significant reduction in their involvement in productive activities. What exactly is personal mastery? It is self-reliance.

A person who takes a passive approach to life and lacks the ability to take action will experience a lack of productivity at any age. Typically, as people age, their belief in their abilities and their power to control their own destiny grows. However, this belief can, if allowed to do so, reach a point of diminishing returns. Experiments and experience have shown that if people are willing to try new things in their mature years, their self-reliance and effectiveness can flourish to all-time highs. Stories abound of people creating new boundaries in their life in their later years—those who are flying on airplanes who have never flown, those who are taking up new courses of study, and those who are dabbling in new ventures and careers at ages others would consider old. Take, for example, Florence, who started driving an 18-wheeler semi at the age of 83 to become the oldest "rookie" in the history of the truck-driving industry!

Habits of the Self-Reliant

What exactly does it take to become more self-reliant and shift our life into a higher state of confidence and healthy, active living? Three important factors come into play:

1. An opportunity to undertake a specific action that challenges one's sense of self-sufficiency without overwhelming it
2. The presence of supporting and reassuring others
3. The experience of succeeding at something with confirming feedback from others

A sense of confidence works on the same dynamics at any age. We imagine ourselves doing something. We muster the courage and abandon our inhibitions to try it. We look for feedback for our efforts from the people around us. A historical pitfall of aging is the narrowed radius of the comfort zones that can control a person at age 65. "I've never done that," or "I don't know anything about computers," or "I'm too old to start that now" are examples of verbal indicators that the fossilizing process is already under way. The fact that you often hear 50-year-old people making such statements is proof that old can start at any age.

Out with the Old

Old itself is on the verge of becoming old. The 65-plus population in this country is no longer content to be defined by classic definitions of *old* and *senior citizen*. With the advent of baby boomers into the ranks of the mature, this trend only promises to continue. A major component in this shifting paradigm of life is the evolving nature and definition of *retirement*. At one time, retirement was the shortest stage of a person's life. Now it may be the longest stage. An individual may now spend 30 years in so-called retirement. I would prefer to call it emancipated living because, for a majority of us, there is going to be nothing retiring about it.

In a study by Peter D. Hart Research Associates entitled "The New Face of Retirement: Older Americans, Civic Engagement, and Longevity Revolution," the reasons for the changing definition of old in our modern world become quite clear. Longer working lives—either paid or volunteer—are a cornerstone of this shifting definition. As long as people are civically, socially, and economically engaged, they will refuse to age as their predecessors in retirement did. The Hart study offered the following profile of older Americans.

Profile of Older Americans

- Education: Seven in ten (70 percent) have some education beyond high school, including one in six (17 percent) who have a college education or beyond. While less than one-third of today's adults 70–74 have some college education, that percentage will rise to over 50 percent by 2015.
- Marital status: Almost six in ten (53 percent) are married; about one in three are widowed (32 percent) or divorced or separated (10.7 percent).
- Income: 50.5 percent have an annual income over $35,000; 32.5 percent have an annual income over $45,000; for one-third of Americans over 65, 90 percent of their income is from Social Security. The major other sources of income as reported by the Social Security Administration for older persons in 2002 were income from assets (reported by 55 percent), private pensions (reported by 29 percent), government employee pensions (reported by 14 percent), and earnings (reported by 22 percent).
- Fitness: More than six in ten (63 percent) are physically active and report participating in exercise or fitness activities on a regular basis.
- Activities: Only about one in five (20 percent) are limited in their daily activities by physical or health conditions.
- Volunteering: Nearly three in four (74 percent) report having been involved in volunteer or community service activities in the past year.

- Lifestyle: About one in three (35 percent) report living or spending time in more than one area.

The numbers in these categories indicate a graying population that is healthy, active, adventurous, and more prosperous than ever before. These numbers only promise to rise with the influx of baby boomers in the 65-plus category between now and the year 2030. In the 1960s, there were 17 million Americans aged 65 and older. Today there are approximately 37 million. By 2030 there will be 70 million aged 65 and older. That number will be somewhere between 20 to 25 percent of the entire population.

As more graying Americans prepare to spend a large part of their life in "retirement," their attitudes toward this stage of life are extremely optimistic; 64 percent say they are currently enjoying either "the best" or "good" times in their life. When you put a magnifying glass on the everyday activities and interests of these so-called retirees, you begin to see why their enthusiasm and optimism flourishes. They are a dynamic and engaged group of people. They object to traditional labels given to their age group, such as "elderly," "old," or even "seniors." They see themselves as experienced, wise, and seasoned.

Today's 70-year-old came of age in a radically changing world. Their experiences were sandwiched between the classic struggles of the Great Depression, World War II, and the rules-breaking, question-everything Vietnam War generation. Today's 70-year-olds don't think like the 70-year-olds of the past, who had depression-era memories locked into their psyches.

> "It seems to me in a way that we are a hybrid generation, sitting between what Tom Brokaw calls the 'best generation' and the 1960s. The previous generation and the '60s were antithetical to each other ... here we sit influenced by both. ... As children at the end of the depression years, things were lockstep and you didn't deviate one bit versus the '60s when you could do anything you wanted. We were exposed to both."
>
> —Retired physician, 67

This generation with a hybrid view is already changing the way people look at "old" and "retirement." Not all are living by the traditionally accepted norms for work and activity for their age group. With the graying of the baby boom generation, we can surmise that the concepts of "old" and "retirement" will be radically redefined or disappear altogether.

Aging Americans are almost unanimous in voicing one conclusion about their later years: their retirement *will not* be like the retirement of their parents' generation. When asked specifically about this issue, 80 percent rejected the idea that "my retirement is or will be similar to my parents' retirement." This generation of retirees is beginning to paint a new backdrop for the portrait of "retirement living."

"Golden, Schmolden"

In the beginning of the retirement concept, the few years remaining were viewed as a fading flame. With the propaganda of the 1950s and 1960s, it was seen as a time for leisure or the "golden years." Today the picture being painted by new retirees is a whole new image. They no longer embrace retirement as a time to just stay busy but rather as a time to engage in meaningful activities that mark a new beginning and not the commencement of a gradual decline. Having a full schedule is no longer enough. It is having a fulfilled life that matters. Today's retirees have learned many lessons from viewing the leisure-focused "golden years" retirees that preceded them; namely, a life focused only on ease and leisure has very short-lived rewards. For many, a life of total ease preceded a life of disease.

> *"I've noticed an interesting phenomenon with my retired friends who have become ill and/or died a short time into their retirement. The physical malady almost always seemed to be preceded by a mental one—boredom. They were disengaged from the part of their being that gave them satisfaction their entire life. They'd try to fulfill themselves on the golf course or through some exotic travel but kept coming back to the same problem. They felt too young and useful to be 'goofing off' all the time. If they didn't respond to this problem with some meaningful pursuit, they just seemed to get sick, and sometimes they died. For these people, a life of ease was really one step from a life of disease."*
>
> *—Art, retired attorney, 70*

It seems as though everyone knows people who fit the description above—retirees who have worked their entire life for a vision of the golden years. They chased an illusion—a life spent in leisure—as a reward for all their years of hard work. It didn't take long, however, for many in this group to discover that boredom was public enemy number one. They then began to focus on being busy. Ask many of today's current retirees or older citizens how things are going and you are more than likely going to hear, "I'm keeping busy." They are conscious of the devil named boredom and are running from him. Eighty-three percent of those surveyed in the Hart study said that they had enough to do to keep themselves as busy and fulfilled as they would like. This sentiment is shared by both men and women and by Americans of every income and education level.

But being busy is not enough. Today's older Americans no longer seem content to simply be busy. They are examining the events of their daily schedule and questioning the personal satisfaction level those activities can deliver. Sixty percent said that they rated "feeling valued and needed" as a 9 or a 10 on a 10-point scale of importance in terms of being fulfilled. Also, 53 percent expressed the same sentiments about "being intellectually challenged."

Bored in retirement is just one of many stereotypes that today's retirees are going to change. They have very strong objections to other ideas that people have about their age group. When asked what stereotypes about the 65-plus age group bothered them most, they expressed a number of concerns, including these:

- Their intellectual abilities are diminished.
- Their activities are greatly limited by physical weakness or poor health.
- They don't really want to learn new things or start new activities.
- Their opportunities to make a difference are mostly behind them.
- They are just interested in leisure activities like golf and bridge.

According to a study by Alexis Abramson and Merril Silverstein, despite having knowledge about many aspects of aging, many Americans are still under the misconceptions that the majority of older people live below the poverty line (64 percent); that older people say they are often angry or irritated (69 percent), bored (64 percent), or lonely (73 percent); that at least one in ten is institutionalized (85 percent); and that the health and economic status of the elderly in the next couple of decades will probably be the same or worse than it is now (77 percent). Many stereotypes are still common. Almost half (47 percent) feel that the majority of older people cannot adapt to change; almost two-fifths (39 percent) feel that older workers aren't as effective as younger workers; and almost one-third (32 percent) feel that older persons have no capacity for sex.

> *"The only thing that has ever made me feel old is those few times where I allow myself to be predictable. Routine is death."*
> —*Carlos Santana*

How Old Would You Be?

The New Retirementality means we keep ourselves connected to the community and the world around us. We do not move out. We do not go south in our lives. Retirement doesn't mean we're tired of living or absorbed in our own decline. Purpose does not leave with age. The flow of activity can someday slow to a trickle but it will not turn off. We can stay engaged to our dying breath, and by virtue of being engaged, we will prolong that breath for many years.

According to the National Center on Women and Aging, we might all be able to learn something about successful aging from older women. Over 50 percent stated that aging turned out to be better than they expected, and older women are no more likely than younger women to report they have a disability. The women in this study offered four keys for successful aging:

1. Stay as active as you can—not just physically but also mentally and socially
2. Be a saver
3. Live within your means
4. Keep the connections to family, friends, and community alive and strong

Women who are working are signficiantly more likely to report that experience with aging has been better than expected (58 percent versus 49 percent).

Aging has far less to do with our age than was previously thought. The longevity revolution is not exclusively attributable to medical breakthroughs, although they are foundational to longer living. This revolution is also the result of people awakening to the self-responsibility aspects of aging. They are discovering that by forming and following healthy habits physically, mentally, socially, occupationally, and spiritually, they can not only increase their years but can multiply contentment in life as well.

There are people who feel old at 37. That aged feeling is the composite view of their habits, attitudes, and approach to life. There are others who feel young and energetic at 75. If old were strictly a matter of age, this paradox would not be possible. In Lydia Bronte's book *The Longevity Factor,* the author wrote:

> The transformation of the life span will almost certainly have a powerful impact in your own life. You may not wake up at fifty and wonder what to do next but you could very easily do so at sixty-five. You won't automatically be "old" when you reach sixty-five, and you won't necessarily be ready to "retire" at that age. In fact, you may not get old physically until much, much later than sixty-five—or you may live into your eighties or nineties without becoming physically old at all.

Older men and women, when given more help than they need, may not be assertive enough in discouraging that help. The more unneeded assistance they receive will eventually take a toll. Older individuals who do not help, or are prevented from helping, themselves edge their way into a state known as "learned helplessness." This is one course the lifetime learner does not need to take. Self-sufficiency, self-efficacy, and self-confidence all play major roles in successful aging.

> *"I am long on ideas but short on time. I expect to live to be only about a hundred."*
> —Thomas Edison

One way to keep these powerful internal forces alive in our life is to continue being engaged in work and activities that place a demand on our physical, mental, and creative resources. As more and more people discover they are not as old as society tells them they ought to be at age

65, they will continue to be engaged in work and society. They will be movers and shakers. Their pace may slow some, but they will still be in the race and not in the bleachers.

It is only when we start looking backward and talking about life in the past tense that we know the process of old has begun in our life. Remember what Satchel Paige said regarding Father Time: "I don't ever look back; he might be gaining on me."

| **The New Retirementality Is . . .** | • Not talking about getting old as if you are used up.
• Marking your age by your physical and mental well-being and not by your date of birth.
• Working until the age you wish to work.
• Planning to be self-reliant and to thrive in later years. |

CHAPTER 8

Staying Connected to the World

> "I think 65 is a phony age. I don't see why we should be losing the productivity of people at a certain age. There is very little reason why there should be an artificial age limitation at all."
>
> —Elinor Guggenheimer, author

> "If Jack McKeon can win a World Series at age 72, I've got to believe I've still got a few wins left in me."
>
> —68-year-old retiree

The modern retiree has no patience with aged stereotypes about aging and is establishing new cornerstones for a redefined retirement living. In the process of doing so, according to the Hart study, "Americans aged 50 to 75 speak with a loud and harmonious voice in describing their approach to retirement and later life and, in doing so, they are laying to rest many traditional clichés." The new definition of retirement overwhelmingly advocated by today's retiree is one that emphasizes activity and engagement over leisure and rest. About 70 percent of those aged 50 to 75 (both retired and not yet retired) who were surveyed said they view retirement as "a time to begin a new chapter in life by being active and involved, starting new activities, and setting new goals." It is a time to break out of the cocoon, not go into one. Only 28 percent of those in this age group preferred the definition offered by traditional retirement as, "a time to take it easy, take care of yourself, enjoy leisure activities, and take a much deserved rest from work and responsibilities."

It is important to note the diversity of the group that embraces this new definition. It appeals equally to men and women, liberals and conservatives, all regions of the country, people in their 50s as well as people in their 70s, people who are limited by physical or medical conditions and those who are not. It is an especially appealing definition to the better-educated and higher-income seniors. Fifty-six percent of those with a high school education chose the new definition of retirement, whereas 73 percent of those with a college education chose the same. The Hart study put it this way, "The better-educated and more affluent older Americans seem to express with even greater intensity a desire to continue to find new challenges in retirement to supplement their hard-sought professional identities."

One way many seniors are incarnating this new definition is by refusing to leave the workplace altogether. They see it as the glue that guarantees an active and challenging life. Forty-two percent of nonretired people aged 50 to 75 report that they plan to work either part-time or full-time, or part-time at another job after retiring from their main job. Currently, almost one in five older Americans who are retired from their principal career continue to work at another job. This number will rise steadily in the next 10 to 30 years. According to a 2003 study by the AARP, nearly 70 percent of workers who have not yet retired (ages 50–70) report that they plan to work into their retirement years or never retire, and almost half indicate that they envision working into their 70s or beyond. The prevailing motive for remaining at work for these people is "to stay active and involved" rather than financial need, although for many, financial need will play a critical role.

Ageism lawsuits are on the rise and will continue to escalate. Americans are beginning to refuse to be defined and categorized as unproductive because of their age. There is a widespread disdain among older people about being shut off from mainstream workplaces and society, and being tagged with disliked titles such as *senior citizen* or *golden ager.* These terms, many feel, are thin veneers for "used up" or "useless."

Today's employer will have to reassess hiring and retirement practices tainted with ageism. Gray hair and wrinkles are no reason to refuse admittance to or invite departure from a workforce. We will be hearing more about age prejudice and ageism settlements in the next few years. Societal and corporate laws and practices will have to change to accommodate updated definitions of old in our society. And have no doubt about it, the 60-plus boomer crowd will have the clout to get the job done. This is a generation that will be defined by their abilities—not by their date of birth.

Other priorities esteemed by this age group underscore the acceptance of the new retirement definition. Their priorities include:

- Volunteering and being involved in community service
- Being involved in sports and fitness activities
- Taking courses for continuing education

These priorities prove that we are preparing for a new era of retirement living. It will be a vigorous and involved stage of life as opposed to a withdrawing and "retiring" stage. The Hart study, "Older Americans, Civic Engagement, and the Longevity Revolution," concludes: "The distinct priorities and values of this generation, coupled with the unique circumstances of their era, will create a new model for retirement—one that places a premium on meaningful and fulfilling activity and engagement in the community and one that creates an enormous reservoir of talent, energy, and experience that the country can ill afford to ignore."

Lydia Bronte, in her book *The Longevity Factor,* made this observation about participants in the "Long Careers Study": "What emerges from their life stories is a view of the long lifetime different from what we might expect: an affirmation of the increasing richness of experience over time, of a deeper sense of identity, of a greater self-confidence and creative potential that can grow rather than diminish with maturity. It is obvious that seen through the eyes of the study participants, chronological age markers (like 65), which have held so much power in the past, are really culturally created—a norm that was accurate only for a particular place and time."

These studies demonstrate the redefining of the age and life stage of 65 plus. Why is it that when we talk of the maturity of money, we think of it as a positive form of growth; but when we talk about the maturity of people, we think of it as a time of depreciation? Within a decade or so we will see many examples of people's greatest harvest of accomplishment and contribution coming after the age of 65. There are thousands of examples out there right now—we just need to take notice.

Do you now see the need for renaming this stage of life something other than *retirement?*

Keys to Living Long

The MacArthur Foundation sponsored an elaborate study on aging that concluded that the three indicators of successful aging are:

1. Avoiding disease and disability
2. Maintaining mental and physical function
3. Continuing engagement with life

Many factors come into play in order to age successfully. The physical, intellectual, social, and spiritual aspects of our being must be attended to equally if we hope to hold back the hands of time. We can readily observe the effect of not attending to one or more of these areas in the lives of people we know who practiced such negligence. It does not take long for the aging process to kick into high gear if we let down our guards of discipline and purposefulness. Jimmy Carter, in his book *The Virtues of Aging,* wrote:

> What should our major goals be as we prepare for our later years? You may be surprised to learn that one of the most important should be our own happiness. I don't think this to be a selfish approach, because it will inevitably open up better relationships with others. It should be clear that happiness does not come automatically, but is something for which we must strive forthrightly, enthusiastically, and with imagination. This engagement in living—successful adjustment to the changing conditions we have to face—will inevitably involve us with responsibilities, challenges, difficulties and perhaps pain. But these experiences will tend to keep us closer to others and allow us to develop more self-respect and mastery over our own lives—crucial elements for a good life.

From Carter's comments you could conclude that the first key to aging successfully is to take an interest in yourself. It doesn't take long in the company of elderly people to figure out which ones are feeling sorry for themselves and which ones are extracting every ounce of life's possibilities. Those who succeed are self-respecting enough to keep their bodies fit, their minds challenged, and their hearts engaged.

The Vitamin Cs of Successful Aging

Aging reflects the relationship of time on our being. Aging describes, in large part, the state of our body. *Old,* on the other hand, describes our state of mind. It has always been a matter of great interest to me to discover the spiritual and attitudinal aquifer that supplies the fountain of youth.

Look around and you will see the role spirit and attitude play in relationship to the concept of being old. Do you know any 75-year-olds who act like they are 35? Do you know any 40-year-olds who act like they are 80? If you answered "yes" to either question, you are affirming the attitudinal and spiritual source of that which separates those who are aging from those who are old. This distinction was well described by the apostle Paul in his letter to Corinth: "Though our outward man perishes, our inward man is renewed day by day."

There is no denying the effects of time on our bodies. Although we can slow certain physical impacts, we cannot prevent them altogether. Hair turns gray or falls out. Skin wrinkles. Senses like hearing and sight can begin to dull—as can short-term memory function. As George Burns once quipped: "You know you're getting older when everything hurts, and what doesn't hurt doesn't work."

Equally immutable as the decaying dynamic of physical being is the constantly renewing and refreshing dynamic of our inner being. This dynamic of engaged living until the day we die is not automatic but is accomplished by the purposeful and intentional discipline of those souls who choose to *live* every day. They accept the inevitability of death, but simply have chosen not to give death a head start in their souls. Attitude becomes a matter of preeminence, for attitude is the rudder that steers the ship on this journey.

Release the rudder for a single day and you can sense a sort of existential seasickness. Release it for a week, and you will drift aimlessly or be tossed on the rocks. Release the rudder for any longer period and shipwreck is inevitable. This is a truth I have witnessed time and again on the retirement landscape.

So, in observing the forever young, forever passionate, and forever engaged, I have come across five internal focuses and patterns that constitute what I refer to as *the attitude instrument*—that which steers our lives safely through the existential seas day-by-day of fulfilled and pleasurable living. These focuses I call the Vitamin Cs of successful aging. They are:

- Vitamin C1—Connectivity
- Vitamin C2—Challenge
- Vitamin C3—Curiosity
- Vitamin C4—Creativity
- Vitamin C5—Charity

Vitamin C1—Connectivity

A study conducted at the University of Michigan found that in retirement, psychological well-being increases for some individuals and decreases for others. The researchers analyzed variables of physical health, income level, traumatic life experiences in recent years, age, gender, and other factors that might affect the psychological well-being of an individual. They found that the most powerful predictor of life satisfaction right after retirement were not health or wealth but the breadth of a person's social network.

The researchers concluded that new retirees need a social network more than they did when they were working. They wrote, "Just having a number of people who provide emotional support, listen to your concerns, and let your know that you're still valued right after you retire seems to make a big difference."

Why do people retire and immediately move away to a place where they have no social connectivity? Not only are they disconnecting from a major lifeline in the science of successful aging, they might also find out they are annoyed with the accents and culture into which they moved. It might be wise to spend some time doing reconnaissance on the geography and culture you plan on staging the next act of your life. Many people disconnect themselves from important social networks when they retire and don't realize it until it's too late.

Stay connected to people you love, people you enjoy, and people that apprectiate you and see value in your presence. Longevity does not favor the Lone Ranger. Both long life and happiness are tied to the quality of your connections.

Vitamin C2—Challenge

The latest Alzheimer research demonstrates that being intellectually challenged and having predictable taxation on our mental acuity literally have the effect of a finger in the dike, holding back the degenerative processes leading to both Alzheimer's and dementia. This research also concluded that as we hit our 50s and beyond, there is an exigency on ensuring that we have riddles to ponder, problems to solve, and things to fix. The brain is a muscle that atrophies without use. One gentleman told me that after six months of retirement, he could literally sense the dulling in his cerebral muscle with signs of slowed thinking and sluggish articulation.

> *"I decided to go back to college part-time when I reached age 62 and study psychology for no other reason than that I was curious about it. I've always wanted to get a better understanding of human behavior and I figured this was one step toward getting it. When I started classes, I was amazed at how many people were there in my age group. I guess I'm not the only curious grandma out there. I spent my career in business management. I got my fill of that. Now I feel like I'm in the middle of an electric storm. My mind is on full alert. I'm in awe of some of the things I'm learning. I have these intriguing conversations with younger people and just doing this makes me feel like I can go anywhere and do anything."*
>
> *—Georgia, student, 62*

The pulsating vein of life that Georgia has tapped into, along with a growing contingent of mature citizens, is that of growth. I hold little hope for the aging individuals who live with the delusion that they have "seen and heard it all." Those who have curiosity racing through their brains are guaranteed an exciting existence. Curiosity fuels both optimism and hope. Lifetime learners have the attitude that their quality of life will rise with their application to learning. This older entrance into new realms of education is, and will continue to be, a growing trend with the end of retirement as we know it. More and more retirees are moving to university towns instead of retirement villages.

It is important to note here that a job of some sort may be the most important source for cognitive demands because it is a primary source of mental stimulation. John W. Rowe, M.D., and Robert L. Kahn, Ph.D., in their book *Successful Aging,* wrote: "Remember the old adage, 'We become what we do'? People whose jobs promote self-direction, use of initiative, and independent judgement tend to boost their intellectual flexibility—that is, their ability to use a variety of approaches in order to solve mental problems." In short, mental flexibility is as important as intellectual curiosity as we age, and being active in challenging work can nurture such mental elasticity. An old and changing stereotype of aging is the old man or woman who won't listen to new ideas. Mental curiosity and flexibility are the answer to that old problem.

Vitamin C3—Curiosity

On a recent plane ride home from Australia, I flew next to a physicist named Ken Clark from the University of Washington. In his late 70s, he is still teaching and researching. I asked him why he wasn't retired, as was expected of a man his age. His answer was, "There's so much yet to learn," and he enthusiastically began describing his latest upper atmospheric physics research project. When I saw the sparkle in Dr. Clark's eyes as he spoke, I realized how good it would be if more seniors had their heads in the clouds of higher learning. Curiosity guarantees a pulse in the brain and a reason to keep our bodies healthy. The role of mental alertness cannot be overestimated and neither can the benefits of a desire to grow. Once a person reaches a point where they no longer want to learn or grow, it is time to order the tombstone. It need not be formal education that one pursues; it can be self-taught or experiential learning. The important thing is to have the curiosity and desire to grow. Age is an uphill road. Learning and tasks that demand mental alertness keep us in gear. Those individuals who stay neutral in this area will quickly find they are going backward. Rigorous mental function helps both to facilitate productivity in later years and to strengthen our need and desire to be active—factors that in turn affect our physical well-being.

Vitamin C4—Creativity

I've long been enthralled by elderly artists in their 80s and 90s who seem as keen and perspicacious as people half their age. I once listened to an interview with a Canadian artist in her 90s whose lucidity of thought and spry articulation was most inspiring. She also confirmed my suspicions about the virtues of creative engagement in our later years. She talked about the aforementioned curiosity being razor-sharp as well. She reasoned that artists have developed a *discipline of observation* that requires seeing what others, less curious, might miss. A creative soul looks at the shoreline and sees something new every day. This might help explain why B.B. King, now over 80, is playing 200 nights a year, and why Peter Drucker was able to write a business bestseller in his 90s. Of course, you don't have to be renowned to be creative and to keep the powers of observation working. You just have to be curious, intrigued, expressive, and intentional. A couple of other gems I heard this elderly artist mention were regularly scheduled, intellectually stimulating luncheons with people younger than herself, a profoundly diminished sense of self-consciousness, and two ounces of Canadian rye whiskey each evening for good measure.

Vitamin C5—Charity

Studies continue to surface around the ameliorative effects of charitable living on quality and longevity of life. Those who think about helping others often talk about how such charitable preoccupations lessen the degenerative effects of stress associated with worrying. Even if we didn't live a day longer because of charitable pursuits, we no doubt would live better.

I'm reminded of a story a financial advisor told about a client in her 70s who had more money than she could ever hope to spend but had no charitable interests. He challenged her to look around her city for places she might like to make a difference. As she began to observe and listen to her heart, a floodgate of generosity and empathy began to open up for her. Now, her life is full of causes she is passionate about—they have put a fresh spring in her step and added adrenaline to her pulse. It doesn't require money to live charitably; it just takes concern, generosity, and self-transcendence.

Pumping Iron at 80

On a recent summer vacation I ended up playing golf with Don. I complimented his tee shot, which went about 180 yards right down the middle of the fairway. His response was, "Well I'm starting to gain a little distance back with my upper body training. But that one there isn't to bad for an 80-year-old man, wouldn't you say?" At first look, you would guess Don to be around 70. I was amused by the irony of Don's telling me that he was gaining yardage on his drives. I have hardly ever played golf with a person over 60 who, at some point in the round, would not begin lamenting the loss of yardage that comes with gaining of years. Yet here was Don talking about a strength-training program he had just begun at age 80! He also told me that he played 18 holes a day as well as walking the two miles to and from the golf course each day.

Is it a good idea to be pumping iron as an octogenarian? Apparently so, according to a gerontological study by Tufts University. The researchers started a weight-lifting program with residents of a nursing home; and the average participant saw his or her strength increase over the testing period by over 50 percent. The average age of the participants was 83. Researchers have seen 90-year-old weaklings restored to greater strength levels than they possessed 30 years earlier. Strength training in the elderly also has been shown to combat osteoporosis in women and depression in both men and women. There are some powerful peripheral, intangible benefits that are observed in people who begin improving their physical state at any age. They become more active, they have more energy, and maybe, most important, they gain self-confidence and a more positive outlook on life.

> *"Much of what we think of as aging is really just a by-product of inactivity and poor nutrition, and it's not hard to change that."*
> —*Miriam Nelson, physiologist, USDA Research Center on Aging*

The MacArthur study on aging found that older people who engaged in strenuous physical activity at home were more likely to maintain their high cognitive function. A cyclical relationship exists between body, mind, and spirit. It is difficult at times to explain, but, once experienced, it is well understood. According to a *Clinician Review* study, cognitive function definitely improves with exercise. The investigators found that, compared with men who walked more than two miles per day, those who walked less than a quarter mile per day were 1.8 times more likely to have dementia, and those who walked a quarter mile to one mile per day had a 71 percent increased risk of dementia. Results indicated that higher levels of physical exercise were associated with better cognitive performance. Women who engaged in the greatest amount of physical activity had a 20 percent lower risk of cognitive impairment, compared with women who exercised the least. Furthermore, researchers found higher cognitive scores among women who walked at an easy pace for at least 90 minues per week than among those walking less than 40 minutes. The apparent cognitive benefits of exercise, observed Weuve et al., compare with "being about three years younger." (McArthur Foundation, 2004) Once lethargy infects a person's body, it seems that within a short time the lethargy invades the mind and spirit as well. Soon energy levels are lower, the mind is less perspicacious, and optimism is affected as well. We cannot wait to feel energy to become fit. We foster a discipline of fitness in order to gain energy. The action precedes the feeling. Positive physical regimens like walking (those who walk just three to five miles a week add five or more years to their lifespan), weight lifting, dietary discipline, and regular physical checkups all add years to the life span. Just as important, these regimens add quality to the years we live. Why live to be 90 if we're going to drag through 30 of those years with low energy and waning enthusiasm? Use your mind, engage your body, and nurture your spirit.

The Soul of Accelerated Aging

"I have probably learned the most about how I will approach aging from the contrast between my two grandmas' lifestyles and attitudes. Both of my grandmas are well into their 80s, but their life contentment factors are like night and day. One is always playing the martyr, poor little me game every time any of us talk to her. Until recently, she has been in pretty good health, but she would exaggerate any symptoms into life-threatening stories to get attention. She has isolated herself socially. When I ask her if she has met any new friends, she says that she is too old to make any new friends. When we visit her, she complains about how short our stay is and tries to manipulate us into staying longer. I hate to say it, but when I think of her, I often think of complaining, whining, and self-centeredness.

"My other grandma, on the other hand, though handicapped in both sight and mobility, is active, positive, and socially engaged. She is active in the senior citizen's center, volunteers as a peer mentor in *an Alzheimer's support group (having lost her husband to that disease), has regular conversations, participates in games and activities—which fills her schedule each day. She loves to talk about the things she is involved in and is looking forward to. She also enjoys meeting new people. To me, her most outstanding attribute is her sense of gratitude. She seems to relish each day and each moment. When I visit with her, she's thankful for the time and conversation, even if it's just a few moments. Rarely do you hear a complaint even though she could list a litany of very real problems. She is a joy to others, and many people look forward to seeing her each day even though as she says, 'They look forward to seeing me and I look forward to hearing them.'*

"The irony of this tale of two grandmothers is that they both have lived long lives so far. But that is where the similarity ends. I want meaningful longevity in my life, not prolonged existence. Living to 90 for one person is a blessing and to another an oxymoron. In my opinion, self-absorption seems to be at the seat of miserable aging."

—Ann, 39

Research from the Cornell study on retirement and well-being indicates that those who give of themselves boost their self-esteem and also gain a sense of more control over their own life. Researchers studied both workers and retirees between the ages of 50 and 72 and came to this conclusion: "Community commitments, especially formal participation, help enhance our sense of identity, promote ongoing networks of social relationships, and foster expectations of what to do when we wake up in the morning." There is an observable difference in the aging of the soul between the self-absorbed person and the selfless one. Giving to others, volunteering, and being a part of meaningful, significant activities seem to help promote healthier attitudes, which in turn improve one's health and contentment in life.

In their book *Successful Aging,* authors John Rowe and Robert Kahn tell the story of Phyllis, who remained productive and engaged in spite of her many functional limitations and chronic diseases. Phyllis, at 80, continued her work as an actress despite three heart attacks, major heart surgery, colon cancer, and a serious fall that led to lung failure and more heart problems. She continues to perform on stage at least two to three months a year. When not acting in a show, she volunteers in the theater world by serving at the box office, doing mailings, and the like. She is also an avid theatergoer as well. Phyllis articulated her secret for being able to move forward and remain productive this way: "Keep your interest in outer things, not inner ones. Keep busy. And always maintain more interests than there is time for."

In the old Greek myth of Narcissus, the man consumed with his own image, he eventually dies of starvation because he cannot stand to leave the pool of water where he beholds his own image. We use the term *narcissism* to describe individuals who are consumed with themselves. In the study of successful aging, a lesson seems to appear later in life, this time as a wrinkled Narcissus beholds his image in the same pool of water. But instead of being enamored with himself, now he becomes self-pitying at the sight of his decline and appearance. He wallows in so much self-pity that he will not leave to do anything to reverse his decline.

Americans generally feel that retirees have too little influence in the country today. This will change as new retirees keep their connections alive, remain relevant, redefine the life stage, and work toward impacting their communities, workplaces, and societies.

The New Retirementality has no time for a self-pitying stare into our aging image. We must follow the ageless image we have within us and stay connected to this world.

The New Retirementality Is . . .

- Leaving the workplace when you are good and ready.
- Continuing your education and mental challenge throughout life.
- Maintaining a positive social network of friends and associates throughout life-stage changes.
- Looking for ways to stay engaged and make a contribution in your later years.

CHAPTER 9

"You Don't Have to Be 62 to Do What You Want to Do"

"Money and contentment are not necessarily linked. If they were, there would be no such thing as a miserable rich man or a happy poor man."

—Mitch Anthony

A wealthy businessman was horrified to see a fisherman sitting beside his boat, playing with a small child.

"Why aren't you out fishing?" asked the businessman.

"Because I caught enough fish for one day," replied the fisherman.

"Why don't you catch some more?"

"What would I do with them?"

"You could earn extra money," said the businessman, "then with the extra money, you could buy a bigger boat, go into deeper waters, and catch more fish. Then you would make enough money to buy nylon nets. With the nets, you could catch even more fish and make more money. With that money you could own two boats, maybe three boats. Eventually you could have a whole fleet of boats and be rich like me."

"Then what would I do?" asked the fisherman.

"Then," said the businessman, "you could really enjoy life."

The fisherman looked at the businessman quizzically and asked, "What do you think I am doing now?"

What do you want to be when you grow up? I began asking that question a couple of years ago, not to children but to professionals and executives between 30 and 50 years old. The answers not only surprised me but the enthusiasm with which they answered the question was the most telling of all. I met a lawyer who wanted to be a fishing guide; a marketing executive who wanted to be an ad man; a corporate communications professional who wanted to be a veterinary assistant; a saleswoman who wanted to be a radio personality; a stockbroker who wanted to be a travel writer; an electrician who wanted to be a private eye; a doctor who wanted to fix old cars; a teacher who wanted to be a musician; a musician who wanted to be a teacher; and on and on the scenarios went. It seemed that almost everyone I talked to was harboring a desire to do or try out something else to see what it was like.

I was most intrigued by how animated these discussions became. A smirk would often break out and their eyes would shine like a child exploring a new playground. People seemed genuinely fascinated with the opportunity to explore the occupational playground that often lies latent within them; the responses were noticeably visceral. While some spoke with enthusiasm, others talked with a tone of resignation, as if they had given up on the idea of ever doing something for a living that was actually fun. This tone of resignation seemed to be rooted in the idea that others had defined for them the path they were following. I do not mean in the literal sense that their parents demanded, "You're going to be a doctor or lawyer," but more in the sense of someone else assigning the values that guided their career decisions.

A Path Paved with Fool's Gold

When I asked the individuals why they chose the path they did, many inevitably pointed to a set of values that led to the axiom, *"Choose the path paved with the most money."* They had contemplated their heartfelt desires in younger days, but those passionate desires to pursue a particular career were mentally dismissed because they would prove not to be materially substantive. These individuals often admitted feeling tacit disapproval and sometimes heard vocal disapproval from family and friends on those rare occasions when they did articulate their "working soul." Material compensation was the be-all and end-all of the career decision for many of these people. What many later discovered was that by not pursuing their working soul, they ended up on a path paved with fool's gold.

When the path was chosen on the basis of material compensation, many said that by the time they realized that they may have traded a calling for a job, they were so far down the one-way street of material reward that turning back or leaving that path would be too materially painful to contemplate.

Others, like the electrician who wanted to be a private eye or the teacher who wanted to be a musician, felt that at the time they chose their career, they were unsure, confused, or pressured as time ticked away. Once these individuals began a job, they often married and then had a family, followed by a mortgage and a world of obligation—and the days of dreaming were over. They had made their employment bed and now had to sleep in it. Their obligations now demanded money, and to change in midstream would cause too much stress. So the life that might have been was put out of their mind in hopes of feeling more content with the life that was. Many of these people told me that they planned on doing what they really wanted when they reached retirement age if they could afford to.

I get the distinct impression from other people that they harbor romantic notions about certain careers. If these people were to do a little due diligence into the day-to-day realities of these pursuits, they might be quickly dissuaded.

It is an odd but impressionable emotional stew that one witnesses when asking the question, "What do you want to be when you grow up?" There is wishfulness and wistfulness. There is passion and pensiveness. There is self-affirmation and self-loathing. There is almost always self-examination, which is why I so enjoy asking the question, with its inference that we have not yet grown up until we express our soul through the work we do. Every soul finds its own expression. Everyone discovers his or her own sense of meaning. It affirms to me that we all like to believe we are constantly growing and evolving.

Discovering meaning in work is a highly idiosyncratic process. Some working souls find expression by fixing things and others by fixing people. Some find expression by connecting people with people and others by connecting people with places, products, or experiences. Some souls find satisfaction by minimizing risks and others by accentuating and enabling risk. The question that we all need to ask our own working soul is: "What is it that I do with my hands and my head that gives my heart the most pleasure?" When we find the answer or answers to that question, we have at least discovered the path we should be on. Many of us possess an eclectic soul that needs to express our head and our hands in diverse ways to give our hearts satisfaction.

Rusty Success Models

I remember well my parents' last words when I left home to go off to school. I'm sure I had dealt their parental hopes quite a blow when I turned down an opportunity to study at a fine liberal arts college in order to take a nontraditional educational path. I remember their last words the day I left: "We need to tell you we're really disappointed in you." At the time, those words stung and disappointed me. Today, however, I do not begrudge either of my parents for saying those words because they were simply articulating the career paradigm of the day. If your child was a good student, he or she should become a doctor or lawyer or business leader and begin climbing the ladder of wealth. If your child did not choose such a path, it was a waste of precious potential (potential defined as talent + intelligence = $$$$$$).

Today, as I look back I can feel for my parents' predicament. One month into my senior year of high school, I was going to go to a good college and study to be a writer; and a couple of months later I informed my parents that I was going to some obscure little Bible college to study spiritual matters. By the looks on their faces you would have thought that I had told them I was going to become an international terrorist. They thought I had lost touch with my sanity. Later, I studied psychology and counseling and, in fact, have never ceased studying matters of human behavior. This matter of perpetual study I will address later in this book. I simply was endeavoring to follow the curiosity of my own heart and in the foolishness of youth didn't give a thought to the material compensation.

My parents and I can laugh and talk today about the irony of my contrarian choice. Because I allowed curiosity to act as my compass, I ended up in a career in which I now consult, speak, and write on matters of human behavior and relational dynamics. I feel as if I get paid too well for what I do because it all feels like experimentation and play to me. None of this would have been possible had I not pursued the holistic path of learning that began with disappointing my parents' hopes at the time. I feel I have ultimately found the greater reward by tracking my heart instead of grinding it out in a career track that would have paid well but would have taken too much from me. This is not to say that I have not taken a career detour or two from my heart and learned some lessons the hard way.

A common philosophical misconception lies just below the surface of many individuals' career choice: you must sacrifice job contentment in varying degrees to have material gain. This subtle myth reveals itself by the fact that people (1) choose to stay in careers they do not enjoy because the pay affords them the material status they desire, and (2) relegate doing the things they really enjoy to a distant retirement date. This subconscious belief is impregnated with such corollary deceptions as "I need to continue doing what I do not enjoy in order to gather enough money to be able to do what I do enjoy." In fact, money is the chief motivation for many people who are saving for retirement. Many see retirement as the time when they can do what they want. This philosophy reveals that material gain has been placed at the true north position on their life compass. If following our heart had been stressed to all of us as the true north on life's compass when we were young, would we have made different choices? It is safe to assume that many of us would have. The underlying deception that many people have unwittingly bought into is "If I do the thing I really desire, I will have to make many material sacrifices." We all need to take a closer look at this assumption before resigning ourselves to a routinized career grind.

I have discovered many people who chose to follow their passions in life and work and who actually made *more* money than they did in previous careers. It was erroneous thinking that led them to believe they would make less money by following their hearts—they had underestimated the economic powers of engagement!

What Do You Have to Lose?

If you were to go through the thought processes of evaluating your present contentment and current level of compensation and then compare them with your desired work scenario and its associated level of potential compensation, would your contentment rise or fall? Notice that I did not ask if your material standard would rise or fall but if your *content-*

ment would rise or fall. One psychological fact of life that all individuals must awaken to if they ever want to grow up into the work of their soul is this: the philosophy of materialism is hinged on discontentment. As long as I believe that what I need most is to be happy, I will never truly be happy. It is well advertised that there is always somebody just around the corner who has more, no matter how much you have, unless you're Bill Gates. If you are serious about treating your life as something other than a dress rehearsal, then you must ask yourself which of the following categories you fall into on the work/contentment continuum. (See Figure 9.1.)

Where do you land on this continuum of contentment? First, place yourself and then ask yourself, "What do I need to do to make my life a 10 or a 9?" God forbid that you should settle for less than you are capable of. Let's take a hard look at what it means to be at different locations on the contentment continuum.

1–2 points: Discontented and poor—"I dread my work and the pay is terrible" or "I dread my work but the pay is decent." To be in this spot, you must have given up, you're apathetic, or you just haven't

FIGURE 9.1 | Contentment Continuum Chart

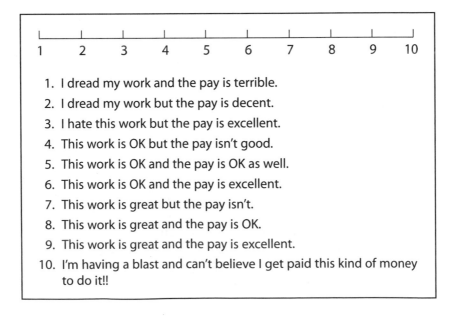

1. I dread my work and the pay is terrible.
2. I dread my work but the pay is decent.
3. I hate this work but the pay is excellent.
4. This work is OK but the pay isn't good.
5. This work is OK and the pay is OK as well.
6. This work is OK and the pay is excellent.
7. This work is great but the pay isn't.
8. This work is great and the pay is OK.
9. This work is great and the pay is excellent.
10. I'm having a blast and can't believe I get paid this kind of money to do it!!

discovered that there are ways to enjoy your working life. The people I have met who placed themselves at this point on the contentment continuum talked about a lack of education and being stuck after they got married and had a family. This group also included those who believed that all work was a grind and you had to just tough it out until you were old enough to collect Social Security.

Some of those I interviewed who placed themselves in this spot expressed regret at not pursuing more education and also at handicapping themselves early in life with suffocating levels of debt. Others felt as if they had jumped on a workplace treadmill and didn't have the confidence or daring to jump off and enter a new arena.

For example, Phil has worked in retail management for 22 years. He bemoans the people he works for, the customers, and many of the people he works with. He says he doesn't like it but what can he do after 22 years. The money doesn't go far (which may have something to do with his spending habits as we noted that the difference between categories 1 and 2 on the continuum—"the pay is terrible" and "the pay is decent"—often had to do with cost-of-living choices) and it's emotionally trying to come to work every day.

Another example is Amber, a 32-year-old flight attendant with a regional airline. On a recent flight in a moment of candor, she told me that she hated everything about the job including the travel. She had taken the job believing it would be a paid sightseeing opportunity. Instead, she found herself trapped in a carousel of homogenous hotel rooms, airplane cabins, and customer complaints. Unfortunately, she has not made any decision to do anything about her discontent other than complain and occasionally act surly to passengers. Amber is at an age where she is still trying to find out what it is she really wants to do. It's early in the game for her. She needs to realize, however, that now is the time to start moving into something that will offer more work contentment. The longer she waits, the more leverage she provides to inaction in her life.

Many people are hearing an inner alarm alerting them that they need to move from a job to a calling. For example, it was recently publicized that by the year 2010, we will have a major teacher shortage in America. How is this problem going to be solved? In large part by people leaving jobs they don't really like to do something they've always dreamed of (teaching). As a matter of fact, this trend is already under way. Five years ago in my city, the people who shifted gears and became teachers in midcareer totaled less than 1 percent. That percentage has now grown to 5 percent. The human resources director of our school system predicts that the total will reach 25 percent by 2010.

The U.S. Department of Education estimates that 2.5 million teachers will be needed over the next ten years, which exceeds the current rate of 200,000 teachers. The "No Child Left Behind" initiative has made finding qualified individuals to fill the shortage much more difficult.

Many people reading this book are "called" to teach but are doing other things, perhaps for economic reasons, from pressure, or because of distractions, but the inner payoff will come when they do work that is in their heart.

If you find yourself in this category, it's time to get a life, get a new job, or get a frontal lobotomy so you stop feeling pain. If you're willing to work for less than desirable wages, which you've already demonstrated, then why not earn them by doing something that you at least halfway enjoy? For example, many people have avoided the teaching profession because they figured they wouldn't get rich. Now that they've gone down another path chasing "rich" and maybe finding the money was just OK, they wonder why they're doing what they do. Individuals could go from a 1 to a 4 on the contentment continuum simply by finding a job that expressed their interests.

If you are willing to labor for less than prosperous wages, then do it on a job you'll enjoy doing. Once people get this low in contentment, they have often lost the confidence to believe they can climb any higher as well as the desire for self-improvement that would spawn such confidence. At this point your problem is not your job; it is either your lack of initiative or lack of self-regard—or both. Every step you take toward self-education, self-improvement, and self-promotion will build your sense of personal confidence, which in turns energizes your willingness to embrace opportunity and challenge. Unfortunately, the opposite also holds true—allow yourself to stay in a place that feels condescending in both task and pay, and eventually your confidence will be depleted until lethargy and numbness set in.

3 points: Discontented and materially satisfied—"I hate this work but the pay is excellent." Individuals who allow themselves to settle into this category (of which there are many in a materialistic culture) are in a place in life where they may have exchanged their life's calling or soul work for an alluring counterfeit—pretty things. Once a person begins to collect pretty things for the purpose of self-affirmation and a sense of identity, it becomes a consuming force of perpetual motion from which few can turn away. If you live in a culture, a city, or even a neighborhood that has embraced the glitter and greed of the materialistic, bling-bling identity, you may suffer from the consternation of trying to turn your back on materialism when surrounded by it.

A friend recently told me about an acquaintance who had struck it rich in his business and is constantly buying new, more exciting cars, boats, planes, and other toys. He uses these high-ticket items a short while and then trades or sells them for something more prestigious. It's obvious to everyone that he is trying to use material commodities to fill a need they cannot fill.

The growing subculture of simplicity seekers affirms this fact in that those who seek a simpler, less hectic, less materialistic, and more balanced lifestyle often find that they must first change associations, locations, and spending habits to achieve a downshifting lifestyle. It is well nigh psychologically impossible to find material contentment when you base your life's work on the money you can make instead of the actual work you do. Those who say they hate their work but stay because the money is excellent put themselves at risk in the following ways:

1. They have chosen to put their dreams of achievement and maybe even their most important talents on the back shelf.
2. Their life and health more than likely suffer from some imbalance as a result of misplaced priorities.
3. Their relationships may be suffering at home and at work because of their lingering distaste for the work they do (it is emotionally exhausting to spend energy on work that drains rather than energizes you).
4. Because they don't care to identify with their work, they may identify with and affirm themselves through the things they buy.

In a study by Aon Consulting ("The America at Work Study: The 1999 Workforce Commitment Index"), 1,800 workers identified "opportunities for personal growth" as a top reason for job loyalty; and they also identified "the business satisfies customer or societal needs" as another top motivation for staying in their job. According to a 2004

WorkZ Staff study, "Top Five Reasons People Stay in Their Jobs," there is a decided slant toward intellectual and emotional fulfillment in why people stay in their jobs. After having a good salary (55 percent), the responses were:

- Good boss (33%)
- Interesting work (53%)
- Varied work assignments (30%)
- Benefits (52%)
- Feel appreciated (25%)
- Enjoy coworkers (45%)
- Education and development (19%)
- Sense of purpose/mission (42%)
- Convenient location (40%)
- Career opportunities (16%)
- Challenging job assignments (39%)
- Autonomy (14%)
- Flexible work hours (38%)

We all want to feel that we are making a contribution, making a difference, or doing something that feels meaningful to us. This need cannot be satisfied by the size of a paycheck. It can, however, be anesthetized by a large paycheck. Under the anesthetic we are able to temporarily ignore the need to do something meaningful and the direction our life needs to take to fulfill it. But this anesthetic eventually wears off.

One does not have to be feeding children who are starving or performing open-heart surgery to be involved in a meaningful career. The definition of *meaningful* is idiosyncratic. For some people it means doing something that has a direct impact on their well-being. For others, it is being part of developing and distributing a product that has an impact in the lives of others. For some, it is a matter of doing something that connects them to a cause, idea, or purpose they love, such as a rancher who loves working with cattle, the ranger who loves working in nature, the physicist who studies the heavens, or the broker who loves the markets and gaining from them.

It is a matter of deciding what interests you most and where your skills and interests can best be utilized. For some, this contemplation may lead to a career change, and for others it may simply lead to a change in career circumstances (continue doing what they are doing but in more tolerable and less stressful circumstances). I have taken many people through a series of questions that are presented in the next chapter in order to get to the heart of this issue of doing work that provides meaning in their life. After answering these questions, many have found that there is meaning in the work they do and that all they need to do is simply change their perspective and purpose in approaching their work each day. Others will look at the following questions on meaningful work and have a sort of epiphany, realizing they are wasting their precious assets, abilities, and energy where they are—and that a change is due. It should be welcome news to all of us that we don't have to be 62 to do what we want to do.

I don't know if everyone can get to ten points on the contentment continuum ("I'm having a blast and can't believe I get paid this kind of money to do it!"), but I'm sure it's not by giving a higher regard to your checkbook than to your heart. Pay attention to both—find out where the two merge in a place of both spiritual and material prosperity. By paying attention to your heart, you can reap more contentment and move yourself toward a satisfied working life.

The New Retirementality Is . . .	• Finding work you can do until the day you die. • Keeping your priorities straight regarding work and pay. • Fully capitalizing on your gifts in the work you do.

The New Retirementality Challenge

Why am I working?

Think about it: What does my family tell me about why I work? How much is money the motivation for my work? How much is money the reward for my work?

Research it: What percentage of my current assets are designated for long-term use? What does that amount to? What does it take for me (us) to live today if we had no children? And the house was mortgage free? Should I count on any inheritance?

Decide and take action:

- Will I continue working in retirement?
- In today's dollars, what will I plan to earn?

CHAPTER 10

Don't Settle for a Lukewarm Life

> *"It's not important to run on the fast track but on your track. Pretend you have only six months to live, and make three lists. Things you have to do, things you want to do, and things you neither have to do nor want to do. Then for the rest of your life, forget everything on the third list."*
>
> —*Robert Elliot*

> *"The key to life is concentration and elimination."*
>
> —*Goethe*

Tom and I went on a hunting trip together and the nine-hour drive gave us plenty of time to explore the landscape of our lives. Tom told me he had a strong inner yearning to do something more or different with his life, but he just couldn't put his finger on it. He thought maybe he wanted to be in sales instead of customer service. He would be more challenged and doubly compensated. I encouraged him to tell the vice president of the company's sales department his desire. He did and was tactfully rebuffed.

A year later Tom told me he was looking into a radical career change by becoming an emergency medical technician (EMT). It would require two years of education and was not an easy proposition at 33 with a family to support. Tom began by taking night classes and interning every other weekend. Tom told me he was having strong second thoughts about six months into his training, wondering if he could pull this off and thinking about giving up the idea when something dramatic happened.

One day the customer service rep next to Tom didn't look or feel well. Tom asked for his symptoms and told him he should get to the hospital. His coworker brushed it off as a temporary problem. Two minutes later this man had a massive heart attack and was lying on the floor without a pulse. Tom called the ambulance and then started administering CPR. The ambulance arrived within ten minutes and informed Tom that he had saved the man's life.

Tom told me that, after that, all doubts about a career change disappeared. He was meant to be an EMT. Tom traded an OK job with an OK paycheck (a 5 on the contentment continuum) for a great job with an OK paycheck (an 8 on the contentment continuum). He knows he'll never be materially rich as an EMT but he's now getting paid in other ways. He also found that his new career allows him time to pursue part-time work, so he is in fact ahead materially as well.

Ironically, as soon as Tom decided on his career shift, his company offered him the sales position he had so desired a year before. He declined. Next, they offered him part-time work where he could choose his own hours while he went to school. That offer he accepted.

Before his change, Tom was living a lukewarm life, which was evident by his energy level and lethargic attitude toward work. Today, he has a vibrancy and a light in his eyes. He's got the life horse pulling the money cart and not the other way around.

This life is not a dress rehearsal. When I meet people who are just showing up, punching the employment clock, and dreaming of a retirement date circled on a calendar a decade away, I want to ask, "How many lives do you have to waste?" Life is too short. The older we get, the more conscious of this fact we become. Do what you want to do before you're 62.

Working It Out

Answer the following questions to give you an idea where you are with your current work. I warn you that this may take some time and thought before you can fill in all the blanks, but the exercise is worth the introspection because of the clarity it provides.

1. What I want out of life is . . .

   _____

   _____

2. Work is . . . (Write your own definition)

   _____

   _____

3. The satisfaction I want from my work is . . .

   _____

   _____

4. The job or work I enjoy most is that which allows me to . . .

   _____

   _____

5. The challenges I enjoy most are . . .

   _____

   _____

6. The most meaningful experiences I have had with my work are . . .

   _____

   _____

7. The stress/pressure I most hate with my current work is . . .

   _____

   _____

8. My dream working scenario is . . .

   _____

   _____

Foolish and Playful Pursuits. When completing this process of work examination, people find either affirmation in the work they do or a disconnection between their work and their heart. My brother, who sells insurance, didn't see an extraordinary amount of purpose in his work until the day he came upon an auto accident on a country road and found a client who had just passed away. My brother had sold life insurance to this client less than a week before the accident. Some peo-

ple who go through this examination realize they have grown tired of
the work they do and it's time for a change. They no longer have the
passion or enthusiasm they once had for their present work. They have
met and exceeded the challenges or realized that the work was not the
best expression of who they really are. Examples are plentiful. It is
fairly common for certain personality types to hunger for some sort of
new and exciting challenge in their life. It is just as common for people
to face up to the fact that they secretly harbor a desire to do something
that would be viewed as a step down in society's eyes, such as the college president who became a golf course ranger, the stock broker who
became a park ranger, the surgeon who became a farmer, or the high-
level management executive who became a specialized auto mechanic.

There are a thousand stories about people who decided there was a
way to unite their heart and their work. All of these people had to negotiate some sort of resourceful transition to get to the place where they
could truly enjoy their playful and foolish pursuits that some would call
a job. The difference is they always wanted to do it and are having the
time of their life (some are also making the best money of their life) by
folding their passions, interests, and dreams into their work.

Out of the Boxes

We need to rid our minds of old, outdated paradigms about how life
should be lived. The passé paradigm is one where education, work, and
leisure are compartmentalized into nice, neat little boxes along the
course of life. This idea of life boxes was introduced by Richard Bolles,
author of the perennial best-seller *What Color Is Your Parachute?* (See
Figure 10.1.)

The desired life course is one that integrates all of these aspects of
life into a balanced approach to everyday living. A great life is one in
which we are constantly learning something new, engaging in work that

FIGURE 10.1 | The Boxes of Life

EDUCATION	WORK	LEISURE
Up to age 22 or so	Age 22 to 62	62 to death

challenges and fulfills us, and reserving time for rest and relaxation. It is a most unnatural life that tries to squeeze these three activities into one box of the lifeline. Happiness and fulfillment for a lifetime come when we learn to fluidly integrate all three.

Education

The only way to keep pace and flourish in the fast-paced information age is to be a lifetime learner. Gone is the day when your diploma defines who you are. If your education stopped when you got a diploma, you're on your way to fossilization. Educational versatility and intellectual curiosity are the hallmarks of today's success story. Make a list of the things you're curious about, afraid of, and need to know, and then begin educating yourself today. Today's world has no patience for the intellectually lazy and lethargic.

Work

Extinct is the 40-year company man. You change jobs and careers many times before you're 60. According to the U.S. Bureau of Labor Statistics, baby boomers held an average of 10.2 jobs from ages 18 to 38. On average, men held 10.4 jobs and women held 9.9 jobs. There's a discovery course for your growing interests and abilities. It is ridiculous that we expect 18-year-olds to decide on a course of study for employment that will engage them for the rest of their life. How utterly delusional to think most people have a clue to what their life will evolve into. Work is simply a testing or plowing ground for finding what fits each individual's own soul and purpose. As many have discovered, if you can't find a job that fits you, then you'll have to go ahead and design one that does. Today, we have thousands of consultants and free agents who have done just that—designed their own working life.

If your résumé shows that you've moved around, be proud and not embarrassed. Your résumé's value is not how long you spent where but what you learned while you were there. Write a résumé that shows where you've been and what skills you've developed while you were there. If you're a lifetime learner, you'll find that you've developed an impressive résumé of skills, competencies, and abilities that you could parlay into future opportunities. Don't allow a job description to limit your personal learning curve. Continually put yourself in positions to learn more. I once read a story of a guy who constantly asked to be moved into new departments, never lasting long at any one job. Some supervisors, while recognizing his curiosity, thought he was a bit flaky and lacked loyalty to one department. This man is now president of the company. He is president for one reason—he knew the business inside and out and has multiple skills as a result of his versatility. In this age it is your curiosity and versatility to try new things that will define you.

Leisure

What's the point of never taking a break? People work like oxen for years with no vacation. In their mind, they relegate leisure and relaxation to retirement years. When they get there, they're miserable because they have no idea how to relax. They can't relax now with their spouse or children. They can't just sit doing nothing but enjoying nature or the thoughts running through their head. They've surrendered their potential for reflective living to a "perpetual motion disease" that they call work. Leisure and relaxation need to be integrated on a regular basis into a healthy lifestyle.

We need to learn to break out of the "boxes of life" and integrate curiosity, work, and leisure into one fluid lifeline. We need to discover a life course that needs no finish line and no retirement date. Then we will be living in the New Retirementality.

What's Stopping You?

The question we need to ask ourselves after we determine what it is we would rather be doing is, "What's stopping me from doing it?" Try articulating what obstacles you would need to overcome to get from here to there. Are you willing to take such risks? If you are not really willing to leap over these obstacles, you have just taught yourself the finite difference between dreaming and daydreaming. If you are able to convince yourself that you are duly motivated to overcome these impediments, then you are ready to define what steps you'll need to take to start your journey.

In Chapters 12 and 13, I present many ideas and strategies that others have utilized (at all income levels) to make the transition into more meaningful work. You may very well be able to use some of the financial and career-switching ideas that worked for them. I have heard many of these individuals say, "I would do this if they paid me nothing," because they now derive such joy and satisfaction from their pursuits. They have found working contentment. Most people can move up to some degree on the working contentment scale unless they are already at 10—"I'm having a blast and can't believe I get paid this kind of money to do it!" If you've settled in at 5 ("This work is OK and the pay is OK as well"), you may be settling for a lukewarm life. Seriously question yourself if there is a way to get your work to follow your soul. There is no greater feeling than to love what you're doing—and to be paid well for it is a bonus.

You can do what you really want to do when you get serious about doing it. For some, the motivation comes from facing the inward loathing they carry toward their work and toward themselves for not doing something about it. They are tired of lukewarm waters. For others, the motivation comes from facing the dreams, passions, and energies they have stored up within themselves that are not being expressed through their current work. I want both sets of contemplators to arrive at the same conclusion: *life was not meant to be a lukewarm experience.* Once you decide to do what you've always wanted, you erase the need to ever fully retire.

The New Retirementality Is . . .	• Not allowing lethargy to creep into your working life. • Taking an honest look at what you put into and get out of work. • Bringing a balance of work, learning, and leisure to your life.

CHAPTER 11

How Much Is Your Paycheck Costing You?

"Fear not that your life will come to an end but that it will never have a beginning."

—*John Henry Newman*

"One day my daughter asked me to come out and play. I said, 'No, Honey, Dad's too busy.' My daughter said, 'You're always too busy' and went out to play. That night I kept turning it over in my head. Why do I work hard? Answer: to get freedom. Why do I want freedom? Answer: to spend time with those I love. When am I going to have this freedom or make getting it a priority? Answer: probably about the time my kids are gone. I realized I had put myself in a vicious cycle of motion and money and had everything turned upside down."

—*Ted, 39*

I went through a period in my own life when I allowed myself to do work I dreaded to gain money I desired. This period came to an end when I received a personal wake-up call and subsequently assessed my entire state of being by asking myself, "How much is this paycheck costing me?!"

My lesson came in a telling set of circumstances that caused me to compare what I gain materially with what I was losing physically, emotionally, and developmentally.

I had done a little consultation work for a start-up company when they asked me if I would consider taking on a consulting contract for 50 to 60 percent of my time for a fee that many would consider a generous full-time wage. On top of this, they offered me options on over 100,000 shares at 2¢ per share. The individual who offered this package had already taken two companies public, which made the offer all the more enticing. I figured I was the great American fool if I didn't take the offer, especially at a time (mid-1990s) when the word *options* was the mantra of a not-to-be-refused opportunity.

I reasoned that with a commitment of only 50 to 60 percent of my time, I would still have time to pursue my other ventures and opportunities, which was quite important to me as I had always been self-employed and diverse in my pursuits. What I failed to calculate into the equation was the toll that the time commitment would exact from my body, family life, and emotional well-being. The first six months were great fun and an adrenaline ride guiding the marketing efforts of a fast-growing enterprise.

The 90-minute commute to and from the office three days a week seemed to whisk by as I schemed new ways to expand the enterprise. Soon, however, some conflicts began to surface. The time commitment was much understated when I factored in my travel around the country. The owner and I operated on wavelengths that were galaxies apart. He was a consummate hands-on-everything microscopic manager, and I am an adventurous, spontaneous, and driving type. Our communication styles were on foreign wavelengths as well. I prefer face-to-face candor, and he preferred avoiding direct confrontation by delivering autocratic messages through third parties. The bottom line was that he was the boss and I wasn't! This was a most difficult spot for my personality. On top of these personality differences, he routinely put in 16 hours a day and I often sensed a tacit disapproval of my insisting I leave at 4 PM so I could be home in time to have dinner with my family.

At first, while our market share was booming, I was allowed to run with the programs I created. With such freedom, I enjoyed the experience immensely (and held out great hope for those options). Soon, however, some company culture issues became apparent. Progress toward changing direction or adopting new ideas was excruciatingly slow and depressing to my vision. By the time a decision could get made, the opportunity was lost or had been accomplished by a competitor. I grew increasingly perplexed at the lack of communication and avoidance of resolvable conflict or disagreements. And although the work itself was challenging, I was not in an area that caused my blood to race. After spending most of my career creating and selling life-improvement ideas, I was now simply selling a product—a good product but a product nonetheless. This differentiation would become the critical catalyst in my self-assessment and eventual transition.

The wake-up call came about 22 months into my consulting job. I had to go to New York to negotiate what potentially looked to be a million-dollar deal. I was encouraged to go immediately and get a commitment. I had reservations about the need for immediacy and timing but didn't want to let the opportunity slip. My reservation about going stemmed, in part, from the fact that this trip would cause me to miss my second son's baseball game, in which he was making his first pitching start. As a matter of priority, whenever possible, I had always tried to schedule my trips to not conflict with significant dates on my children's schedules.

I told my son I regretted missing his start but I had to go to New York to do a really big deal (with a child you might as well say you are going to the moon to gather cheese). I told him I would call right after the game to see how it went.

True to my word, I called after the game. "How did it go, buddy?" I asked. There was an eerie silence on the other end of the line.

"Dad," he said wistfully, "you should have been here. I threw a no-hitter *and* hit a home run and a triple!"

The longing in his voice echoed in my ear long after that call ended. It wasn't just the fact that I had missed his moment for a deal that might never transpire that bothered me the most; it was that I missed his moment doing something I no longer enjoyed. That night I began to assess the impact of my consulting work on all aspects of my life. I began to ask myself just what this paycheck was costing me and why I was still hanging around to collect it. It was a difficult introspection that forced me to take an honest look at my priorities in every realm—from the material to the spiritual. What I discovered was that I had made some compromises that were now taking a depreciating toll on my life.

Finding Breathing Room

During the two years of my consulting contract, my health had disintegrated to an all-time low. I became chronically asthmatic, prone to injury, and suffered chronic fatigue and spells of depression. It seemed as though I was always struggling for breath and short of energy. I knew the asthma was the result of breathing excessive molds in the air of the company's office, which had a debilitating effect on my respiratory system. The growing stress and tension of the working environment no doubt compounded my asthma. I was tired and cranky to my wife and children after driving 90 minutes home three days a week.

The aspect of this scenario that caused me to reach the tipping point, however, was that I had become bored with the work. Although I always gave my best when talking distributors into buying our product line, I felt that I was running on automatic pilot while doing it. I was doing work that didn't bring fulfillment to my soul. The greatest thrill in my working life has always been a result of doing things that are related to convincing people to improve the quality of their lives and relationships. This mission can be fulfilled for me through a number of expressions such as writing, speaking, consulting, and media productions of the messages. Whenever I drift too far from this personal mission, I feel the anchor line grow taut in my soul—articulated emotionally by a sense of dissatisfaction and a frustrated sense of creativity. There is also a pervasive sense that I lack the necessary challenge needed to force me to keep myself sharpened in mind and daily approach. Through my introspection, I realized that I was driving down the wrong way on the road to fulfilling my personal potential. The paycheck was costing me too much.

Figure 11.1 is an introspection, a mental journey, I like to guide those on who find themselves anywhere below a 7 on the contentment continuum. If you have an intuitive sense that you are not fully utilizing your talents and abilities, or if your work does not draw on the things you do best, you are ripe for such an introspective examination. Grappling with these questions can be a humbling but liberating process.

FIGURE 11.1 | Fulfillment Questionnaire

Directions: Rate yourself on these issues with 1 being the least and 5 being the most.

1. I feel as though my natural talents and abilities are expressed through my work: 1 2 3 4 5
2. I have a continuing enthusiasm about the work I do: 1 2 3 4 5
3. I have a sense of serenity and fulfillment regarding my work: 1 2 3 4 5
4. I enjoy the people I work with: 1 2 3 4 5
5. I feel my work helps me to grow intellectually and personally: 1 2 3 4 5
6. I feel that I bring some benefit to others through my work: 1 2 3 4 5
7. I often feel energized by the work I do: 1 2 3 4 5

Add Total: _____

The lowest you could score on this self-assessment is 7 and the highest is 35. If you scored anywhere below 28, I would like you to consider the following questions:

1. Is there some sort of work you know of that may give greater expression to who you are?
2. Could you raise your sense of fulfillment by taking your talents to another company or realm?
3. Is it the things you do or the people you work with that rob you of a higher sense of fulfillment? Or both?

If you scored below 21 on this self-assessment, I would like to pose some even tougher questions:

1. What kind of work gives you the greatest satisfaction?
2. What do you do in your work now that gives you a sense of satisfaction?
3. Are you willing to sacrifice fulfilling who you are for predictability and material safety?
4. Do you lack fulfillment because of the attitude you bring to your work?

As a result of hundreds of such discussions with people, I cannot help but believe that responses to these questions are signals from our souls guiding us to choose, change, or alter our mind-set and the application of our abilities. Answering these questions positively is a signal that we are following the work path that our soul requires for contentment. When we answer negatively, however, it is a signal that we are on an unrewarding work path or are bringing the wrong attitude to the right place. As Stephen Covey so succinctly asked in *The Seven Habits of Highly Effective People,* "What's the point of climbing the ladder of success if it is leaning against the wrong wall?" I might add a question that pertains to those who bring the wrong attitude to the right kind of work: "What's the point of climbing the ladder of success if you're only going to look down?"

Bloom Where You're Planted

Career coaches like Laura Berman Fortgang confirm that a majority of the clients they see end up staying right where they are after a consultation on work-fulfillment issues. Fortgang, author of *Take Yourself to the Top,* says, "Nine out of ten people who call me, desperately looking to change their careers, wind up staying in their jobs." How do you know if you're one of the one in ten who needs to move on? Fortgang suggests looking for these three telltale signs:

1. Your work doesn't mesh with your life. If the work severely clashes with the rest of your life, you need to move on.
2. You've outgrown your job; your job needs to jibe with who you are today.
3. You've fixed the things that drive you nuts. And you're still miserable. Your job dissatisfaction has become chronic. You won't get better without a change.

Many people—nine out of ten—who were suffering much discontentment and job-related stress discover that they begin to see their work through a new set of eyes when they shift from a mind-set of expecting happiness to looking for growth. It is easy to grow disturbed and agitated in our work when we are constantly looking around at what others make and what others get to do instead of trying to capitalize on the growth opportunities that our job offers us. When we are driven by a sense of psychological entitlement that demands things go our way, it doesn't take long for ingratitude, envy, and stress to dominate our mental realm. On the contrary, when we shift our focus on growing and exceeding the various demands of our work, we begin to discover a new sense of anticipation and fulfillment in our work.

It is quite easy, however, to let the annoyances of frustrating personalities and circumstances at work rob us of the joy and growth we could harvest from our work. It doesn't take long for stress to get the best of us and for our mind to start wandering by wondering if we would be happier doing something else somewhere else. When career coaches guide their clients through a thorough examination of that question, they often find the clients realizing that their work does, in fact, have many opportunities for growth and satisfaction—and maybe isn't such a bad deal after all.

> *"The last of our human freedoms is to choose one attitude in any given circumstance."*
>
> —*Victor Frankl*

A periodical attitude evaluation usually helps to pull us back to the reality that there is no perfect world and that familiar and predictable trouble is always preferable to unfamiliar and unpredictable trouble. A simple attitudinal exercise you can do is to take inventory of the opportunities for personal development that your current job affords you and determine what skills you *are* developing and *can* develop that will make your résumé look that much better tomorrow.

Personal Development Inventory

- Does my work provide the opportunity for desired intellectual growth?
- Am I forming valuable relationships and contacts in this work?
- Can the tribulations of my current work contribute to needed skills in future work?
- In my response to current conditions, am I rising above it or living under the circumstances?
- Am I seeking the company of the groaners or the growers?

If opportunities for growth still exist, it might be best to bloom where you're planted. If such opportunities do not exist and you're beginning to feel like you're going in circles, it might be time to uproot.

Calling In Sick

I learned in my personal wrestling match with the issues described above that I would never feel a higher sense of work fulfillment until I cut my ties to the work that required less than my highest level of interest and ability. I decided that I needed to dedicate myself to the philosophy I had already established, which was doing work that challenges people to think about their relationships and their quality of life. This book is an expression of that philosophy. I sense that as long as I follow this direction, I have the inward contentment of being on the right path. There are always risks associated with such decisions, but, in my opinion, these risks are far less dangerous than the risks of compromising deeply seated visions and desires for your own life. The risk of ignoring those desires is the depletion of your physical, emotional, intellectual, and spiritual strength. Once these precious resources are depleted, you find yourself getting sick in both a physical and emotional sense.

Dr. Paul Stepanovich, who teaches community health at Old Dominion University, advises people to give their employer a fitness test. Stepanovich says there are certain warning signs he wishes he had been aware of when he was climbing the corporate ladder in the 1980s. He states, "It struck me that although I had read about stress in my MBA program, I couldn't believe that I could visually see the effect on people's health" (as quoted in Carla Bass, "Give Your Employer a Fitness Test").

When Stepanovich went back to school to earn a degree in epidemiology, he decided to dedicate his research to uncovering the prevalence of unhealthy work environments. Stepanovich says, "I don't think we have any idea how sick some organizations are." He recommends giving your prospective employer a fitness test before jumping aboard. If you don't, your new job may end up costing you more than you're paid. Where you work can affect not only your quality of life but how long you live as well. Stepanovich has developed a list of vital signs to measure a company's emotional healthiness. The health of any organization seems to hinge on five characteristics: *vitality, integrity, tolerance, appreciation,* and *latitude/empowerment.*

A Company's Vital Signs

Vitality. Employees are interested in what they are doing and they care about it as well.

How to test for it: You can learn a lot simply by shadowing current employees for a day or even a few hours. Check to see how involved they are in their work. Are they intellectually and emotionally involved with their tasks or are they just going through the motions in a detached sort of way?

Integrity. Current employees have a high level of trust in their employer.

How to test for it: Talk to current employees to see if the company "walks the walk" as well as "talks the talk." Does it promise training and growth opportunities to prospective employees that it fails to deliver? Ask current employees what they were promised and see how much integrity the company demonstrated to these individuals.

Tolerance. The company demonstrates equal opportunity for advancement for all races and both genders as well as the acceptance of differing viewpoints.

How to test for it: A quick perusal into the management offices will give you an idea of the type of individuals that get promoted. Sitting in on a meeting will give you a good idea of the tolerance level toward different viewpoints and conflicting opinions.

Appreciation. The company demonstrates a high level of appreciation and recognition for achievements and rewards a job well done.

How to test for it: Check to see if current employees feel like their job is highly important to the success of the company. Companies that promote an ethic of appreciation and recognition foster a higher self-image in every department of the company. Every employee has the feeling that his or her performance is crucial to the company's success.

Latitude. The company empowers employees to take risks and exercise a reasonable degree of autonomy.

How to test for it: Talk to both managers and employees to see if they have the space they need to do their jobs. Working for people who drive you crazy with control tactics and job interference causes the worst sort of workplace stress. Punishing people for results out of their control and micromanaging every detail will cause the sort of tension that can make working life miserable.

This acid test for a prospective employer is just as relevant when measuring your current employer. How does your current employer stack up from an A to an F on the vital signs report card? (See Figure 11.2.)

If you are a manager, you may be interested to know that you can bring a great degree of influence to the vital signs of your particular department or team. When it comes to rating their bosses, most people say that their leader's attitude is what matters most. A national survey of 1,000 people chosen randomly by Personal Decisions International, a global management and human resources consulting firm, found 37 percent of the people surveyed identified communication skills or interpersonal skills as the most important quality in a good boss. The ability to understand employees' needs and help in developing skills came in second (19 percent). In an article entitled "Trouble Finding the Perfect Gift for Your Boss—How About a Little Respect?" an Ajilon Finance survey reports that most people agree they want a boss they can respect. When people were asked to select one trait that is most important for a manager, more than one-fourth of American workers selected "leading by example." Of all qualities from which they could choose, employees ranked the most important as follows:

1. Leading by example (26%)
2. Strong ethics or morals (19%)
3. Knowledge of the business (17%)
4. Fairness (14%)
5. Overall intelligence and competence (13%)
6. Recognition of employees (10%)

FIGURE 11.2 | Corporate Vital Signs Report Card

Vitality	A	B	C	D	E	F
Integrity	A	B	C	D	E	F
Tolerance	A	B	C	D	E	F
Appreciation	A	B	C	D	E	F
Latitude	A	B	C	D	E	F

This need for the opportunity to achieve growth was confirmed by the Aon Consulting survey of 1,800 employees that found the opportunity to grow as the top reason for employee loyalty.

When people assess the emotional well-being of the company they work for, many find that their workplace is "calling in sick." Many companies still get away with abusing employees—simply because they can. A company is usually doing something well, whether it is in a specialized market or a key technology or has some other advantage that makes it competitive. Stepanovich witnessed many corporations where "[p]eople were horribly unhappy but were getting paid so much money that they would get the mortgage and the family commitments and they would just kind of get stuck." This common phenomenon of prosperous discontent is the result of allowing ourselves to compromise what we want to do with our life for what we can accumulate with our labor. In such a case, our paycheck has proceeded to rob us blind.

Subtle Counterfeits

One of the first signs that this process of compromise may already be under way is when you derive material satisfaction only from your work. Once this happens, people begin to measure themselves by their possessions rather than their contributions. They have exchanged their work fulfillment for a counterfeit, material significance. The ultimate scenario we can achieve is to do fulfilling work and be rewarded materially in such a way that causes us to feel truly grateful. This is not to say that gratitude is not possible at various levels of compensation. This sense of gratitude has much to do with a person's level of material wants and preferences. Once a person opts for the counterfeit and makes material gain the sole purpose and not the result of meaningful labor, it's only a short time before workaholism and neglect of relationships begin to surface.

> *"My friend runs a nanny service in the Midwest and serves clients in big cities. She told me that many of the people who employ her service work from 7:00 AM to 9:00 PM, even on weekends, and rarely see or interact with their children. Yet these people specifically call my friend's service because they want an Iowa girl with 'good Midwestern values.' How ironic."*
>
> *—Connie, 35*

Many of those who have children struggle with maintaining the balance between practical material needs and family needs. Nowhere is the dilemma between material progress and relational priorities greater than with working mothers. Studies show that many mothers carry a significant sense of regret and guilt to work each day over the absence of time with their young children. In one study, 38 percent of working moms said they would take a new job with less pay if it meant they could spend more quality time with their families. One-fourth of working moms would accept a pay cut of over 5 percent, and 15 percent of working moms would accept a pay cut of over 10 percent. I have interviewed many who began to question the wisdom of working as many hours as they do when almost half of what they earn goes toward paying someone else to watch their children.

This issue of spending more time with the family is not restricted exclusively to the female gender. A recent study by the Radcliffe Public Policy Center revealed that younger men were the most willing to give up some pay to have more time with their families. Over 70 percent of men 21 to 39 said they would give up pay for family time. Employers are now seeing more fathers who telecommute, attend parenting classes, and take time off for family.

Paula Rayman of the Radcliffe Public Policy Center calls it "an evolutionary shift in gender expectations," adding that "men are saying they want to be in their children's life the way their fathers and grandfathers couldn't be."

Another factor involved here is the number of men who are now primary caregivers. According to the U.S. Census Bureau, there are now (2004) more than 3.3 million children living with their fathers, which is three times the number there were in 1980.

When Charles Schwab held classes on balancing work and family, more men than women attended. Because of the tight labor market, employees have been feeling bolder and more secure asking for accommodations for family life. It is also apparent that women's expectations of their partners have changed. It is no longer assumed that the male is the principal wage earner.

Peter Baylies, who writes a newsletter for at-home dads and who left a programming job in 1993 to care for his children, sums it up this way: "A lot of dads don't want the stress anymore of staying at the office until 10 o'clock. . . . Now, a good family equals success."

A friend of mine, a working mother, told me the following story:

> *"In the last year I have grown weary of watching a day care center raise my children. My youngest girl has one year left before she's off to full-time school. I sat down one night and figured out that I was working one-half of my hours just to pay for the day care. It made no sense whatsoever but I had been doing it while my two children were growing up. I assumed that I had no other option with my job, which I had held for 13 years. I had approached my supervisor before about possibly working part-time or designing hours that fit better into what I wanted in my life, but she said it wouldn't be possible. I finally made up my mind that I would leave and go somewhere else where I could get the flexibility I needed. When I went in to inform my supervisor of my decision, she had a whole different posture in the situation. Suddenly, she could find a way to accommodate me with the hours I wanted. I'm now staying put with hours that fit my life, and I am at home with my youngest child in the morning. I have never been happier. I guess I had no idea that I could make my life this much happier just by asking."*

Man's Search for Meaning

My friend's story illustrates just the tip of the iceberg when it comes to the work scenarios that cause people to feel as though they are missing something meaningful in their life. It may be the career they've chosen that causes these feelings, or they may be in the right career but pursuing it in the wrong place. In the above example, it was a case of being in the right career in the right place but working the wrong hours for the stage of life she was in. It is important to pay attention to this feeling of purpose and meaning and whether it is being fulfilled in your present circumstance. As great as money is, no person was designed to simply make money. People are designed to make a difference, and material gain is simply a chief by-product.

Counting the Cost

We are often quick to calculate the material benefits of the work we do but are reticent to calculate the emotional, physical, and relational liabilities we may have to trade to receive those benefits. Every inch we gain in this world costs us something. The question to be answered: "Is this paycheck taking away more than it is giving?" When I realized that the work I was doing was chipping away at the energy, creativity, and optimism that had made me what I was, I knew that sort of paycheck deduction was too high a price to pay.

What does all this have to do with the New Retirementality? Everything! Many people's retirement fantasies are fueled by the idea of escaping employment that has had an eroding effect on their person over the years. Some people feel at 50 that they are just a shadow of what they were at 38. This is a sad statement about life and employment. Retirement from a career that has robbed us of personal qualities, irreplaceable relationships, and prime years of physical health will not replace what is lost. Retirement, for some, has given them time to repair their health, relationships, and desire to follow their soul's work.

Taking Time Out

Denny Stone was once ensconced in a high-pressure management job with a computer company. His life fell apart when his wife of two and one-half years died of cancer. Stone felt his foundation crumbling beneath him. He sold his house and left his company in a quest to figure out what was important.

His sabbatical lasted two years, and he eventually returned to the same company, albeit in a different job. Stone's time away convinced him of three principles regarding his work:

1. *Reconnect with your passion.* Why work on things that don't matter to you?
2. *Take on new experiences.* You'll surprise yourself at the undiscovered aptitudes you possess.
3. *Listen to people you trust.* Ask the people around you what you're really good at to get better direction for your efforts.

Stone's time-out paid a lasting dividend. According to Stone, "I don't check my life at the door when I go to work anymore and then pick it up on the way out. Life and work are no longer separate."

"If you've been mentally or emotionally detached from your work, it's time to reengage. First, rededicate yourself to your job. Determine to give it an appropriate amount of your undivided attention. Sec-

ond, figure out why you have been detached. Do you need new challenges? Are you in conflict with your boss or coworkers? Are you in a dead-end job? Identify the source of the problem, and create a plan to resolve it."

—John C. Maxwell, author

Don't just look in the mirror; look around you. Look at the price some people are paying for a paycheck. There is something to be learned by observing what people allow themselves to trade for their paycheck. I have made notes of the people I have met over the years who have made inequitable trades. I have seen firsthand what people have chosen to trade for their paychecks:

- A redeemable marriage or relationship
- Meaningful relationships with children
- Personal dignity
- Dreams and ideas
- Physical well-being
- Optimism for life
- Balance and relaxation

No paycheck on the planet Earth is worth any of the aforementioned trades. When we find work we love and carry on that work in balance with the rest of our life, we eradicate the need for retirement. Life was not designed for us to work myopically for 40 years to the neglect of all else and then try to catch up for lost time in retirement. With some introspection, proper guidance, and persistence, we can find work we will always enjoy. If we find that this work comes with a good paycheck, we will enjoy it even more.

The New Retirementality Is . . .

- Finding a sense of self-expression and satisfaction in the work you do.
- Not allowing work to depreciate your physical and psychological health.
- Seeking employment that offers vitality, integrity, tolerance, appreciation, and latitude.
- Counting the cost of your paycheck as well as its benefit.
- Getting your head back in the game.

CHAPTER 12

More Than an Economic Event

> *"I have come to the conclusion that more retirements will fail for non-financial reasons than for financial reasons."*
> —*Michael Stein, author,* The Prosperous Retirement: Guide to the New Reality

> *"Alice came to a place where there were many roads. She stopped and asked the owl for directions.*
> *The owl asked, 'Do you know where you want to go?'*
> *Alice said, 'No.'*
> *'Well then,' the owl said, 'it doesn't make any difference which path you take now.'"*
> —*Lewis Carroll,* Alice in Wonderland

What difference will all our financial planning for the future make if we have no idea what kind of life we want to purchase with those finances? Money has no value in and of itself. Money is only useful in terms of what you can do with it. Just as important as saving for our future is having some sort of vision of what that future will be. An inspiring vision of what you might be and do if you were financially emancipated must accompany all the number crunching if you hope to have a successful transition into whatever your next phase of life may be. Millions are saving for what might be a 35-year journey with absolutely no idea where that journey might take them. These individuals will have a ticket but possess no road map.

Although your freedom to make a transition depends on having your financial house in order, it also hinges on much more than financial factors. Author Michael Stein, in his book on prosperous retirement, talks about the prosperous retirement wheel. A prosperous retirement is at the hub of Stein's wheel, but eight spokes come out from this center—physical health, mental health, diet, exercise, social relations, personal relations, intellectual stimulation, and spiritual balance. (See Figure 12.1.) Many retirement transitions are less than wonderful and fulfilling for the simple reason that preparation was myopically focused on only the financial aspects of retirement with little or no regard for the issues, stresses, and challenges of a radical life transition.

FIGURE 12.1 | Prosperous Retirement Wheel

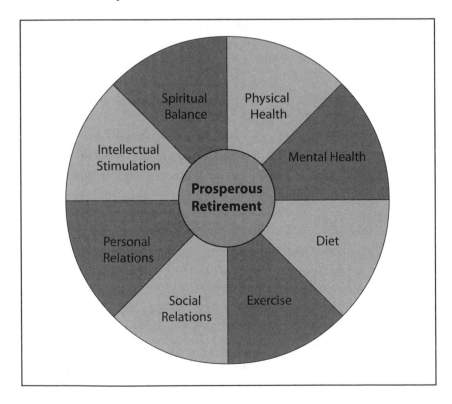

This fact is beginning to be recognized by the financial industry. The National Endowment for Financial Education convened a thinktank to discuss retirement planning in the 21st century. This think tank was not limited to financial professionals but included gerontologists, researchers, a social worker, and a psychologist as well. Some of the strong points of agreement that these varied professionals developed included the following:

- The picture of retirement is changing dramatically.
- Consumers must become more responsible for the success or failure of their own retirement.
- The financial services industry must do a much better job of educating the public about the features, possibilities, and parameters of this new retirement.

> *"Many people are so occupied with getting out of a career trap that they seem to care little about what happens after they leave their jobs. Despite the fact they have planned other aspects of their lives, they seem to feel retirement will take care of itself. The opposite is often true."*
> *—Elwood Chapman and Marion Haynes, authors,*
> *Comfort Zones: Planning Your Future*

Many members of the think tank felt that financial planning in the 21st century is going to be more about personal issues than about financial issues—it will be about generating a new identity, a new you, for a new phase of life. Although money is a primary concern in this new phase of life, it is just one of many. This report on the future of retirement planning states, "Future retirees need to be asking what they want to do with their life during retirement, and what the personal implications of retirement are for them. Baby boomers are looking for a meaningful role in their later adulthood. Money is important to them, but so is the quality of life in their retirement."

> *"My wife and I got a financial advisor in a rather unusual way. I called up a financial services firm and told the woman who answered the phone, 'My wife and I are into the outdoors, hiking, volunteering in our church, that kind of thing. If you have an advisor who's into that kind of stuff, we'd be happy to talk to them. If not, fine.'*

> *The woman said, 'We have just the person who is an advisor here. He's an outdoors nut and probably shares some of your values.'*
>
> *We made an appointment and came to see him a few days later. Did we ever hit it off! What most impressed us about him was that after about an hour of him inquiring into our lives and background, I finally had to say, 'Aren't you going to ask us about our finances?'*
>
> *We ended up having a really good relationship with him and trust him with our money and the future our money will buy."*

I am assuming, because you have read this far, that you have already settled in your mind some basic ideas about retirement, namely:

- Retirement at any particular age is an outdated concept.
- The age at which to retire or the decision to retire at all is based on an inner desire and not outer resources.
- Work can and should be an expression of one's soul and a means for making a meaningful contribution to the world we live in.
- Much of the aging process hinges on choices we make regarding activity, involvement, and attitude.
- I can do what I want with my life when I get serious about doing what I should with my time, energy, and resources.

Issues for Our Middle Years and Beyond

Now we come to all the issues that will accompany our progression into middle and later years. We may never fully retire but we will, nonetheless, still need to deal with these issues. Because most people have only been presented with retirement as some sort of economic cliff that they will jump from in their 60s, they have consequently only looked at preparing a fiscal parachute to carry them through those years. Most people have only done sketchy work on the financial issues, and little or no work on all the life issues that will accompany such a transition. This is about your money and your life. Later chapters of this book will help you to identify some of the financial, legal, estate, and taxation issues that you will need assistance with. The goal is to get you to start seeing your future life in a more holistic sense instead of monomaniacal obsessing over having enough to retire.

If people focus only on having enough money, then the owl's advice to Alice in Wonderland will apply to them. It won't matter what road you take because you haven't given enough thought to where you're going. Life will eventually take us through some very predictable phases. The phases I refer to I borrow from author Michael Stein: the "go-go" phase, the "slow-go" phase, and the "no-go" phase.

The "go-go" phase is the second childhood, the time when you achieve your financial emancipation and can do all the things you wanted to do but couldn't because you were too busy working. Stein characterizes this period as "a second childhood without parental supervision, potentially the most wonderful time in a person's life."

The "slow-go" phase is a more passive phase that is marked by time for more quiet introspection and getting life straight.

The "no-go" phase is defined by the need for medical and possibly nursing care.

There is no guarantee that we will spend any certain amount of time in these particular phases, but chances are that we will end up with experience in all of them. My personal fantasy is that I will live the rest of my life somewhere between the slow-go and the go-go and die in my sleep at 99 (or die of a heart attack from the excitement of a hole-in-one at the same age). I would prefer to live out my emancipated years at a pace that will be both challenging and enjoyable, somewhere between go-go and slow-go. If the slow-go years were marked by introspection and increased spirituality, I would prefer to have them in my current phase of life. It would seem to be a critical step to slow one's pace to a degree if there is a desire for balanced living. From my conversations with those closer to the last phase, it has become apparent to me that I must ponder both the possibility of spending some time and money in the last phase (no-go). At some point, we'll have to make some contingency plans. These contingencies include long-term care insurance, charitable trusts, and the like.

When we achieve our emancipation, we will live most of that emancipated life somewhere in the slow-go to go-go range, but we will still be confronted with issues that come with retirement. These issues are manifold and include the following:

- How we will best occupy our time and energies
- How we will address our personal health and well-being
- How we will continue to challenge ourselves
- What role we will play in our parents' future
- What role we will play in our children's future

- What kind of legacy we will leave in this world
- How we will define success once we have already met our financial goals

Lessons from the Sudden Retiree

"In addition to difficulties relating to lack of preparedness, sudden retirees are in the often unwelcome position of having to redefine themselves."

—Susan K. Bradley, CFP, author

If you want to get an accurate picture of what retirement might feel like, it is better to learn from someone who has been suddenly retired at an early age as opposed to learning about it from someone who worked for 40 years in a job they didn't particularly like and then retired at 65. Sudden retirees are those who are young but ended up in a retired state because of unexpected events such as the merger or sale of a business, downsizing, injury, sickness, caregiving for a family member, or the death of a breadwinning spouse. Some fortunate souls enter unexpected retirement because they come into wealth through the sale of a business, the exercise of stock options, or ownership of a company that goes public. The experiences of these individuals might be a better looking glass for previewing some of your concerns in an early retirement. The people who have been cast into unexpected retirements are often still young, energetic, and full of vision for their future; and this description may apply to you no matter your age.

Once individuals enter retirement, they are suddenly confronted with such issues as cash flow, tax and estate planning, the impact of inflation, insurance, and spending limitations that earlier seemed irrelevant. These issues are just as relevant to the person who has received a windfall as for the person who lacks adequate assets.

Mental Challenges of Retired Living

According to Susan Bradley, a certified financial planner and author of the book *Sudden Money,* the immediate challenge of retirement is the element of surprise. People often aren't mentally prepared for this radical change-of-life pace and direction. Although each person reacts uniquely to surprises, Bradley says there are a few things you can count on. "Whether the impact is positive or negative, it is probably unsettling at first. And people tend to make bad decisions, rash decisions and generally operate with less clarity when they are unsettled."

Sudden retirees find themselves having to make many life decisions before they are ready. Bradley defines "ready" as "the development of money maturity that comes from many decades of consciously saving and investing, the experience of dealing with the expansions and contractions of the markets over the years." This sort of experience helps individuals find insight into their personal levels of risk tolerance. It is hoped that all people understand before they reach retirement stage how to live within their financial limits, what their tax position is, and exactly what financial literacy is. Chapter 16 gives a detailed picture of what financial literacy is all about.

"Who Am I?"

Bradley notes that new retirees are challenged to find a way to redefine themselves in their new state of life. They often find themselves asking soul-searching questions such as, "What is the purpose and meaning of my life?" If the new retirees are relatively young, they still see their peers finding meaning and purpose through the challenges of life and work. The emancipated retirees must now navigate through this maze of finding a sense of personal significance. Bradley thinks that advisors, if they are comfortable, can help people work through this emotional/intellectual/spiritual evolution. At the very least, you want to work with someone who recognizes and acknowledges these issues that are so pertinent to the retirement life stage. By being aware and discussing such issues, advisors can help people avert the potential damage any rashness or confusion may cause.

If individuals are down-and-out about their lack of career identity, they may not be in the mood to vigilantly deal with their many money issues. This is where good advisors are worth their weight in gold. Having a money coach or a life coach who specializes in money gives sudden retirees someone to hand their financial baton over to, which helps them to keep their sanity and balance—while working out how to express their working soul in this new stage of life. Good planners work to empower their clients by providing them greater knowledge of life-stage issues affecting their money. You want an advisor who is interested in your thoughts and feelings, concerns and worries, as well as the management of your money.

Money, Money

A practical issue the starry-eyed candidate for early retirement often overlooks is the impact of inflation over time. If a 65-year-old has a $1.5 million nest egg growing annually at 9 percent, she can expect a cash flow of $100,000 per year for the next 40 years, when adjusted for 3 percent inflation. This is a healthy projection for individuals entering the final quarter of their life, especially if they expect their discretionary spending to decrease over time.

But what if that retirement with the same amount of money came at 40? This same projection would result in running out of money at 80. What happens if that someone lives to be 95 (a very likely possibility in our age)? This would mean a transition from 40 years of financial cruising to the poorhouse overnight. This sort of opportunistic plan leaves little room for unexpected expenses and may not be realistic about the amount of money individuals really want to spend to enjoy their new lifestyle. Factor into this scenario the eroding effect of inflation over time on the spending power of the $100,000. We're talking 40 years here, which is very realistic today for someone taking retirement at the early age of 50 or 55. What did a postage stamp cost 40 years ago? What will it cost 40 years from now? Do you remember when $100,000 sounded like a ton of money? I distinctly remember about 30 years ago a picture of Jack Nicklaus on the cover of a sports magazine with a headline about his winning $100,000 in a year. Players today win ten times that in one tournament. What will that $100,000 represent in another 25 years? The poverty line? Who knows?

When people are not financially or emotionally prepared for a new lifestyle they, being a bit disoriented, tend to get into trouble. The trouble they most commonly get into is mental as well as monetary. They either spend more than they should or they obsess over financial details and investment returns and drive their family and their advisor crazy. These sudden retirees now have the time and opportunity to delve into the minutiae and can't stay away from it. The sudden reliance on investment income as opposed to earned income can quickly trigger such an obsession. Now the dream life of sitting on the beach and drinking Mai-Tais is in reality obsessing over *Investor's Business Daily* and drinking Pepto-Bismol.

The emotional and financial shortsightedness that often crops up with the sudden retiree can act as the arrow on the compass for our own life transitions. What we once called retirement, because those who retired stopped working, we now see as a life transition to other work, less work, or very little work. Money issues and emotional issues accompany this transition—and need to be dealt with. Today, a growing number of advisors recognize this fact and are developing their own competencies and practices to help people through these transitions in a more holistic manner. They are life planners, money coaches, consultants, advisors, and planners. Although these individuals may go by different names, when you meet a good one you'll recognize him or her.

Whether you engage professional help or do it on your own, it is vital to your future to recognize that retirement is not just an economic event. If you do choose to retire, financial preparation becomes just one aspect of a life event. Your life is more important than your retirement.

The New Retirementality Is . . .	<ul><li>Making plans to occupy your mind, time, and energies in retirement.</li><li>Doing all you can to maintain personal health and well-being.</li><li>Deciding how you will define success once your financial goals are met.</li><li>Preparing for the roles you will play in our children's and parents' lives.</li></ul>

The New Retirementality Challenge

Is my financial house in order? What about the rest of the house?

Think about it: How will inflation affect my life in the future? Are there health or relationship issues that will have an impact on my future? How much risk am I willing to take?

Research it: What is the risk level of my current invested assets? How much more or less am I willing to take? What is the risk level of my current lifestyle, including health? How much more or less am I willing to take?

Decide and take action:

- Organize finances and lifestyle to align with long-term goals.

CHAPTER 13

Making a Meaningful Transition

The story is told of Harry Houdini, the famous escape artist who issued a challenge everywhere he went. He claimed he could be locked in any jail cell in the country and be able to free himself in a short time. He had never failed in this challenge except for one isolated incident. One day Houdini walked into a jail cell and the door clanged shut behind him. From under his belt Houdini removed a strong but flexible piece of metal. He began to work, but something seemed odd about this particular lock. He worked for 30 minutes with no results. Frustrated, he labored for another hour and a half. By now he was soaked in sweat and exasperated at his inability to pick this lock. Completely drained from the experience, Harry Houdini collapsed in frustration and failure and fell against the door. To his surprise, the door swung open—the door had never been locked! The door was only locked in the mind of Houdini.

We would all do well to pause for a moment from our work and lean against a philosophical door that can free us from feelings of futility, frustration, insignificance, and even failure. We lean against this door by asking ourselves what we must do to bring a greater sense of meaning to our working life. Once that door is unlocked, everything else, including our material management, can be ordered in such a way as to accelerate and accommodate that meaningful existence.

What can you do to make a meaningful and resourceful transition in your life? You can begin this transition by following these three steps:

1. Decide what it is going to take to define *meaningful* in your life.
2. Begin looking at innovative ways to use your resources (money, time, and ability) to purchase the life you want.
3. Partner with those people who can help you articulate and achieve your goals.

In this chapter I will help you first define what it is that you find meaningful in your life, and in the next chapter I explore some of the innovative transitions others have made to reach that place where they are making a life rather than making a living. In Chapter 20, I explore the process of finding partners to achieve those goals.

In the course of asking people what it is in their working life—and life in general—that will give their life meaning, I often hear such answers as happiness, fulfillment, balance, satisfaction, security, significance, and success. When people use these words, are they simply using different terms to talk about the same thing or do their answers reveal unique elements to a meaningful life? I believe they are unique elements that, once understood for what they are, will add a great degree of clarity to our life. Success is not the same as significance. We can be enormously successful by world standards and feel that what we do is not significant. Happiness can easily be differentiated from security, and it is possible to have one without the other.

As we look forward to a meaningful transition in our life, we need to understand how these seven elements together can define a meaningful and contented life. A meaningful life is a life full of meaning. There are many aspects of our life that give us a sense of fulfillment—family, achievement, exploration, freedom, and altruism are some of the more important aspects. For the sake of clarity, I would like to take a stab at defining these seven meaningful words. Many times people can have an inward revelation when they come to understand these intangible goals for what they are and stop looking for them in the wrong places.

The Seven Intangibles

1. *Happiness* is wanting what you already have. This is not the Madison Avenue definition of happiness. In fact, this definition is the polar opposite of Madison Avenue's mantra that happiness is having more than you have now. It is an old and worn sermon we have heard a million times that things won't make us happier. Yet we watch the ads and begin to accept the underlying message that possessions define the person. We begin to develop a keen sense of peripheral vision regarding our neighbors' homes and the possessions that fill those homes. Soon, we too have assumed the definition of happiness that Madison Avenue has designed for us: the more you have, the happier you'll be. You really won't be happy until you get the things you want.

But the true key to happiness is not getting those things; it is in changing what we want. If you cannot sense the emotion of contentment with your current circumstances, what makes you think you will feel it with your desired circumstances? Your desired circumstances will only change your view. Once you get there, you will be subjected to a whole new and higher realm of advertising proclaiming that you can have more than this.

"Money won't make you happy, but neither will poverty."

These comments are not pious rantings against possessions and a home on the hill. Possessions can be personal rewards for significant labors—and there is certainly nothing wrong with that. Where many individuals go wrong, however, is in believing that things, once possessed, will make them happy. Ultimately, they will not. In fact, as many of those who possess the things you may think you want will tell you, these things have the potential to make you unhappy because all things of value require responsibility and insecurity. A bigger house means more work, more maintenance, and more things that can go wrong—and at a bigger price tag. Part of the price tag of that shiny new car, boat, or other luxury item is insecurity, because now there is worry about damage and risk.

It's important to settle in our minds that happiness is a state of mind and not a state of material ownership. If we do not settle this fact, we are destined to a maze of futility at a very high price.

"When I started making really good money, I decided to buy myself a really nice watch, something in the Rolex genre. In the midst of my search I stopped myself with the thought that I wasn't really

being honest with myself as to why I wanted this watch. I came to the conclusion that the motive I was articulating didn't agree with what I was feeling. I said I wanted the watch because 'I wanted a nice looking, dependable timepiece.' But what I was feeling inside was that I simply wanted to impress others with my achievements. I asked myself if I really needed to spend $7,000 to tell everyone I had made it. I thought of some of my family back home who wouldn't know a Rolex from a Timex. I came to a compromise. I decided I did indeed want to reward myself with a fine timepiece but that I would not choose a brand that was a blatant advertisement of my achievement. I bought a brand every bit as beautiful and dependable as a Rolex but far less recognizable to the masses. This decision started a very powerful line of reasoning that, so far, has kept me from buying a bigger house and more expensive car than I need and has helped to keep my materialism in check. It's like the old saying, 'We buy things we don't need with money we don't have to impress people we don't like.' And I'm trying not to go down that path."

—Doug, financial professional, 35

Happiness is easy. Don't complicate it. If you want what you have, you are happy.

2. *Fulfillment* is optimizing the use of your abilities. Fulfillment is easy too. It is doing the things you love to do. It is expressing your working soul. It is engaging in work that energizes you rather than depletes you. It does not necessarily come from success in your career because the career you are in may not be the soul-felt expression of who you are. When you are expressing who you are with your work, you have shaken hands with fulfillment. Once you discover this relationship between who you are and what you do, it is awfully difficult to go back to work that engages the hands but not the heart. Taste of this water and you will no longer be satisfied with simply making a living.

I remember well the lack of fulfillment I felt at one point in my career because I was doing the same routine over and over. I knew I needed an outlet for the creative impulse within me. I wasn't fulfilled until I found ways to express that creativity. I now know that I can never go back to work that clogs this creative expression. My first criterion today when I am offered work is not how much I'll make but rather will it be a creative challenge. Once you discover the work that fulfills you, it will be hard, if not impossible, to disengage yourself from it.

3. *Balance* is walking the tightrope between too much and not enough. Work, family, and leisure—when we get them in balance we enjoy life. Feeling as if we're having fun in life is a good indicator that we have achieved some degree of balance. How many people do you know who have worked hard for so long that they no longer know how to relax when they get the opportunity? How many people do you know who are so busy supporting their family that they never see their family? What do they achieve by neglecting the very people that motivate them to earn a good living? People today are aware of these issues and are no longer as willing to put their personal life in a deep freeze for the sake of their company's goals. It is becoming quite frequent in interviews to hear the applicant ask, "Will I have a life?" A growing percentage of employees are willing to trade more income for more time and flexibility.

At the other extreme of the life balance pendulum are the individuals who have so much time for leisure that they have lost their sense of purpose and significance, and, consequently, their fun is no longer fun. There is a fine balance to be achieved in attending to the physical, emotional, social, and spiritual sides of our being. There is also a fine balance to be achieved in attending to the working, familial, and frolicking sides of our being.

4. *Satisfaction* is improving the quality of our efforts and relationships. I believe that satisfaction is a quality issue. If we are constantly seeking to raise the level of quality in the products and services we are involved with, if we are constantly striving to improve key relationships in our life, and if we are living a thoughtful, self-examined life, we will feel a sense of satisfaction.

When talking to those who feel a sense of dissatisfaction in their life, I see a recurring pattern of lukewarm relationships and a lack of conviction about the impact and meaning of their daily work. It is important to look for opportunities to satisfy your need for inner satisfaction at the place you are today before you start believing greener grasses elsewhere will fill that appetite. I recently talked with a woman who told me she needed to get back to helping the homeless so she could feel a greater sense of satisfaction about her life. She felt her life was too self-absorbed at the time. I began to ask her what she did in her job that helped others. She thought about it and said that she gave seminars that helped women discover financial independence. After she said that, she suddenly realized she was ignoring a great source of inner satisfaction right under her nose. Satisfaction can often be fulfilled by appreciating the things we do now and by striving to do them better. Satisfaction revolves around the quality of our efforts and our relationships.

5. *Security* is possessing the freedom to pursue our goals. Whether our goals are anchored in work, family, leisure, or all of the above, we only feel a sense of security when we know we will have the freedom to continue pursuing those goals. People may feel insecure about their job for fear of getting laid off and not being able to pursue the work goals they desire. Others fear they will not have enough assets to be able to pursue the lifestyle they want in their retirement years. Possessing adequate finances can unquestionably provide a great degree of security because it can give us a material guarantee of sorts that we will be able to do what we want with our life. This is the security that modern retirement represents for most people. Life will always present us with opportunities to feel insecure because very little in this world is guaranteed. We may have the money to do what we want, but our health could diminish and rob us of our mobility and activity. We can make all sorts of plans for our future, but we have no guarantee that those plans will pan out.

Security hinges on more than just the health of our assets; it is also affected by the health of our body and close relationships. As billionaire Warren Buffett put it, "The only two things that can make you truly happy in this world are people that love you and being healthy, and money can't buy you either one of those." We can however build on our sense of security by staying close to those who love us, form good physical habits, and keep putting away all we can toward our financial emancipation.

6. *Significance* is making the best use of our time. The famed psychiatrist and philosopher Victor Frankl stated that man's chief motivation was the need for significance. People are motivated by a need to make a difference somehow in others' lives—to feel they are making a contribution that is significant. Many people erroneously believe that a sense of significance will be satisfied by the acquisition of power and control over others. It cannot. This inward sense of significance is satisfied by the best possible use of our most valuable resource: time.

Why do so many retired police officers have such a short life expectancy (many die within one year of retirement)? Could it be because they no longer feel significant and this feeling quickly leads to their demise? Quite possibly their life expectancy could be lengthened by spending retirement time on activities of personal significance.

We all have only so many days on this earth, and those days are fleeting. Look at how fast the last decade has seemed to pass. Parents get a magnified perspective on the fleeting nature of time as they watch their children sprout and exit while they feel almost the same as they did 15 years ago. People want to make a difference in other people's lives. People want to make a difference in the work they do. People want to make a difference with the wise distribution of their time, energy, and resources. Money has the power to feed this significance only when it is shared or emancipates us to share our time and skills. Charity and volunteerism can be crucial to a sense of significance in our life.

A person who works in a job but doesn't see the benefit of that job to the end user will lack a sense of significance. He will feel that he is wasting his time. A person who is a workaholic and misses all her children's meaningful activities will feel she is abusing the short time she has. Significance is closely related to how we manage the time we have.

7. *Success* is the satisfaction of reaching our goals. Success is a sense that relies heavily on moving toward or achieving personal goals. But the term *success* must be broadened beyond the material to have real meaning in our life. The truly successful individual has goals involving who they are (character), what they do (career), and what they possess (wealth)—and, more than likely, in that order of importance. How successful does an individual who is garnering riches but failing in the personal character department feel? It is a truth that our reputation is worth its weight in gold. Financial success could be defined as having enough to meet your own needs and the needs of those you choose to help. This is a worthy financial goal. Career success could be defined as having the opportunity to pursue your career goals. We feel most successful when we are actively pursuing our heartfelt goals. As long as we are actively pursuing personal goals and making progress toward them, our sense of success and confidence will be fed.

A sense of success starts with first having a goal. Many fail the financial success test at this point because they have no clearly defined financial goals. Having enough to retire is not a goal; it is a vague desire, a dream. Wanting to have financial assets of a million dollars by the time you are 55 is a clearly articulated goal. Now we have a standard against which we can measure our success. Having a clearly defined goal to feel successful holds as true in our career and character as in our finances. *Studies show that the majority of us do not have clearly defined financial goals, and I would assume this to be true in other areas of life as well. In the financial realm, this problem can be easily remedied by partnering with someone who can first help us articulate those goals and then help us stay the course in achieving those goals.*

The Meaningful Transition

These seven intangibles cannot be satisfied simply by a job or a certain amount of material possessions. Happiness, fulfillment, balance, satisfaction, security, significance, and success should not be the by-products of our life; they should be the goals! When we myopically focus on money or work or leisure at the expense of other areas of meaning in our life, we deny ourselves the fulfillment that comes from these seven intangibles, the things that define contentment. Remember, your life is not about making money—*your money is about making a life.* These seven intangibles cannot be bought, but you can easily sell them out.

The New Retirementality Is . . .

- Deciding what it will take to define "meaningful" in your life.
- Looking at innovative ways to use your resources (money, time, and ability) to purchase the life you want.
- Partnering with people who can help you articulate and achieve your life goals.

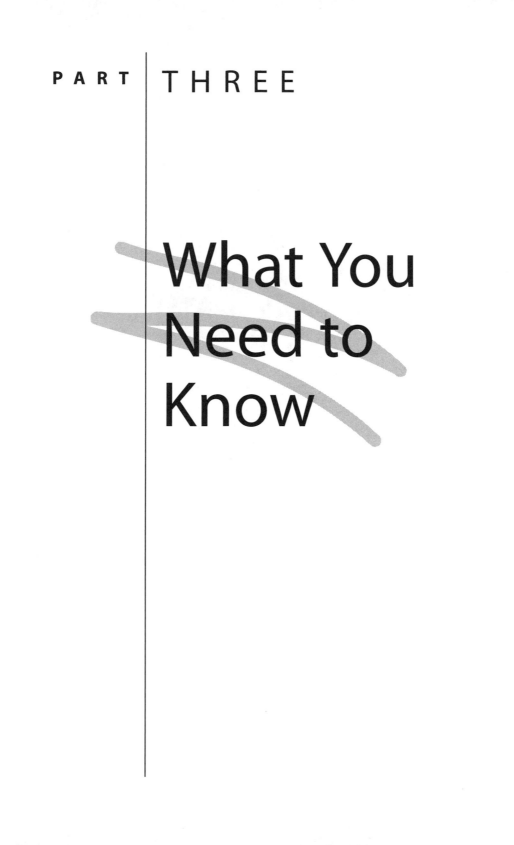

PART | THREE

What You Need to Know

CHAPTER 14

Your Money and Your Life

> *"Money is a terrible master. If it gets over you and you get under it, you become its slave."*
>
> —*E. Stanley Jones, theologian*

Dr. Gordon Allport, in writing about the characteristics of healthy personalities, offered these six traits:

1. A positive concept of self
2. Seeing value in people as human beings
3. Enjoyment in helping others
4. A realistic perception of the world
5. A sense of humor
6. A unifying philosophy of life that defines purpose for living

I can't help but wonder, when considering these characteristics, how much bearing our money life has on the health of our personalities. For example, do you have a poor self-image because you feel you don't make much money or manage money well? Have you ever met individuals who, rather than valuing people as humans, view relationships as stepping stones on the path to material achievement? Have you ever wanted to help someone but couldn't afford to? Do you know anyone who is living a champagne lifestyle on a seltzer budget? Has your sense of humor been dampened by financial frustration and strain? And finally, do you ever feel that your financial situation is keeping you from fulfilling your sense of purpose in life?

Most of us can probably answer "yes" to one or more of these questions. The quality-of-life issue I'd like to focus on here is the last—*a unifying philosophy of life that defines purpose.* I have witnessed a great disconnection in people between their money and their lives and sense the need for a unifying dialogue. I call this dialogue *Financial Life Planning.*

Financial Life Planning clearly addresses the uniqueness of each individual's life issues as they relate to investments and financial decisions. Too often we deal with money issues in a quantitative vacuum and leave the life ramifications to chance.

I believe that no financial or investment decision should be made outside of the context of how it can and will implicate our lives as a whole. On the other side of the financial/life coin, I believe that no life decision should be made without contemplating the impact on our financial situation. There is an umbilical connection between our money and our lives, an inextricable connection where every money decision has the potential to affect the quality of our life, and every life decision has the potential to impact the quality of our financial situation.

> *"Jesus talked more about money than about heaven. Maybe that's because he understood that money, if not respected for what it is, can turn our lives into a living hell."*
> —The author

We don't achieve financial/life success by engaging in a numbers-driven money discussion and hope that it fits our lives. We experience financial/life success by taking a closer look at our lives—what we are experiencing, what we hope to experience—and by designing a financial plan around those life factors. In this chapter, I will share some of the tools you can use to help align your life and money. Once you take this step, you may find a new sense of wholeness and peace surrounding your financial and investment decisions, *because you are engaging in a unifying philosophy of life that defines purpose for your money and your life.*

The Money/Life Puzzle

I have met a number of competent and caring financial planners who are engaging in this sort of life-focused dialogue as a preface to financial planning—and they have profound stories to tell. Clients are experiencing life-changing epiphanies when engaged in dialogues that cut to the core of what money is all about—quality of life and a sense of purpose.

I have found that the financial professionals who are most eager to adopt the Financial Life Planning approach are highly competent, possess great integrity, and are extremely caring about the well-being of their clients. No coincidence there. One such planner, Elizabeth Jetton, CFP, of Atlanta, shares a beautiful metaphor of this unifying philosophy of money and life: "You have a 200-piece jigsaw puzzle scattered on the table in front of you. What is the first and most important piece?" Most people will say the corner piece. Elizabeth answers, "No, it's the picture on the cover of the box. If you don't know what that picture is, you're just moving pieces."

Too often, when it comes to our financial lives, we fail to step back and look at the big picture. Instead, we move pieces around, replacing investments, insurance policies, etc., and paying too little attention to the long-term and holistic perspectives.

> *"Some people know the cost of everything but the value of nothing."*
> *—Oscar Wilde*

The general public has been universally informed that every money issue should and can be solved through a myopic focus on mathematics: "Let's take your age, the amount of money in your portfolio, run some calculations, and presto! Here's the answer for your life." The financial services profession and its practitioners share some responsibility for this perception (along with the media), as too often we rely exclusively on calculators to solve problems that are better weighed by conversation and conscience.

The overweighting on quantitative factors results in a process that is skewed more toward *what we have* instead of *who we are*. How do we begin to balance the books between quantitative and qualitative factors in developing a financial plan? By engaging in the Financial Life Planning, or FLP, process.

The goal of quantitative inquiry is to establish objectives as expressed in mathematical terms (i.e., amount needed, return expected, time needed, time for accumulation, etc.). These calculations are necessary and good but are not "waterproof," unless we have also performed sufficient qualitative inquiry into what is going on in our lives and what financial needs arise from that inquiry.

Moving from Financial Planning to Financial Life Planning

In the financial planning model in Figure 14.1, I seek to address issues in the areas of asset management, risk management, debt manage-

FIGURE 14.1 | Financial Planning Model

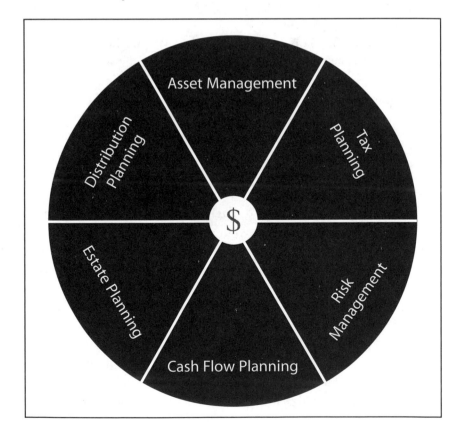

ment, tax planning, estate planning, and income planning. Although each area is meaningful and critical to financial well-being, there is an underlying assumption inherent in the solely quantitative approach used to perform these functions. The tacit and unwitting assumption communicated by many financial professionals in developing a financial plan is that everyone is essentially the same, and the only thing that really needs to change from one person to the next is which numbers get plugged into the formula. Is this an assumption you would want someone to make about you?

As good as your principles may be, I am not comfortable with the assumption that my values and principles with money are the same as everyone else's. Neither am I comfortable with the assumption that my history, present circumstances, and future hopes are the same. Yet, by virtue of a process that leans heavily on mathematical function, these assumptions are made thousands of times a day across the financial planning landscape.

> *"If I were a client and the financial professional I went to visit asked me in the first five minutes about what I had and where it was, I would run for the exit, because it is obvious that that advisor is more interested in my money than in me."*
> *—Roy Diliberto, CFP, selected as one of America's top financial planners by several consumer financial magazines*

The numbers are important only from the standpoint that they deliver the quality of life that we desire. The numbers should not exist to drive the life but to support it. If we believe this, we must place primary emphasis on life issues before we address our financial issues. This, in a nutshell, is the philosophical footing of Financial Life Planning.

It's More about the Who Than the What

At the core of the financial planning process is the life of the unique human being for whom that process is being utilized. Financial Life Planning recognizes four critical life arenas that need to be understood in order for the financial processes to be "spot on" and lead to the kind of fulfillment that comes from material/philosophical harmony. These four life cornerstones are:

1. Your history (including your history with money)
2. Your principles and values toward life and money
3. Your present life transitions
4. Your hopes and goals

These four areas are the corner pieces you'll need to start with to put together the puzzle of your financial life.

At the qualitative level, the financial industry's inquiry process historically has been largely focused on "goals." Inquiring only about goals without balancing history, present circumstances, and the value set of the client can, and often does, lead to disappointment. What is the point of building a plan around a goal, only to see that goal usurped by a circumstance you are facing and possibly not disclosing?

The Financial Life Planning process starts with your life, helps you examine your greatest needs and priorities, and then moves to financial adjustments to facilitate the needs in your life—rather than making financial decisions and then crossing your fingers and hoping that these dollar decisions fit what's happening in your life.

For the past three years, I have been developing tools and teaching the Financial Life Planning process to both consumers and professional financial planners. What I have discovered is that, since the events of 9/11, the market downturn of 2000–2002, and the reports of corporate corruption, people are more than ready for a financial process that revolves fully around the needs in their life, not around what a company wants to sell or the ever-elusive goal of getting rich or becoming a millionaire.

Figure 14.2 is a sample of one of the FLP tools, the Life Transitions Profile, that will help you examine the most pressing issues in four areas of your life: family, work/career, finances, and charitable/legacy issues. Check off the transitions that you are dealing with now and assign a priority (high, medium, or low) to them. If the transition does not apply, then check NA.

You can get your personalized Life Transitions Profile based on the transitions in your life by visiting http://www.flponline.net. This report includes:

1. Questions you need to answer about each transition
2. Financial implications related to your particular transition(s)
3. Educational resources (books, articles, and Web sites) that will help you navigate successfully through each transitions

FIGURE 14.2 | Life Transitions Profile

Life Transitions Profile				Financial *Life* Planning

① FAMILY

Priority Code: **H** = Highest **M** = Medium **L** = Low **NA** = Not Applicable

Life Transitions	H	M	L	NA
Getting married	○	○	○	○
Going through a divorce or separation	○	○	○	○
Recent loss of your spouse (widowhood)	○	○	○	○
Expecting a child	○	○	○	○
Adopting a child	○	○	○	○
Need to hire child care	○	○	○	○
Child entering adolescence	○	○	○	○
Child with special needs (disability/other)	○	○	○	○
Child preparing for college	○	○	○	○
Child going away to college	○	○	○	○
Child getting married	○	○	○	○
Empty nest	○	○	○	○
Family special event	○	○	○	○
Providing assistance to a family member	○	○	○	○
Concern about aging parent	○	○	○	○
Concern about health of spouse or child	○	○	○	○
Concern about personal health	○	○	○	○
Family member in need of professional care	○	○	○	○
Family member with a disability or serious illness	○	○	○	○
Family member expected to die soon	○	○	○	○
Death of family member	○	○	○	○
Other	○	○	○	○

② CHARITABLE LEGACY

Priority Code: **H** = Highest **M** = Medium **L** = Low **NA** = Not Applicable

Life Transitions	H	M	L	NA
Monthly stipend to parent(s) (parental pension)	○	○	○	○
Gifting to children/grandchildren	○	○	○	○
Develop or review an estate plan	○	○	○	○
Develop an end of life plan	○	○	○	○
Create or fund a foundation	○	○	○	○
Create or fund a scholarship fund	○	○	○	○
Give to community causes / events	○	○	○	○
Give to church or religious organizations	○	○	○	○
Give to other charitable organizations	○	○	○	○
Other	○	○	○	○

(continued)

4. A "next steps" area, where you can define your action plan (self-directed or with the help of a financial planner)

Figure 14.3 shows the summary page from my personal FLP report.

FIGURE 14.2 | Life Transitions Profile, *continued*

Life Transitions Profile

Financial *Life* Planning

3 **WORK / CAREER**

Priority Code: **H** = Highest **M** = Medium **L** = Low **NA** = Not Applicable

Life Transitions	H	M	L	NA
Contemplating career change	○	○	○	○
New job	○	○	○	○
Job Promotion	○	○	○	○
Job loss	○	○	○	○
Job restructuring	○	○	○	○
New job training / education program	○	○	○	○
Starting a new business	○	○	○	○
Gaining or losing a business partner	○	○	○	○
Selling or closing a business	○	○	○	○
Transferring business to family member	○	○	○	○
Downshift / simplify work life	○	○	○	○
Taking a sabbatical or leave of absence	○	○	○	○
Phasing into retirement	○	○	○	○
Full retirement from current job / career	○	○	○	○
Other	○	○	○	○

4 **FINANCIAL**

Priority Code: **H** = Highest **M** = Medium **L** = Low **NA** = Not Applicable

Life Transitions	H	M	L	NA
Selling a house	○	○	○	○
Refinancing your mortgage	○	○	○	○
Purchase a home	○	○	○	○
Relocate	○	○	○	○
Reconsidering investment philosophy and risk profile	○	○	○	○
Significant investment gain	○	○	○	○
Significant investment loss	○	○	○	○
Concern about debt	○	○	○	○
Considering an investment opportunity	○	○	○	○
Receive an inheritance or financial windfall	○	○	○	○
Selling assets	○	○	○	○
Considering change of financial service provider	○	○	○	○
Other	○	○	○	○

The high priorities in my family life are "children going to college" and "concern about aging parents." My transition issue in work/career is "starting or purchasing a business." My priorities in the arena of charitable/ legacy are "increasing charitable giving" and "developing an estate plan."

FIGURE 14.3 | Personal FLP Report

Financial Planning
FLPinc.com

Life Transition Summary Report
for Mitch Anthony

FAMILY

Selected Transitions	Priority Code
Child going to college	High
Concern about aging parent	High

WORK/CAREER

Selected Transitions	Priority Code
Start or purchase a business	High

CHARITABLE/LEGACY

Selected Transitions	Priority Code
Increase charitable giving	High
Develop estate plan	High

We have one child going into his final year of college, and another getting ready to enter. (Is that ingenious family planning or what?) We also have two more children who will both be ready for college within the next seven years (nothing ingenious about that). You'll remember from an earlier chapter that I'm on the hook for half the college bill. Some of you may even be doubting my true motives for the "Anthony family matching-grant college savings" program. The net/net is we need to do some serious planning for both the short term and the midterm to meet our obligations.

The next family issue for us is concern about aging parents. One parent was swindled out of his pension by a company he served for 25 years. One parent sold her business in the year 2000 and invested in a stock market that ebbed both her assets and hopes. We decided that it was in our power and in accordance with the principles of gratitude to do something about both these situations. So we created a "parental pension" for both parents (I will describe that in more detail in Chapter 15).

In addition, another parent needed financial assistance in building a "retirement residence," to be able to reside near lifelong friends during the autumn years. We consider these transitions as worthy investments and had to make a number of financial adjustments, investments, and maneuvers to facilitate them (this is where we learned the value of a competent and caring advisor).

Under the category of business transitions, I am in the throes of creating a new business that is loaded with financial implications for my current business, lifestyle, and future.

The final category on my personal Life Transitions Profile is charitable and legacy transitions, which is as near and dear to my heart as the family transitions, because it fulfills my heart's deepest sense of purpose. My wife and I agree that the most gratifying contributions on this planet are the lines of support we are able to provide for friends who are doing the difficult (and scarcely recompensed) works of mercy in this world. We want to increase our support for those we know who do excellent works in caring for orphans in China, supporting single and abandoned mothers around the world, aiding in suicide prevention efforts, and as missionaries who live and breathe the love of God. This component also plays into our need for developing an estate plan as well as our longing to leave the right legacy to our children someday (and not see corruption infect our family as a result of inheritance). Most important, I know that my wife, after losing her first husband whose estate was not in order, does not need to see an encore of that event in her life. I have some financial arrangements that I must continue to revisit to properly manage this transition in life.

Figure 14.4 is an example of one of the worksheets I (and my financial planner) received when I completed the Life Transitions Profile. We received similarly customized worksheets for each aforementioned life transition.

FIGURE 14.4 | Life Transitions Profile Worksheet

FAMILY
Concern About Aging Parent

1. Describe the current physical and mental health of your parent(s): _____
   _____
   _____

   What are your concerns for the future? _____
   _____
   _____

2. Describe your parents' income sources (i.e., Social Security, pensions, VA benefits, personal savings and investments):
   _____
   _____

3. Describe your parents' insurance coverage (i.e., long-term care, health insurance, Medicare, Medicaid):
   _____
   _____

4. Do you anticipate that your parent(s) will require special care or living arrangements? ☐ Yes ☐ No ☐ Unsure
   If yes, have you researched availability and costs? _____
   _____

5. Do you anticipate that it will be necessary for you to subsidize the living expenses or special needs expenses of your parent(s)?
   ☐ Yes ☐ No ☐ Unsure   Explain: _____
   _____
   _____

   If yes, what assets or income do you plan to use for this purpose? _____
   _____

   Do you have family members who could help share these expenses?
   ☐ Yes ☐ No ☐ Unsure   Explain: _____
   _____

6. Will it be necessary for you or your spouse to change your living and/or working situation to care for a parent?
   ☐ Yes ☐ No ☐ Unsure

   If yes, how will this affect your personal/family financial situation, financial goals, retirement plans, and long-term financial security?
   _____
   _____

(continued)

FIGURE 14.4 | Life Transitions Profile Worksheet, *continued*

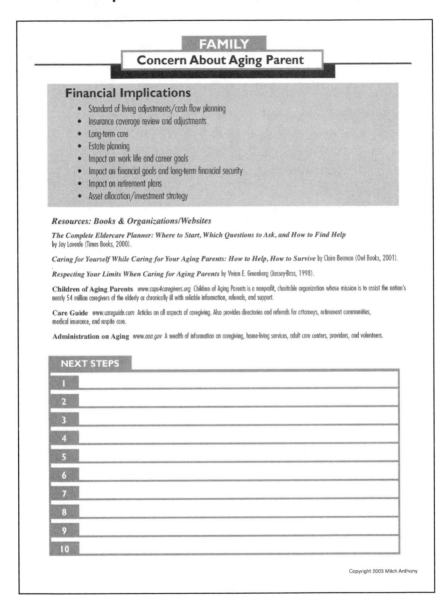

FAMILY
Concern About Aging Parent

Financial Implications
- Standard of living adjustments/cash flow planning
- Insurance coverage review and adjustments
- Long-term care
- Estate planning
- Impact on work life and career goals
- Impact on financial goals and long-term financial security
- Impact on retirement plans
- Asset allocation/investment strategy

Resources: Books & Organizations/Websites

The Complete Eldercare Planner: Where to Start, Which Questions to Ask, and How to Find Help by Joy Loverde (Times Books, 2000).

Caring for Yourself While Caring for Your Aging Parents: How to Help, How to Survive by Claire Berman (Owl Books, 2001).

Respecting Your Limits When Caring for Aging Parents by Vivian E. Greenberg (Jossey-Bass, 1998).

Children of Aging Parents *www.caps4caregivers.org* Children of Aging Parents is a nonprofit, charitable organization whose mission is to assist the nation's nearly 54 million caregivers of the elderly or chronically ill with reliable information, referrals, and support.

Care Guide *www.careguide.com* Articles on all aspects of caregiving. Also provides directories and referrals for attorneys, retirement communities, medical insurance, and respite care.

Administration on Aging *www.aoa.gov* A wealth of information on caregiving, home-living services, adult care centers, providers, and volunteers.

NEXT STEPS

1	
2	
3	
4	
5	
6	
7	
8	
9	
10	

A Healthier, Wealthier, Happier You

These questions will help you and your mate (and advisor, if need be) think through each issue and get your arms around the implications of this particular transition in life. The financial implications illustrate the fiscal tether between this event in your life and the impact or adjustments within your financial situation. The resources listed are like navigational instruments—you can study the notes of those who have traversed these waters before you.

In this simple exercise, the power of unifying our money and our life is apparent. I have seen enough evidence of the ameliorating effect of this simple exercise and dialogue to convince me that *this is the future of financial planning*. The day is coming when financial conversations will not commence around numbers, balances, and account whereabouts, but in the only place of real relevance to our heart and soul—at the core of what is happening in our lives.

Both emotional and financial ledgers can and should be settled into one action plan. This sort of process brings about a unifying effect that results not only in more positive personalities but in more balanced and fulfilling lives as well.

The New Retirementality Is . . .	• Understanding the impact of money on every area of our lives. • Engaging in a financial process that commences around what's happening in our lives, and then making financial adjustments to facilitate those happenings. • Using our money to fuel a sense of purpose.

The New Retirementality Challenge

Have you ever engaged in a Financial Life Planning process?

Think about it. Do you have a financial plan in place that covers all the family, work, financial, and legacy transitions you will navigate in your life?

Research it. Get your own Life Transitions Profile by logging on to Financial Life Planning online at http://www.flponline.com and begin researching the steps you need to take.

Decide and take action. If you have a trusted financial advisor, make an appointment to review your Life Transitions Profile and decide the financial steps that need to be taken.

CHAPTER 15

It's Not Just about You

> *"No one ever wishes on their deathbed that they had spent more time at the office."*
>
> *—Anonymous*

Not only can we not "take it with us," but neither can we recapture the time we spent gathering it in the first place. Richard Wagner of Worth Living, LLC, contends that people in his profession need to go beneath the surface of the answers people give when asked about their financial goals. For example: When a client says, "I want to retire at age 65," the advisor should ask, "Why?" When a client says, "I want to ensure my family's financial health," the advisor should ask, "What does that mean?"

It's about getting past the merely quantifiable to questions that engage issues of life purpose, duties and responsibilities, and spiritual imperatives. Or, as Wagner puts it, "confronting the essence of money and soul" by asking questions such as:

- What's the money for anyway?
- How much is enough?
- What do you think you are supposed to do with the money?

- When and where do your most deeply felt concerns and values come into play, and how do they relate to your financial resources?
- If you had all the money you would ever need, how would you live your life differently?
- If you knew you were going to die in six months, what would you change?

These sorts of questions instigate conversations that help people differentiate quantity from quality in money issues. Wagner asks his peers, "What exactly is quantity if we can't acknowledge and identify quality?" These conversations inevitably lead us to other people.

Other People's Money

Is all that money you're saving exclusively designated for your personal ride into the sunset? Or will you find other obligations laying a claim to some of your retirement savings? Today's prospering baby boomers will have more responsibilities to consider than the retirees of the past and may find that those responsibilities provide due incentive to redefine retirement at a personal level. Do I support my children or my parents? My children *and* my parents? My parents and then my children? Today's contemplators of retirement living have more to consider than whether they live on the gulf side or Atlantic side of Florida. One of the realities of increased longevity is increased responsibility for the children and grandchildren of the entire octogenarian to centenarian population. The reality check that a lot of people in their 50s and 60s are now experiencing has to do with the time and attention they must pay toward aging parents. The freedom they dreamed of and saved for was cruising down the highway in their Winnebago with not a care in the world. This freedom in many cases has been seriously restricted by caretaking responsibilities for aging parents. A growing number of these parents prefer to live in their home, but are frail, in failing health, and require increased degrees of vigilance. For many, the carefree drive down the freeway in the Winnebago has been supplanted by a ride that is interrupted with three calls to the ailing parent a day and an abiding sense of anxiety over the parent's well-being. For others, the ride down the freeway has been postponed indefinitely.

"My wife and I always thought we would sell our business, retire at 62, and travel the country and take our sweet time wherever we wanted. When we were 50 and my wife's mother was 83, we really didn't expect that she would be around for another 12 years with the health problems she had. Now we are 62 and she is 95 and quite vulnerable to accidents and injury. It's touch and go every day. We're putting off our plans and have resigned ourselves to whatever hand fate deals. Sometimes we feel a bit selfish for thinking about what it would be like to get out and see the world a bit, but you can't help but dream when you saved so many years to be able to do it. We don't blame my mother-in-law for wanting to live at home as long as she possibly can. We certainly don't want our children to convince us to live in some sort of nursing facility unless it was absolutely necessary."

—Darrell, architect, 62

The Baby Boomer's Crunch

A fact of life those of us aged 30 to 55 must face today is that our society's great strides in longevity will have a long-term effect on our economic and life planning. Many of us can plan on having parents living until they are 90 to 100 years of age. Many will be self-sufficient but many will need our time, attention, and resources. Here I want to address the issue of resources for those whose parents may be facing a financial shortfall in their retirement years, my motive being the wide economic disparity I often see between prospering baby boomers and their mature parents.

Many of today's baby boomers are caught in a crunch between their parents' longevity and their children's entitlements. I recently met a gentleman in his 50s who said he probably could have retired a couple of years ago but he is supplementing his mother and father's Social Security by $800 a month, and he has a ten-year-old son whose college costs he estimates will tax his nest egg. His scenario is not all that unusual and will become all the more common in the next 20 to 30 years. His child is the result of a second marriage, so the child from that marriage will enter college when the father is 61 years old. His parents didn't have a pension to supplement their Social Security; they are in their late

70s and would have an uncomfortable existence were it not for the subsidy their son is providing. Many people reading this book are facing or will potentially face similar circumstances.

Some people facing this financial crunch between parents and offspring will not be able to support both. To maximize their potential to meet these obligations requires ingenuity, discipline, and a possible redefinition of retirement living. A primary question many will have to ask themselves is, "What is my first obligation?" Is subsidizing an aging parent's financial shortfall an obligation of adult offspring? If so, what compromises in our own spending and planning will be necessary to accomplish such a subsidy? Is paying for my children's college expenses an obligation? If it is, how do I do it without sabotaging my own hopes for financial liberation? If I don't feel it is a mandatory obligation, how do I help my children get through the college years? These questions raise some sharply divided opinions on what our moral and financial obligations are and are not. These questions also reveal that many of us have failed to prepare adequately from a financial planning perspective.

Mom and Dad

"My experience has shown that it takes somewhere between $250 and $400 per month in additional income to give most retirees the comfort level and peace of mind they need. A surprisingly large deal of good can come from a modest sum of additional income."
—*Bruce Bruinsma, financial planner/retirement specialist*

Do you have a parent whose life would derive a margin of comfort with an additional $300 to $400 per month? Is it in your power or your power combined with that of your siblings to provide this margin of comfort? While doing research for this book, I met many people who have found creative ways of giving their aging parents additional peace of mind in their mature years. Following are some of their stories.

"One year at Christmas my brother, who has made a great deal of money, got all seven of us siblings together and suggested a way to help our parents enjoy their retirement. They still lived in the big old house we had grown up in. Mom was tired from all the upkeep. It was too much house just for the two of them. But they stayed

because the mortgage was paid off. My brother suggested all seven of us chip in what we could and build them a smaller, more appropriate retirement home. The proceeds they received from the sale of their current home could then be put in a fund or annuity that would provide them additional monthly income. They were both on Social Security and didn't have enough money to freely pursue some of their travel interests. We all thought it was a great idea, and though we couldn't contribute in equal amounts, we did what we could. The seven of us came up with a budget of $150,000. The brother who brought up the idea donated half of that amount. We sat Mom and Dad down that holiday and told them our intentions and advised them to start planning their new home. Needless to say, it was one unforgettably joyous holiday for all of us."

—Marlene, 37

The Parental Pension

Some, whose parents were subsisting on Social Security, part-time earnings, meager pensions, savings, or a combination of these, created annuity-type funds that paid their parent(s) a monthly subsidy. I like the concept of a *parental pension* for these types of situations. Many would agree that we owe a great deal to our parents for the sacrifices they made for our benefit. I think of my own father's decision to turn down higher-paying, more prestigious jobs in many cities because those cities were experiencing racial tumult in the late 1960s. He chose instead to restrict his career advancement so he and my mother could raise us in a small, quiet midwestern city. Many of our parents are stunned at the financial opportunities we have access to today. The kind of money we take for granted was rare in their prime working years, even when adjusted for inflation. Some of you reading these accounts may be inspired to do something of this sort for your own parent(s).

"My sister and I had talked many times about how unjust our father's retirement situation was and wondered if there wasn't something we could do to make his retirement years more enjoyable. He had worked loyally and earnestly for the same company for 30 years. Because of numerous ownership changes over those 30 years, the end result was that his pension was basically worthless, something

like $60 a month. Now Dad is 65 and working odd jobs (some he likes and some he doesn't) to make ends meet. We could see the anxiety in his eyes even when he said he was quite content. My sister and I talked together about the fact that we had both prospered in our respective professions. Neither of us was yet at the point where we were set for life, but we figured out a way we could help. We had agreed years ago that we would take care of Dad's needs in his later years should he become ill or frail, but now we realized that the best thing we could do was contribute now while he was still healthy, vibrant, and full of life. Why wait until a parent's life is limited before you help?

"What we came up with was the parent's pension. It worked this way. We both contributed $30,000 of our own savings for a total of $60,000 into a mutual fund that had averaged 15 percent returns over the last 15 years. We had it arranged for a disbursement of $500 a month to be sent to our father's checking account. Even though our father receives the distributions, the fund itself is in our names so we, in effect, both still own the $30,000 we contributed. This was all quite easy to arrange. The fund will need to average a net return of 10 percent a year to keep up with the $6,000 yearly distribution to our father. My sister and I agreed that if the returns did not keep up, we could add more principal down the road. But we think there's a pretty fair chance the returns will keep up. Basically, all we are sacrificing is the interest on our savings to help our father rid himself of his financial anxiety. We feel it was the best thing we ever did."

—Andrew, 41

In the preceding example we see how two people discovered a way to give a parent a margin of comfort and security while he is still vital and mobile enough to enjoy it. Many baby boomers have already prepared themselves, at least mentally, for the possibility that they may need to subsidize and support their aging parents' later years. Some of these people, like Andrew and his sister, have decided to accelerate that subsidy to lessen the economic anxiety of their parent's retirement years. Bruce Bruinsma, founder of the Christian Retirement Coalition and Life Stages, Inc., says that the children of retirees would be surprised to learn how far a little extra income can go for most retirees. The $250 to $500 per month, more than anything, buys peace of mind.

It really isn't important what parents do with the money; they may even put some of it in the bank. What is important is that they feel a sense of security and a margin of safety in their retirement years.

I have met those who took a portion of the windfall they received from the bull market run of the 1990s and created an annuity for parents who were living exclusively on Social Security payments. These parents had already adapted their lifestyle to the level of income they were forced to live on and enjoyed great freedom and liberty with the added income.

Hiring Your Parent

Recently, I needed a house repair and the servicemen that came were a 40-year-old and his 74-year-old father. I told them what a great thing I thought that was. The 74-year-old said, "All my friends at the retirement community are jealous. I have something meaningful to do. I still get to fix things and be productive. If I didn't have this, I'd probably end up dying like a lot of my friends who had nothing to do."

It is becoming all the more common to see children hiring their retired parents into their business. Both sides win. The parents get meaningful work, extra income, and a chance to do something that contributes to their child's success. And the child gets help they know they can trust. My father has been working with my company part-time for the last few years, and it has been a great reciprocal arrangement in both tangible and intangible terms.

Hiring a parent can be the saving grace for many retirees who want either extra income or meaningful work, or both. If you have a business, it can be the optimum way to give back, while parents get the chance to contribute to your life. I have found out it's not just about money and being able to work. It can add a whole new and intriguing dimension to a parent-child relationship as you build an enterprise together.

Grandpa or Junior?

From a philosophical and values perspective, the decision to support a parent or a child can create a dilemma for those who don't have the material substance to do both. For example, financial services companies have been promoting college tuition as a chief motivation for investing to baby boomers for many years. How much should you provide for your children's education? Can you divide support between a parent and a child? Who needs or deserves the support more at their respective stage of life? Opinions and views on these questions are as varied as the individuals being asked. One clear trend I picked up is that not everyone is buying into the establishment view that we should provide everything we possibly can for our children.

Karen Ramsay, in her book *Everything You Know about Money Is Wrong,* states that we don't need to buy into the idea that we should provide all the college tuition and expenses for our children. The baby boom generation is notorious for giving their children everything they want—and the best of everything. Some would say that we have created a generation of ingrates with an entitlement mentality. They expect to get what they want without any special effort on their part. Whether your children have this entitlement mentality depends entirely upon the values you have promoted regarding money, self-initiative, the work ethic, and responsibility. In Chapter 18, I share some examples of very wealthy people who have discovered crucial keys to raising financially responsible and industrious children.

> *"My husband and I were facing a financial dilemma between our high school–aged child's upcoming college costs and finding a way to help my mother, who had raised our family as a single mother and was struggling in her later years. She worked long hours in jobs she didn't particularly enjoy while most of her friends were enjoying more relaxed lifestyles. All of our friends took it for granted that they would supply every penny of their children's education. Some of them were planning on sending their kids through private schools that would cost over $100,000 for a four-year degree.*
>
> *"My husband and I felt like we were the oddballs in these conversations because we never fully bought into the idea that we should provide every penny of our children's preparation for the future. Because of our experience (both of us had worked and paid our own way through college because our parents couldn't afford to pay our way), we felt we had gained some valuable character development and a strong work ethic by having to plan and work our way through our college years. We both had witnessed many college classmates on what we called the 'Budweiser scholarship'—those*

whose parents paid every penny and didn't seem to take the educational opportunity all that seriously. This experience, combined with our increasing concern about my mother, caused us to rethink the idea of following everyone else on the 'pay your kids way' path.

"If we did what everyone else was doing, it would be at the expense of my mother, who we thought had done more in life to deserve a financial subsidy than our children had. We decided to offer our children the family matching grant tuition program. We told our children, 'For every penny you save toward college, we will match. If you save $1, with our contribution you will have $2. If you get really serious about work in the summers and save $4,000 each year, we will match that amount. We also expect you to pursue any kind of grant and scholarship you can, and we will be happy to help with that process, but we will not do it for you. If you are still short after this, you may have to look at a student loan.'

"We decided to take this path to teach our children that all goals worth pursuing require hard work, discipline, and determination. We also explained the economic and moral realities of balancing their needs with their grandmother's. We were quite pleased with their response to our proposal. One, a junior in high school, got a job working 20 to 25 hours a week and opened a savings account. His brother, 13, started investing the money he earned on odd jobs along with the birthday and holiday monies he received. Within a year, he had saved over $1,000.

"We are now sending a monthly check to my mother, which has allowed her more free time and greatly reduced her stress. We feel good about these decisions all the way around. We feel that both my mother and our children are getting what they deserve."

—Sandra, 44

When considering a life transition that could last up to 30 years, or roughly one-third of your life, it would be foolish to consider that transition through a selfish lens. Although financial support for ourselves is crucial, it is no more crucial than other considerations that successful living demands. We must consider this transition through many lenses: a philosophical lens, a family lens, a values lens, a spiritual and ethical lens, and a personal fulfillment lens. This is not about retirement planning; it is about life planning.

Our decisions go beyond ourselves. Others are and will be affected by the decisions we make. Whether it is our own family members or those affected through our charitable efforts, the decisions we make with our money and life can send ripples that are felt by many others for many years.

If you have been thinking about retirement planning, start thinking about the responsibility that you believe comes with your money. Your life is bigger than the balance of any account you own. And the fact that you own it doesn't mean it will benefit you alone.

The New Retirementality Is . . .	• Using your prosperity to express gratitude for the sacrifices your parents made.
	• Including the possibility of parental aid in your financial planning ($300 to $400 a month can make a difference for most).
	• Making sure you don't give your children so much that they fail to learn life's larger lessons about initiative and self-reliance.

The New Retirementality Challenge

If you plan to take it with you, the weight of the money will hold you down, not lift you up.

Think about it: Who has helped me to live rather than just exist? What can I do to lift them up? Where can I make decisions that will make a difference for others?

Research it: How can I organize my assets to make it easier for those who survive me to deal with the grief rather than the money (perhaps a living trust)? What amounts of money today will have a positive impact on those who have helped me? How can I organize my assets to make a positive impact on those in need after I die?

Decide and take action:

• Set up an estate plan for later.
• Implement a helping plan for now.
• Maintain a giving plan forever.

CHAPTER | 16

Maslow Meets Retirement

> *"Self-actualization is the desire to become more and more what*
> *one is, to become everything that one is capable of becoming."*
> —*Abraham Maslow*

At the age of 52, Briggs Matsko was about to retire from his financial planning business. A friend heard about Briggs's plans and sent him a copy of this book. Briggs said that reading *The New Retirementality* not only changed his life but also gave him a new passion and mission for the work he thought he was going to leave.

I had the pleasure of meeting Briggs over breakfast while in California on a speaking engagement. He shared this story with me: "I had a real epiphany when I read *The New Retirementality* and realized that the most foolish thing I could do is retire early and go into a life of wondering how to make a difference. The opportunity for making a difference was right there in front of me in every client conversation. I just needed to change the conversation from being a numbers conversation to being a life conversation."

Briggs began by telling clients about his awakening and then giving them a copy of *The New Retirementality* to read before they came in for their appointment. He told them to come prepared to discuss the sort of life they were desirous of living before they entered a conversation on what to do with their money. When they came for their appointments they already were primed to talk about the life they wanted to live.

Briggs has been quite generous in sharing with me some of the testimonials that his clients shared with him as a result of reading the book and engaging in a conversation with him. One client comment to Briggs stands out to me: "I need your help to start living the life I want to live and not wait any longer." This woman realized that she needed a relationship with a financial planner who would invest in her life and help her arrange her finances in a way that would lead to true self-actualization.

The New Retirementality conversation has not only transformed Briggs's life but the lives of his clients as well. Briggs quickly realized how hungry people are to enter a dialogue about how to bring their life into balance and stop delaying their dreams. Once this dialogue regarding lifestyle takes place, we are ready to move to the conversation of *how to pay for the lifestyle we desire.* But we are not really ready for the money conversation until we have experienced the dialogue about what we really want from our life. Money can either serve or impede a life worth living.

During our inspiring breakfast conversation, I mentioned to Briggs that, subsequent to the publishing of *The New Retirementality*, I had created a financial conversation called "Income for Life," where I overlaid Abraham Maslow's Hierarchy of Needs with a financial inquiry. When I mentioned Abraham Maslow, I thought Briggs was going to jump out of his chair. His eyes got as big as the over-easy eggs on his plate, and it was obvious that he just had to tell me something.

"What is it Briggs?" I asked. "Are you familiar with Maslow?"

"One of the first things I did when coming back to work with my new vision," Briggs spilled out, "was to create an income dialogue with clients that I called "Matsko's Hierarchy of Needs," where we look at a client's emotional needs before making financial decisions. "I just couldn't resist," Briggs confessed regarding the play on Maslow's name with his own, "with our names being so similar and all."

Briggs had intuitively settled on the same solution as I did after engaging in the New Retirementality conversation; namely, that we need to design an income plan that simultaneously settles both emotional and financial ledgers.

Briggs and I had both independently observed that, too often, financial advice and financial planning are based on numbers and strategies outside of the very context they are intended to address: our quality of life and our sense of emotional well-being. You cannot simply number-crunch your way to emotional well-being and quality of life, but neither can you achieve these ends without crunching the numbers and making the necessary adjustments. There is a need for a Financial Life Planning approach that amalgamates both realms into one conversation.

Income for Life

According to studies by Cerulli and Associates, seven years ago the greatest fear of Americans was dying. Today, Americans' greatest fear is *living*. People are mortally afraid of living to be 100 and being poor. I call it the "bag-lady/poor-old-man syndrome." This socioeconomic anxiety is deeply rooted in the fear of outliving our money. With the confluence of an aging revolution, rising healthcare costs, and the erosive power of inflation on our money, it is easy to see how people may not be optimistic about their later years.

As a young man in Iowa, I remember vividly working with a social worker named Jeannie to create a charity for widows in our town who were living on minimum food and heat in the winter months. Jeannie discovered the problem by talking to grocery store clerks who said little old ladies were buying dog food when it was known they did not even own a pet. Jeannie walked the streets and when she found an older house in somewhat disheveled condition, she would knock on the door and ask to visit. What she found was appalling.

Little old ladies would answer the door in winter months in full winter gear, because they had to turn their heat down to 55 degrees or risk having it turned off by the power company for nonpayment. Those who chose to heat neglected to eat, or they ate dog food, as Jeannie stealthily discovered by checking their cupboards. These women were too indoctrinated in depression-era self-sufficiency to ask for assistance, and so we had to find creative ways to help them (e.g., anonymously paying their heating bills). This experience has stayed with me 25 years later in a visceral way—I don't want to be old and poor. None of us does.

Our Hierarchy of Financial Needs

We will all eventually need to engage in a conversation about developing an income stream that lasts as long as we do, and that outpaces the inflation that threatens to "rot" our nest egg slowly but surely. The best way I know to accomplish this task is to work Maslow's Hierarchy of Needs (with money in mind) and walk through the process of designing an income for life. I have developed a financial rendition of Maslow's Hierarchy of Needs for this purpose. (See Figure 16.1.)

Maslow taught that human beings are motivated by unmet needs, and that lower needs must be satisfied before the higher needs can be addressed. We must meet people's most basic needs (like physical survival) before they will be able to address other needs (like love or actualization). Rather than study rats (like Skinner) or the mentally ill and

FIGURE 16.1 | Maslow Meets Retirement

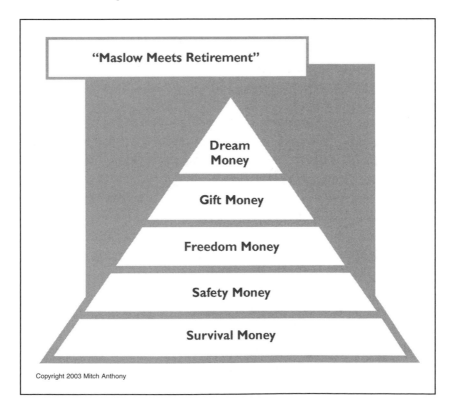

"Maslow Meets Retirement"

Dream Money

Gift Money

Freedom Money

Safety Money

Survival Money

Copyright 2003 Mitch Anthony

neurotic (like Freud), Maslow developed his theory by studying people such as Albert Einstein, Eleanor Roosevelt, and Frederick Douglas. The hierarchy Maslow offered was physical survival, safety, love, esteem, and self-actualization.

For the purposes of a financial/life discussion, I have taken the liberty of renaming and juxtaposing two categories, love and esteem. Love, in Maslow's definition, had to do with belonging—to a mate, to a family, to a community, or to a group. For a financial discussion, I have titled this area, "gifting," as this is most often the material expression of love.

What Maslow called esteem, I have called "freedom" in the financial/life hierarchy. Maslow was referring to the self-esteem that results from doing things well and being recognized for the doing. In the Income for Life model, this is categorized under "freedom money," because unless people have the freedom to do what they want with their occupational lives, they will be missing the esteem and satisfaction that come from doing what they are best at. How many people do you know who long to apply themselves occupationally to something they are naturally good at?

There is also an aspect of financial freedom that allows us to address not just esteem but enjoyment as well. Hobbies and trips and exploration cost money, and if we don't prepare an income stream to address these costs, we may not realize those experiences.

I have placed freedom below gifting on the hierarchy, because from a financial point of view, it is quite unlikely that we will give money away to others *before* we are free to pursue a fulfilling life ourselves. However, there are exceptions to this rule; such is the case of parents who slave at jobs they hate in order to pay for a college education for their children. I happen to believe, however, that it is far healthier— from both emotional and financial perspectives—for people to secure their own freedom to pursue the lives they want. The kids can help with their college expenses by working and saving also.

Following are the phases of financial preparation we need for Income for Life planning.

Survival income. *This is money that we have to have to make ends meet.* How much do you need simply to survive each month? $3,000? $7,000? If you stripped away the frills and thrills and just paid the bills of survival, what would it cost? The majority of people have never taken the time to answer this most basic financial question: What is the cost of survival? The money needed to pay for your basic necessities is your survival income.

Safety income. *This is money we must have to meet life's unexpected turns.* What if everything doesn't work out as you hoped and imagined it would? In life, the one thing we can predict with great assurance is that things will rarely go exactly as planned. We are surrounded by risks—physical, familial, financial, circumstantial, and relational. Financial risks exist in every category of our lives. Look at the financial risk associated with a divorce—a path that hastens financial ruin, guarantees your assets will be cut in half, and diminishes your saving capacity.

Look at the risk of being disabled for a prolonged period of time. Forty-eight percent of mortgage foreclosures are due to the disability of the chief breadwinner versus only 3 percent due to the death of the breadwinner. If you are 35 years old, the chances that you will be disabled are six times greater than the odds you will die before age 65.

A leading risk in the minds of those individuals approaching retirement is the risk of outliving their money. Other top-of-mind risks are health and paying for health care, investment risk, loss of income, and financial needs within the family. As much as is possible, we want to protect ourselves against catastrophes to our bodies, our money, and our material things. The money needed to guard against these risks is your safety income.

Freedom income. *This is money to do all of the things that bring enjoyment and fulfillment to life.* What is the exact cost of the activities and indulgences that bring pleasure and relaxation into your life? Some people engage in low-cost relaxation activities (like walking), and others engage in high-priced activities (like walking after a golf ball). Travel, adventure, and personal growth/education are also some of the considerations to include when calculating the amount needed to fund your freedom.

Gift income. *This is money for the people and causes that we care deeply about.* As we move up Maslow's pyramid—securing our survival, safety, and freedom—our money can be utilized in the higher calling of bringing blessing to those people and causes we care deeply about. If you are a part of what has been characterized as "the sandwich generation," you are experiencing financial concerns on both ends of the generational spectrum. Many of us would love to do something for our parents *and* our children. Many of us also have aspirations to support causes and charities that connect with our heart and purpose. The money needed to pay for these gifts and benevolent annuities is your gifting income.

Dream income. *This is money for the things we've always dreamed of being, doing, and having.* What do you want to be? What do you want to do? What do you want to have? These are all part of the financial conversation necessary for paying the bills of self-actualization. For some people, only a career change will bring them to this place. For others, it may require part-time involvement in activities more closely aligned with their sense of passion and purpose.

The cost of self-actualization is the time it takes to do the things that bring meaning into our lives. If we do not own enough of our own time to engage in these activities, then we must negotiate with our work schedule and personal finances to make the time available. There is often a cost associated with being what we want to be.

There are also costs associated with doing what we want to do and having what we want to have. Some of us dream of owning a sailboat and spending a year sailing from port to port. Others dream of owning a recreational vehicle and seeing America. Whatever dreams and adventures have surfaced in your own musings on self-actualization, there will be bills to pay in the process. The money needed to pay these bills is your dream income.

In Chapter 17, I will introduce you to worksheets you can use to calculate the income needed to live the life you desire. I will share stories of people who have used this process to begin developing an income stream that helps them pay for the life they dream of living.

To complete this process (after sorting out all your income needs), you will need to examine your income sources to see how much you can address on Maslow's Hierarchy of Needs and determine the preparations and self-negotiation necessary to cover every level. Potential income sources include income from work, retirement funds, income-earning investments, Social Security, rentals, and/or other sources of income.

Paying the Bills

The final phase of the Income for Life discussion is to match your income sources against your income needs—which sources will pay for which needs. (See Figure 16.2.) If it's a case of only having enough to

FIGURE 16.2 | Income/Outcome Worksheet

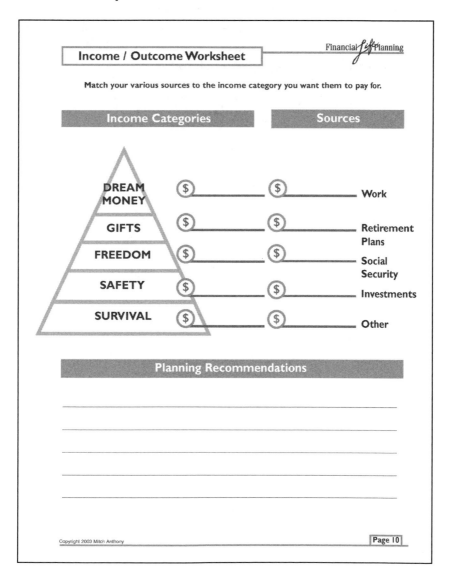

pay for survival and safety at this point, then you will at least have the comfort of knowing those two critical bases are covered.

You will also have a clear picture of how much you will need to meet your other needs. You can then set goals around saving and budgeting to expedite achieving the income necessary for funding these important needs of freedom, gifts, and actualization. As one financial planner stated: "If your outgo exceeds your income, you may need to downsize to realize your upside." In other words, if your income isn't enough to meet your needs, you may have to negotiate with your needs.

By working through the exercises in the next chapter, you can bring both clarity and hope into your financial life. Get a handle on what you need and what you have. This exercise produces clarity. Get a handle on what you need to do to get what you want, and how long it will take to get there. This exercise also brings hope. Begin to view your income not as just a way to pay the bills but as a means to funding a life—the life *you* want.

The New Retirementality Is . . .

- Developing an income plan that addresses both emotional and financial needs.
- Understanding the relationship between well-invested and well-being.
- Ordering our finances to meet life needs: survival, safety, freedom, love, and self-actualization.

CHAPTER 17

Calculating
Income for Life

Working Through
Maslow's Hierarchy
of Needs in Your
Financial Plan

"There is in the act of preparing the moment we start caring."

—Winston Churchill

Locate Yourself

We have come to the place where our money meets our life and heart, where we organize our financial expenses and income sources and attempt to bring them into alignment with our hierarchy of needs. By going through this brief financial planning exercise, we can synchronously settle the emotional and financial ledgers.

In this chapter, I have provided simple worksheets for organizing your finances in a way that puts first things first, clarifies what you can and can't pay for at this time, and offers peace of mind for the needs you can meet.

Many people have told me of going through life with a haunting, eerie feeling about their financial lives. They are afraid of those aching questions that never quite make it to the surface of a conversation: Am I walking a financial tightrope with my debt and spending? What if my income took a hit, would my lifestyle fall like a house of cards? Is it OK to spend some money to have fun once in a while? Am I really living within my means? Am I going to be financially stressed and miserable in my later years?

Like a lost hiker in the mountains who discovers a GPS instrument, just discovering where you are brings a degree of comfort—especially compared to the grinding fear in your belly that you are miles from safety. The exercises in this chapter will act like a financial global positioning instrument. You will gain clarity on where you stand with regard to funding your personal survival, safety, freedom, loved ones, and self-actualization. No more wandering and wondering.

Even if this exercise reveals that you still have a ways to go, there is newfound hope in finding clear direction to your destination. It helps you locate yourself.

Paying for Survival

How much money do you need each month to survive? Many of us have a general idea of how much it takes each month to make ends meet; however, making ends meet can include many items outside the purview of survival, such as dining out, club memberships, extra vehicles, and expensive toys.

I was surprised to discover while conducting Income for Life dialogues, that the majority of people (over 80 percent) had never bothered to calculate their "survival" expenses. Top financial planners across the country have affirmed that because of disorganization, lack of initiative, or just plain denial, most people wouldn't think of calculating survival costs unless they were suddenly put in a position where survival was an issue (e.g., loss of a job with no good prospects on the horizon).

Some people act like they aren't sure they would want to know. Like someone with a nagging pain resisting a doctor's appointment, it may just be too depressing to find out. But after calculating survival costs, most people feel illuminated and comforted for knowing. Those who calculate and do not like where they are begin to see the relationship between their chosen survival lifestyle and the stress they are experiencing in their lives. Many of these people become more resolute to take steps to bring peace of mind to their financial life.

The Good Old Days

Getting by isn't cheap these days. Of course, it all depends on where and how you live. We all remember the days where we got by on next to nothing. The funny thing is, when I converse with people about those days, many say that, although they had less, they felt more content. Even though many were "just surviving" at some point in their life, they felt they had enough.

I called my son at college the other day to see what his survival budget was. He's 21 years old and living in a beautiful cabin on a lake in the boundary waters, a scene many middle-age men dream of and will pay dearly for in their retirement years. My son informed me that it took a total of $450 to maintain this lifestyle. I asked for the details of his monthly survival ledger. They were:

- Rent: $250
- Groceries: $40 (Yes, you read that right—that is *per month.* "How can that be?" I asked. He informed me, "I buy potatoes, onions, flour, and staples, and catch and hunt the rest. We make up big pots of deer stew and ice-fish with a sense of purpose.")
- Gas: $50
- Utilities: $50
- Bait, beer, and babes (his description): $60

Oh, for the ingenuity, resourcefulness, and contentment of youth. I remember stringing together such an existence myself—surviving off tips from waiting tables over lunch. It was refreshing for me to hear his budget. It highlighted how inflated with luxury is our modern definition of survival. We could get by with much less if we really had to, and even with a breakeven survival cost many thousands beyond my son's, it brings my soul comfort to know that my family and I could survive with much less and still have one another. We will continue to enjoy the existence we have as long as we can, but there is solace in knowing we could be content in a place where we may never have to go.

Like me at his age, my son dreams of someday having a new(er) truck, a house to call his own, a spouse, and children after that. His survival costs will escalate, as will the need to earn more. Hopefully, he will heed my lessons on debt management, living below his means, and paying his bills on time. Hopefully, he will never talk himself or be talked into a survival budget that strips away the joy of living, the joy of working, and the joy of building for the future.

There is comfort to be found in financial clarity. Take time to fill out the "Survival Money Worksheet" in Figure 17.1. Discover your finan-

FIGURE 17.1 | Survival Money Worksheet

Survival Money Worksheet		Financial *Life* Planning
Home / Utilities / Related Needs		
Description	Monthly Need	Yearly Need
Total		
Food / Health / Medical Needs		
Description	Monthly Need	Yearly Need
Total		
Clothing / Personal Care Needs		
Description	Monthly Need	Yearly Need
Total		
Transportation Needs		
Description	Monthly Need	Yearly Need
Total		
Taxes		
Description	Monthly Need	Yearly Need
Total		
Other Needs		
Description	Monthly Need	Yearly Need
Total		
Monthly Survival Total		
Survival Money $		

cial location in monthly and yearly terms. If you are married, discuss your survival situation (if you believe you both can survive the conversation, that is) and talk about how your current survival budget could be adjusted, should you ever face the prospect of having to do so.

Once you have added up your survival expenses, place the total in the total box at the bottom of the worksheet.

Safety Money

Once you ensure that you can meet your survival needs and those of your loved ones, it is time to think about protecting that survival: "Me build hut, me build fence around hut to keep out thief and tiger." Inflation is a thief over time. If you are 50 and live to 100 and inflation continues at the same rate it has for the last 50 years, it will have taken 86 percent of your spending power in the next 50 years. As Figure 17.2 illustrates, predators such as disability or long-term care for a loved one—exposures in our risk protection—are waiting to pounce on us at vulnerable moments in life:

- I get paid to give speeches and have been for the last 20 years. What if tomorrow I lost my ability to speak publicly? How would I replace that income for my family? That is a safety issue.
- Fred's mother is showing signs of decline at 75 years of age. Her home and life savings would be consumed if she were placed in an assisted living facility. This is a safety issue for Fred's entire family.
- Bob has longevity in his genes. His father is 92 and going strong. His mother is 90. His grandparents all lived into their late 90s. Bob's finances, invested as they currently are with his current rate of withdrawal, will disappear when he is 83. This is a safety issue for Bob and his children.
- Jerry has worked hard and saved a lot of money in his professional career. He's two years from eligibility for his pension. His daughter, a recent graduate from college, can't find employment and has no health coverage. If a catastrophic illness or accident should happen, Jerry could be wiped out, erasing the 35 most-fruitful earning years of his life. This is a safety issue for Jerry and his wife heading into the next phase of their life.

Many of the safety issues can be addressed through insurance products such as long-term care, health insurance, health insurance supple-

FIGURE 17.2 | Safety Survey

Safety Survey		Financial *Life* Planning
Scenario		
I Live Past 100	○ Current Concern	○ Future Concern
Serious Family Illness	○ Current Concern	○ Future Concern
Family Needs in Case of Death	○ Current Concern	○ Future
ConcernParents Need Advanced Care	○ Current Concern	○ Future Concern
Child Needs Financial Assistance	○ Current Concern	○ Future Concern
Uninsured Family Member	○ Current Concern	○ Future Concern
Lose Ability to Earn Income	○ Current Concern	○ Future Concern
Lose Job	○ Current Concern	○ Future Concern
Income Reduction	○ Current Concern	○ Future Concern
Major Home Repair	○ Current Concern	○ Future Concern
Need to Replace Vehicle	○ Current Concern	○ Future Concern
Major Vehicle Repair	○ Current Concern	○ Future Concern
Other	○ Current Concern	○ Future Concern
Other	○ Current Concern	○ Future Concern

Notes: Gather risk protection quotes to calculate your **SAFETY TOTAL** _____

_____

_____

_____

_____

	Monthly Safety Total
△ **Safety Money**	$

Page 4

ments, disability coverage, life insurance, and homeowners coverage. Many people also choose to use insured investments that guarantee their principal and a rate of return that outpaces historical inflation rates to address their long-term income needs such as the possibility of living to 100.

Insurance companies are in the business of helping people manage their risks. Exactly how much risk you can tolerate is up to you. Each individual has a distinct and individual tolerance for risk in his or her life. For the sake of awareness, it's important for every one of us to have a conversation about the exposures and vulnerabilities in our life and in the lives of our family members. At the end of that conversation, we can each decide where we desire protection and, ultimately, how much protection we can afford.

Another factor that impacts your need for safety is whether you feel your best earning years are ahead of you or behind you. If you feel they are behind you or you currently are at your peak, safety will assume a more prominent position in your mind.

How Much Risk?

The fact that people continue to build homes on fault lines proves that everyone is unique in his or her response to risk. Some people are comfortable with the risk of living to 100 and trusting that income will be there, and others are not. Some people are comfortable dealing with aging and long-term-care issues when they arise, while others would rather prepare ahead and remove future exposure. As with all risks in life, we must first acknowledge that the risk is there, then decide how to respond to that risk.

A friend of mine who spent 30 years in the insurance industry put it this way: "No one buys insurance wanting to use it. It's a lot like a plunger—nobody ever buys one hoping they get to use it, but should they ever need one and don't have it, they'll find themselves knee deep in it and wishing they had one then." Risk protection is not something you get excited about having, but according to Maslow it is a basic emotional need in our lives. There is some peace of mind in knowing that, if life or Mother Nature brings adversity, we will be safe.

Go through your "Safety Survey" worksheet in Figure 17.2 and note where your vulnerabilities exist. Are there cracks in your financial foundation? What coverages do you have in your work benefits? You may need to sit down with an insurance provider to calculate long-term-care, disability, or other coverages. Take the time to calculate the monthly cost of building a fence of emotional safety around your survival.

Freedom Money

What are the things you do that make life worth living? What are the activities and places that bring joy to your life? What is the reward you look to after long hours, weeks, and months at your job? (See Figure 17.3.) These hobbies, pursuits, and adventures are the engagements that motivate us and energize us to keep our hand to the plow. Without such weekly, monthly, or yearly rewards, life becomes drudgery and Jack becomes a dull boy.

A friend recently told me about a neighbor, a dairy farmer, who at the age of 48 was diagnosed with cancer of the colon. This man had not taken a single day off, including holidays, in 35 years. My friend commented that his neighbor was, as expected, quite miserable, but in all the years he had known him he had always been quite miserable.

How happy could any of us be without taking a cathartic break in more than 10,000 days? The human species was not made this way. "And, on the seventh day, God rested from all his labors."

I know many people in the cattle business, and they tell me that cows don't take days off—and neither can the people who care for them. Some have been fortunate enough to find people who could fill in for short periods, so they could experience the occasional rest and relaxation. What great dividends short periods in diversion of leisure can pay.

My wife Deb and I share a similar philosophy in life—work hard and play hard. My wife's play happens to include horses (I play golf and basketball), and so her freedom bill is a lot higher than mine—but it does motivate me to keep working hard! We both work out of our home and try to work efficiently to leave time for play. The opportunity for fun is a constant motivation in our working life. We treasure our leisure pursuits enough that we will pay the price of labor to ensure that the opportunity for fun is always there.

Adding Up the Fun Bill

Our fun bill can run rather high. A friend once warned me to never get a hobby that eats. I didn't understand his point until I married a horse lover. Horses set off a financial domino effect that simply starts with the purchase of the horse: food and board, training, vet bills, farrier bills (new shoes every seven weeks), horse accessories, truck and trailer to pull said horsey, and did I mention horse insurance? Can you

FIGURE 17.3 | Freedom Income Worksheet

Freedom Income Worksheet			Financial Life Planning
Leisure / Hobbies	**Monthly Need**	**Annual Need**	**Lump Sum**
Club Memberships			
Primary Hobby			
Secondary Hobby			
Other			
Total			

Notes:_____

_____

Travel Adventure	**Monthly Need**	**Annual Need**	**Lump Sum**
Second Home			
Vacations			
Family Visits			
Recreational Vehicle			
Other			
Total			

Notes:_____

_____

Personal Growth / Education	**Monthly Need**	**Annual Need**	**Lump Sum**
Education			
Developing New Skill for Income			
Developing New Skill for Pleasure			
Health and Fitness			
Other			
Total			

Notes:_____

_____

Monthly Freedom Total
Freedom Money $

Page 5

Copyright 2003 Mitch Anthony

tell I like to whine about the horse bills? I often threaten my wife that I am going to start a new national support group called "Equini-non" for men who love women who love horses. Did I also mention that my wife has now thoroughly indoctrinated our daughter in this deception as well? (Multiply the above freedom expense by a factor of two.)

Not that my fun doesn't cost something as well: a golf membership at a good golf club, the early spring golf outing with the boys, and Titlelist Pro V1 balls that I have no business buying given their short life expectancy in my golf bag.

Then there is the family trip each year to an exotic spot like Mexico or the Caribbean. We decided some time ago after watching how fast the kids were growing up that we needed to make a conscious effort at creating some magical travel memories together.

It all adds up, but in our life it adds up to fun—and balance. We have a sense of balance in our personal and family life that keeps us all looking forward and staying out of ruts along the way. It was well worth the exercise for us to sit down and figure out how much these freedoms are costing us and how we will continue to pay for them.

Free to Grow

For some, freedom money is about more than leisure. It is about the freedom to pursue personal growth and expanding their capabilities. These pursuits also come with a price tag, whether it be pursuing a degree, taking language lessons, or embarking on a self-improvement course. These freedom initiatives can also bring great joy into our lives, as we sense ourselves expanding and growing. The cost of these pursuits needs to be calculated into our freedom income ledger as well. Tally up your freedom costs on the "Freedom Money Worksheet" and calculate the monthly income needed in the total box at the bottom.

Money to Give

Once we pass survival, safety, and freedom in our financial hierarchy of needs, we come to the place of giving to others. (See Figure 17.4.) This is not to say that we can't do any giving along the way while we pay our bills related to survival safety and freedom. Many people form the "charitable habit" and systematically give 10 percent of their income in tithes to their church, 5 percent to charities, or periodically support causes that come around asking for help.

I believe that the *ultimate intention of wealth* is to eventually give back all that was gathered—and to do this in ways that will improve

FIGURE 17.4 | Gifting Income Worksheet

Gifting Income Worksheet

Financial Life Planning

	Monthly	Annually	One-Time	Amount
Parents				
Income Subsidy	☐	☐	☐	$________
Long-Term Care	☐	☐	☐	$________
Purchase Their Home	☐	☐	☐	$________
Other________	☐	☐	☐	$________
Children / Grandchildren				
Education	☐	☐	☐	$________
Marriage	☐	☐	☐	$________
First Home	☐	☐	☐	$________
Other________	☐	☐	☐	$________
Others				
Support for Family Member	☐	☐	☐	$________
Support for Close Friend	☐	☐	☐	$________
Other________	☐	☐	☐	$________
Charities / Causes				
Local Causes	☐	☐	☐	$________
National Causes	☐	☐	☐	$________
Scholarship Fund	☐	☐	☐	$________
Create Scholarship Fund	☐	☐	☐	$________
Other________	☐	☐	☐	$________
Other________	☐	☐	☐	$________

Notes:____

____

____

____

Monthly Gifting Total

Gifting Money $

Page 6

lives and meet real needs in our world. Naked we came, and naked we will leave. I'm reminded of the old joke of the wealthy man who left an equal third of his wealth to his banker, doctor, and lawyer with the agreement that they would place it in his casket before his burial. The banker and doctor grudgingly dropped in their share and watched with horror as the lawyer dropped in a check for his share. He knew the old boy would have no use for it now. And neither will we one day. Take the case of the McDonald's restaurant fortune left by Ray and Joan Kroc. At the end, all those billions of burgers sold ended up being billions of dollars in the hands of the Salvation Army and other charitable organizations funding their noble efforts at helping the less fortunate. This is a picture of wealth as it should be.

First People First

Many people who have found wealth in modern times have taken instruction from the lessons of spoiled and shiftless trust-fund babies produced by inheritances and have decided to place no such curse on their own children. Because of the expenses of longer life expectancies for our parents and protracted tenures in retirement for us, it is inevitable that the expenses of our predecessors will take precedence over the expenses of our progeny. After all, our children have more earning years ahead of them. You might also consider the example you set for your children by stepping up and helping, if need be, your parents. This is an example they may someday need to repeat.

In America, when I talk to audiences about gifting to their parents, creating parental pensions, and the general attitude of dismissal and neglect that suffuses our culture's approach to aging, I'm either met with knowing nods or shamed avoidance.

A financial planner from Asia recently told me that when he sits down to talk with clients in their 40s and 50s, one of their first concerns is creating "pocket money" for their parents. This is the first concern, because Asians place a premium on experience and age over youth. Our culture worships beauty and youth—albeit ephemeral beauty and ignorant youth. In Korea, the birthdays most worthy of celebration are the 1st and the 70th. Here, we are supposedly over the hill at 50. Whose hill? Does this mean we expect to go into decline after 50? Many people are still ascending at age 80.

Your "Gifting Income Worksheet" in Figure 17.4 takes into consideration parents, children, extended family and friends, and causes near and dear to your heart. Some issues you will need to sort through, prioritize, and calculate around are:

- Subsidizing a parent's survival or freedom costs
- Contributing toward children's education
- Contributing toward children's "getting started" costs (i.e., wedding, first home, etc.)
- Creating income streams for your favorite causes
- Creating a scholarship fund for youth facing hardships and/or pursuing careers you are familiar with
- Giving one-time gifts to a project or cause

Give While You're Living

My Friend, Roy Diliberto, CFP, an exceptional financial planner in Philadelphia, loves to tell the story of a woman in her 70s who came to see him who had over $2 million and a cost of living that was minimal. Roy asked her if she was charitably inclined. She replied that she was not. Rather than just letting it go, Roy challenged her to take a closer look at her neighborhood and community and look for areas where her gifts might make a difference right away. In their next meeting, she told Roy she had found three causes she wanted to start supporting immediately. She had a new energy and excitement in her voice as she described the work of the three causes she had located. Now, many years later, Roy reports that all this client can ever talk about are the causes she supports. She has added a few more to the original three, and has added a new layer of meaning to her own existence.

Roy believes that we make a big mistake when we relegate talk of charitable giving to estate planning conversations. By doing so, the giver misses out on the joy of giving. *The New Retirementality take on gifting is to be giving while you're living.* Be a firsthand, rather than posthumous, witness to your charity.

Tally up the gifts and income streams you'd like to create. How much will it cost each month or each year? Place your gifting total at the bottom of your gifting worksheet.

> *"Do something you love and you'll never have to work a day in your life."*
>
> —*George Burns*

The last income category to evaluate is the expenses associated with our dreams, or to borrow from Maslow, the cost of self-actualization.

Self-actualization takes a different form for every individual. Here are some of the dreams I've heard from individuals:

- Starting and running my own business
- Taking a year to travel the world
- Working for Habitat for Humanity
- Writing a book
- Going back to school to be trained as an artist, teacher, musician, etc.
- Trying different forms of volunteer work
- Owning a boat and sailing around the world
- Restoring old cars
- Woodworking
- Giving time and talents to a ministry
- Building a dream home
- Taking children and grandchildren on a long European vacation

The list is as endless as the number of people who dream. The worksheet in Figure 17.5 is about being, having, and doing. We dream to *be* someone. It is that wistful seed that lives unsprouted within us. There will most likely be costs associated with planting that seed. We dream of having and doing things. Maybe we want to have and do just for a while or maybe permanently, depending on whether we decide we like the having and being enough. But there are obvious costs to having (like owning the boat or RV) and less obvious costs to doing (like owning the time needed to do what we will with it).

Owning one's own time is at the core of the need for self-actualization. How can we be and do what we dream of being and doing if our time is owned by another? Or consumed with simply paying bills? There are many in our culture whose dreams are drowning in inflated survival costs. They have some decisions to make.

There are many others who would be doing better economically if they pursued their heart's passion, but just don't realize it. (I've always been bothered by the assumption that if you follow your heart, you'll make less money.) If, on the other hand, you know what you really want to do will pay less, then a negotiation with your lifestyle will be necessary to get you to the position where you can begin collecting a "playcheck." Remember, a "playcheck" is when you have so much fun doing what you're doing that you can't believe someone is paying you to do it.

FIGURE 17.5 | Dream Worksheet

Dream Worksheet

Financial *Life* Planning

If I had the Money...   **Cost**

Things I've dreamed of owning:

Places I've dreamed of going:

Adventures and goals I've dreamed of accomplishing:

Notes: Research costs associated with your dreams and goals to calculate your **DREAM TOTAL**.

Monthly Dream Total
Dream Money $

Page 7   Copyright 2003 Mitch Anthony

Paying for Your Life

Tally up your totals for each need on Maslow's hierarchy and you are now ready for working out the income side of your life ledger—how to pay for the life you need and want. (See Figure 17.6.) At some point,

FIGURE 17.6 | Income/Outcome Worksheet

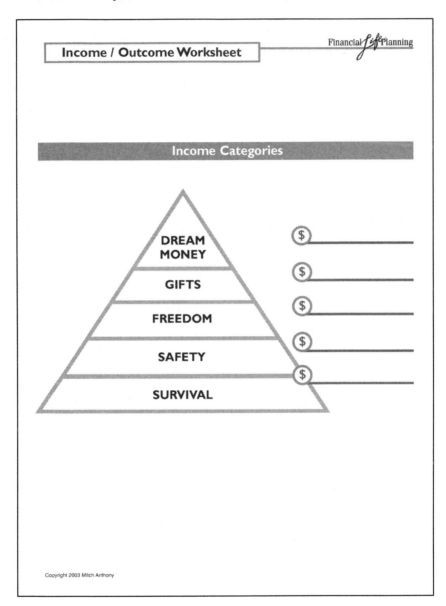

we all will need to engage in the process of figuring out how to make our income provide the lifestyle we want *and* last a lifetime. It is time to tie our assets to our liabilities. Financially speaking, all the totals you have factored into your Income for Life plan are financial liabilities. Peace of mind and contentment enter the picture when we designate exactly what assets will pay for which liabilities.

The New Retirementality Is . . .

- Taking the time to calculate my bill for monthly survival.
- Knowing what are the associated costs for safety, freedom, love, and actualization to materialize in my life.
- Realizing that life is not a dress rehearsal. I need to use what I have to live the best that I can.

CHAPTER 18

Making Your
Money Last

"More people should tell their dollars where to go instead of asking where they went."

—Roger Babson

"A nickel ain't worth a dime anymore."

—Yogi Berra

"In 1975, Joe retired early at the age of 55 so that he could go fishing. He started receiving a pension check for $352.75 per month. Seven years later he started receiving Social Security. Today at the age of 85, Joe, who is in relatively good health, is still receiving his pension check of $352.75 each month and continues to go fishing almost every day. What I want to know is this: Is Joe going fishing these days because he wants to or because he has to?"

—Dave Zander, retirement consultant

According to an Employee Benefits Trends study by MetLife, 48 percent of employees rank "outliving their savings" as their greatest retirement fear. Other fears loom on the retirement horizon as well, with 48 percent saying they feared they would have to take on full-time or part-time jobs to maintain financial stability. Forty-three percent are also concerned that during their own retirement, they will need to provide for the long-term-care needs of others, such as a spouse or relative. According to a study by Merrill Lynch and Ken Dychtwald/HSBC/Prudential Retirement, the greatest fears felt by the next generation of retirees are:

- Being unable to afford health insurance (53%)
- A major illness (48%)
- Going to a nursing home (48%)
- Not having enough money (46%)
- Being bored (23%)
- Dying (17%)

A fair number of these people caught up in trepidation are consequently caught up in procrastination, as these fears do not necessarily translate into action. Of the employees surveyed, 26 percent have done absolutely no retirement planning. Thirty-nine percent have no idea how much might be their annual income needs for retirement, perhaps because 44 percent do not know how many years they need to plan for living beyond retirement. Why not plan on living to 100 and develop a plan that guarantees that the only check that bounces is the one written to the undertaker?

The next step in your Income for Life planning process is to look at your sources of income, your life, and your money management, and then match what you have (or will have) against what you will need going forward. And, unless you want to be like Joe in the example above who retired to what seemed to be a nice little pension in 1975, you need to be realistic about what the costs of living (surviving) might be 30 years down the road.

Looking Forward by Looking Backward

How have the expenses of daily living changed in a generation? The U.S. Bureau of Labor Statistics recently published a study of expenses in retirement that compared the expenses of a retiree in 1949 to a retiree in 2003. The following table shows some contrasts I have organized from the study:

1949	Retirement Expenses	2003
33%	Food, tobacco, and alcohol	15%
15%	Household operation	16%
14%	Clothing and accessories	5%
11%	Transportation	17%
10%	Housing	18%
6%	Recreation	8%
5%	Medical care	13%

The most notable changes in retirement living expenses in the last 50 years are the expenses for food, tobacco, and alcohol, and medical care. What is going on here? In 1949, more was spent on eating, smoking, and drinking than on medical care, and in 1999 half as much was spent on these three and almost 200 percent more on medical care. Is there something we are not being told about the benefits of eating, smoking, and drinking? Or are today's retirees being taken for a ride by drug companies and health insurers?

Congressman Gil Gutknecht of Minnesota claims it is the latter. His findings inspired him to sponsor the Pharmaceutical Market Access Act of 2003. While at a metropolitan pharmacy at the Munich, Germany airport, he discovered that the prices for popular drugs are up to 600 percent *more* in the United States! Two examples are: Glucophage, which cost $29.85 in the United States and $5 in Germany, and Tamoxifen, which cost $360 in the United States and $60 in Germany. No wonder so many U.S. seniors go to Mexico or Canada to purchase their drugs. Who can blame them?

Health Care or Health Scare

"This is the true joy of life: the being used up for a purpose, recognized by yourself as a mighty one: being a force of nature instead of a feverish, selfish, little clot of ailments and grievances, complaining that the world will not devote itself to making you happy."
—*George Bernard Shaw*

Going forward, it will be more beneficial to choose a posture of proactive health rather than get caught up in the health scare. We can make the preparations we feel are necessary (such as long-term-care insurance), but the greatest impact to our health will be rendered by the New Retirementality decisions we make, such as:

- *Work out your heart on a regular basis by walking, jogging, or some other aerobic exercise.* One study showed that walking three times a week for two miles adds five years to your life expectancy and decreases depression, diabetes, and cancer rates, and helps you sleep better.
- *Engage in regular, light weightlifting.* Lifting holistically produces not just physical strength and resilience but attitudinal and internal strength as well.
- *Maintain physical intimacy.* The head actuarial at a leading insurance company told me of a conversation he had with a 75-year-old woman who was rated for a 20-year life insurance policy by his company. Having never seen this happen before, he called the woman to ask for her secret to her great health. Her reply, "Frequent and frantic sex."
- *Schedule charitable and altruistic activity into every week.* Those who feel a sense of purpose live longer and better.
- *Don't join the "moan and groan" sorority or fraternity.* Pessimism leads to an expedited health decline.
- *Engage in work or activities that utilize your talents and challenge your brain.* "Continuing to work keeps the mind sharp and the body healthy, which aids in maintaining a positive attitude."—Dr. Russell Clark, 103-year-old real estate developer
- *Drink a little coffee to start your engine and a little red wine to wind it down.* You've seen the studies. Cheers!

If you have spent any amount of time in a nursing home, you know you don't want to go there—or at least you want to do your best to delay a stopover. I like to visit occasionally because I draw personal motivation and insights from talking to residents, and because I steel my own resolve toward healthy living.

By the way, the estimated cost of an annual nursing home stay in 2034 is expected to be $190,000, according to the *Journal of Financial Planning* (July 2003). And, you don't get a lot of room for your money. If you have to end up in a nursing home, it's better to reside in Jackson, Mississippi, than in New York—the New York last-stop costs three times more than in Jackson.

Stay focused on healthy living and follow some of the great examples of active and vibrant 80- and 90-year-olds (see the Web site http://www.experience.com for hope and inspiration). Your health habits will have a major impact on both your quality of life and the quantity of income available for that life. Think of health habits as an investment . . . in yourself.

Financial Disconnect

As baby boomers move closer to their 59½ birthday party, they are becoming increasingly aware of financial issues tied to enjoyable retirement years. But there may be a "disconnect" with money focus and money habits, as patterns with self-directed retirement and investment accounts seem to indicate. First, let's take a look at the change in financial focus, and then we'll explore the self-sabotaging patterns.

Attitudes toward retirement saving have changed dramatically, according to a study by AXA Financial. The study contrasted the focus and attitudes from 1993 with those of 2003 and discovered the following:

	1993	2003
Use IRAs	17%	40%
Concerned about adequate resources in retirement	26%	43%
Live within means/lower debt	81%	90%

Protect Yourself . . . From Yourself

Although the focus of the baby-boomer crowd seems to be changing, prudent money behavior is not keeping in step with the new focus. Two examples are 401(k) cash-outs and individual returns over the last decade compared to fund and index returns. According to a study conducted by Hewitt (a global outsourcing and consulting firm) of 200,000 workers who changed jobs, far too many people are cashing out of their retirement funds while in transition

Forty-five percent of transitioning workers cashed out their 401(k) accounts when they changed jobs. Whatever the reasoning was for cashing out would likely not hold up as a sound financial rationale. Making a purchase with tax-advantaged funds and paying a 10 percent penalty on top of the new taxes is not a good move. If the reasoning was that the amount in the account was inconsequential, then this can hardly be perceived as good news either. This study is especially troubling because 39 percent of the people who cashed out were *60 years old and older!*

Why would we need *less* tax-deferred savings as the result of losing or changing jobs? If we needed the money to simply survive, that would be understandable, but to take the money now and rob ourselves of future earnings proves that many of us may simply need to be protected from ourselves. Lack of restraint in the present can cause long-term financial problems.

A case in point is the story of why the State of Nebraska jettisoned its 401(k) plan (see "Riding Herd" by Steven Neff King, *Investment Advisor,* August 2003). While the average pension in Nebraska returned an average 11 percent over 30 years, the average return for individuals was 6 to 7 percent. The Street.com reported, "Nebraska's decision offers proof that the average investor lacks the knowledge, and perhaps just as important, the interest necessary to invest for retirement on his own."

It seems that the problems in Nebraska were not confined to that area of the country but are universally hinged to human nature. A recent Dalbar study exposes the shocking results of the do-it-yourself and self-directed retirement approach. Here are the annual averaged returns for equities, pensions, and individual investors from 1984–2004:

- Equities—12.9 percent
- Pensions—13.1 percent
- Individual investors—3.5 percent

Yes, you read it right: *3.5 percent!* Over a 17-year period, how much retirement lifestyle impact is there between 3 percent and 13 percent? It's the difference between building a penthouse and an outhouse.

The self-directed, do-it-yourself approaches were motivated with good intentions, but time has shown that most of us have neither the expertise (or the time to gain the expertise) nor the needed attention span to manage successfully such a proposition. Another revelatory fact of the Dalbar study was that "market timers" in stock mutual funds (those trying to predict highs and lows) lost an average of 3.3 percent! My advice? Hire a competent, caring, and honest professional. Pay him or her the 1 percent management fee and get on with your life. If you don't know how to find a financial professional who fits that description, read Chapter 20, "Finding the Right Wealth-Building Partner."

When we look at the difference between returns on equities (12.9 percent) and doing it yourself (3.5 percent), most of us could have hired a negligent manager who charged 5 percent and did nothing but throw funds into stock indexes—and we would have done better. We would have suffered much less damage than what we did to ourselves with ill-timed moves and very bad Warren Buffett imitations.

The point is to have as much money as possible available for you to do with what you want. We can be our own worst enemy when it comes to reaching this point. Know your ability, availability, and attention span, and do what is best for you in the long run and get help where you need it.

Working It Out

> *"If you had ever told me that I would be working in retirement, I would have told you that you were crazy. After being a pilot for many years, I figured I would spend my days golfing and taking it easy. Now, I'm 72 and I'm driving a limo three days a week . . . and loving it!."*
>
> —*Fred in Ft. Lauderdale, Florida*

As a result of shrinkage in 401(k) and 403(b) accounts, many people are planning to work longer than they had originally anticipated. If you have the New Retirementality, this can be a good thing, because it means you are going to be doing work you feel good about, at a pace you can easily keep. Also, if you have the New Retirementality, you know that the elements of challenge, networking, and usefulness tied to your work are going to ameliorate your aging prospects.

A recent study by the Congressional Budget Office, titled "Baby Boomers' Prospects in Retirement" (November 2003), illustrated how much impact one to five extra years of work can have on the economics of retirement. Consider a couple, Bobby and Brenda Boomer, both in their 60s with a household income of $62,000 per year. After taxes, this couple typically takes home approximately $49,000. If we assume an 80 percent retirement income replacement rate (a rate promoted by many financial professionals), then this couple will need $39,000 per year to live on.

If both were to retire at 62, they would receive almost $18,000 in Social Security benefits, which leaves a balance of $21,000 needed per year for the next 21 years, assuming the age expectancy for people retiring at their age and a 3 percent real (inflation-adjusted) rate of return on their assets. To produce the additional $21,000 would require an accumulation of just over $330,000 by this couple at the time of retirement.

However, if Bobby and Brenda waited three years to retire, they would receive almost $23,000 in Social Security benefits and would need to finance the balance of $16,000, which would require $225,000 at the time of retirement. By working three years longer, not only would they have more tucked away, but they also would actually need less. This sounds like a much more comfortable position to be in—a position with some breathing room.

At this point, if Bobby and Brenda decided to work part-time after their retirement for reasons of purpose, passion, activity, and sanity, they would have even more financial latitude. They may be in a position to finance all the activities and expenses listed in their hierarchy of "financial" needs.

According to the chart in Figure 18.1 (borrowed from the Congressional Budget Office study), if Bobby and Brenda were really enjoying their work and wanted to continue until they were 70, they would be even better off with a bigger nest egg to fund their future. Working until 70 would reduce the needed nest egg to $77,000 from the $330,000 needed at age 62. Their Social Security benefits alone at age 70 would be $32,000.

Each additional year of work provides the following financial benefits:

- Increases your Social Security benefit.
- Reduces the amount of wealth needed at retirement.
- Increases your time to earn returns on your savings.

According to the CBO study, if Bobby and Brenda Boomer had arrived at age 62 with only $26,476 but continued to work to age 70 and saved 10 percent of their income per year during the additional working years, they could still retire at 80 percent of their working income.

Following is a case study I have borrowed from a certified financial planner who uses the Maslow dialogue to help her clients calculate their income needs. Mark, age 58, wants to work full-time until he is at least 62, and then hopefully consult on a part-time basis after that. Bon-

FIGURE 18.1 | An Illustration of How Retirement Age Affects The Total Assets Needed in Retirement (in 2003 dollars)

	80 Percent of Preretirement After-Tax Income	Annual Social Security Payments*	Additional Retirement Income (Besides Social Security) Needed to Achieve 80 Percent of Preretirement Income	Assets Needed at Retirement to Produce That Additional Income**
Retirement Age				
62	39,154	17,735	21,419	330,170
63	39,154	19,279	19,875	295,680
64	39,154	20,958	18,196	260,630
65	39,154	22,770	16,384	225,330
66	39,154	24,591	14,563	191,740
67	39,154	26,517	12,638	158,740
68	39,154	28,593	10,561	126,080
69	39,154	30,832	8,322	94,010
70	39,154	31,908	7,246	77,060

Married Couple Earning $62,000 per Year before Taxes

*Taken from the Social Security Administrations "Social Security Quick Calculator" (available at http://www.ssa.gov/OACT/quickcalc/calculator.html)
**Assuming a real rate of return of 3 percent

Source: Congressional Budget Office.

nie, age 59, enjoys her part-time work as a real estate broker, has a nice network of customers established, and would like to continue as long as is possible.

Their survival expense is $2,700, which is easily met by Mark's take-home pay as a business manager ($4,600 a month). The additional $1,900 income can be used to pay Safety expenses, which come out to $1,800 monthly and include long-term-care insurance for Bonnie's mother and a policy they are paying for themselves.

Bonnie's part-time work as a real estate broker brings home an average of $1,500 monthly. Bonnie's income is applied to the Freedom expenses, which include a golf/tennis membership, time-share fees, and two annual vacations. The Freedom expense is $900 a month. They are using the $600 balance from Bonnie's income to eliminate debt, which will be cleared in two years' time.

Bonnie is eligible to begin taking distributions on her IRA in a few months, and their planner has calculated they can begin taking $600 a month out of a balance of $140,000 and still have a comfortable margin of safety. They plan to use this $600 per month for their gift needs ($500 monthly) and for miscellaneous expenses and entertainment. Their dream is to build a summer home on the Oregon coast (approximately $1,500/month), which they believe they will use earnings from approximately $175,000 in investments for about a year. At that time, they will begin using distribution from Mark's IRA (approximately $340,000) to make the monthly payment.

In seven years when Mark takes his retirement, they plan on selling their current home and transferring the equity to pay off most of the balance on their coastal home. They also plan on using the proceeds from their investments and Mark's IRA along with Mark's Social Security to make up the income needed as he transitions into a part-time consulting career.

Mark and Bonnie's accountant has suggested a number of income-providing investment tools, including real estate investment trusts, instant annuities, and corporate bonds, that they can utilize when they come to the point of needing to guarantee income from their accumulated assets. Their insurance agent has worked with them to make sure that their Safety expenses regarding long-term care will be paid up before they make their big transition to the coastal home.

If you work with a financial professional, it would be important to consult with him or her on these important calculations to ensure that your retirement plans and investments are invested in such a way as to provide maximum income with the greatest degree of safety possible. (See the sample in Figure 18.2.) You don't want to run out of money because of an unrealistic, assumed rate of return on investments or because of a lack of hedging and protection against the next bear market.

Everyone's Income for Life plan will be unique, because we all have needs particular to our situation and income sources that vary and fluctuate as we pass through various transitions.

Beware of singular-focus solutions promoted by people with self-interest at heart. Systematic withdrawals from mutual funds or equity

FIGURE 18.2 | Income/Outcome Worksheet

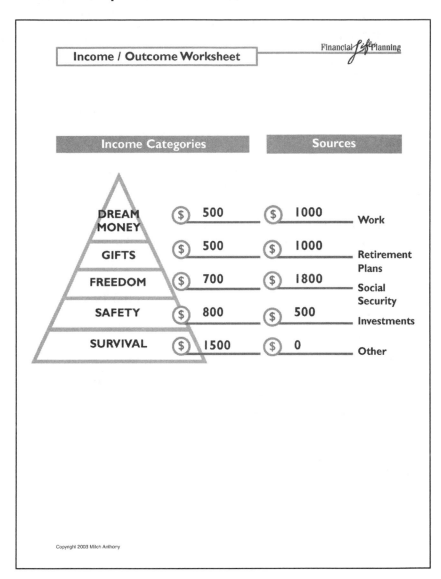

accounts, bonds, and annuities can be good strategies when properly utilized, but rarely work as a total solution. Systematic withdrawals can turn into "dollar loss averaging" that causes you to run out of money in a hurry when the market takes a dip like it did in 2000–2002.

Bonds can put you in a bind when interest rates go against you. And the wrong annuity will not only lock you in to a rate of return but also can lock you up as far as access to your money goes. Remember, a guarantee of 5 percent looks awfully nice when the market is losing money, but it doesn't look so great when everyone else in getting 12 percent out of the market. It's great to get locked in, but it's not so great to be locked up.

A competent, caring, and trustworthy professional worth his or her weight in gold discovers the intricacies of your situation and researches the products most appropriate for your situation. Additionally, you want someone who keeps a regular pulse on the events and transitions in your life to make necessary adjustments along the way. Rarely is a financial plan implemented that does not require tweaking. Some life transitions may call for a complete overhaul. In these moments of stress, duress, and even grief, the last thing you want to be mucking through is who you can trust with your money decisions.

If you are going to handle all these matters on your own, it is paramount to develop not only an income plan for the present but also contingency plans in the case of extended illness, accident, loss of earning ability, and death.

The idea is not just to live long; it is to live well. To do that, you'll need to make sure your money lives as long as you do.

The New Retirementality Is . . .	• Organizing my resources and developing an income plan for my future. • Taking a proactive role in improving my personal health. • Knowing my limitations regarding managing personal financial matters. • Engaging in some "retirement" work, because I add value to society and I can always find good use for the income.

CHAPTER | 19

Wealth-Care Checkup

Facing Investment Reality

> A boy with a cocoon came to a farmer. "Look," he said, "the moth is trying to get out. I think I'll help him."
>
> "Don't do it," the farmer said, "let nature take its course."
>
> An hour later the boy returned with a dead moth in his hand. "Why did he die?" he asked through tears.
>
> "Because you gave him too much help," replied the farmer. "The moth gets his strength for life through the fight out of the cocoon. He needed to do it on his own."

Getting our financial wings is not going to be easy. We make mistakes, we struggle, we question ourselves. There are hard lessons to learn, but those that come the hard way seem to have the most sticking power. Anyone who tells you building wealth is easy hasn't lived outside a raging bull market.

If mastering the stock market and making our money grow were easy, we would all be multimillionaires. It is possible to become a successful investor if we can avoid some of the self-sabotaging mental traps that deceive today's investor. The saboteurs are an overconfident mind-set, a vulnerable emotional state, and a naïve psyche. Following are five common mental errors that have infiltrated the modern investor landscape like a plague.

Investor Error 1: People Think They Are Smarter Than They Are

The bull market provided fertile ground for feeding into the hubris of individual investors. If the stocks they picked skyrocketed, they were geniuses; if the stocks they picked tanked, it was the market's fault. This logic provided a convenient excuse for investor foolishness. It is also just this sort of hubris that led thousands of once-rational people to quit their jobs and become day traders. It was once said that failure is always a bastard while success has many fathers. Today's investors can raise their financial well-being by facing the fact that they are responsible for their successes and failures, or by realizing that they may not be responsible for either. Warren Buffett once said that everyone thinks he's a genius in a bull market because "a rising tide lifts all boats; it's not until the tide goes out that you find out who's swimming naked."

Most behavioral finance experts agree that today's investors are far too optimistic and smug about their ability to pick stocks. I had a personal epiphany during the market correction of April 2001. I had just mentioned to a colleague that my personal stock portfolio, which I was managing on my own, was up 120 percent for the year. That was before the correction took the air out of the Internet stocks. After the correction my portfolio was up 20 percent for the year. The quick collapse of my portfolio value motivated me to take a closer look at what was really going on with my stock-picking ability. I learned some hard, costly, but valuable lessons about the reasons that I had bought certain stocks. I learned that many others had (have) been making the same misjudgments as me. Here is what I found out about my ability to pick stocks when I took an honest look at how I arrived at my choices.

I invested in a new theory. Remember all the hype, articles, and books about the new rules of the new economy? Ideas circulated that earnings numbers were basically irrelevant in the new marketplace and there were novel means for valuing a stock in this new world. I was in Silicon Valley giving a speech when I heard people from Internet companies bragging about their "burn rate," which is how fast their companies were going through investment capital. Companies that were bleeding money were watching their stock prices skyrocket. It was confusing to watch for anyone who believes in the fundamentals of valuing a company's stock.

Nobody will be heard bragging like that again because the other shoe (of earnings' reality) finally fell. They said all the measurements for success had changed from earnings and net profits to other nebulous quantifiers of success that only the person who speaks the language of HTML could understand. But in business, one number that will always be important is earnings; and sanity was finally restored with a flushing out of companies that couldn't produce earnings. Many investors, myself included, believed all the "new rules" tripe and hype, and paid a heavy price for it. We were buying stocks because they were going up. Those who did got quickly reacquainted with the law of gravity. Don't ever forget this mathematical fact; a stock that falls 50 percent must now rise 100 percent to reattain its former value.

I invested in companies and industries I knew nothing about. I live in Rochester, Minnesota, home of the Mayo Clinic and a large IBM facility. I have always marveled at the doctors who were investing in computer stocks they know nothing about and the IBM engineers who were investing in biotech companies they know nothing about. I made the mistake of trying to pick winners in sectors where you could fit the knowledge I had in the belly button of a gnat and still have room for a new boat and an SUV. Don't fool yourself. Each industry has idiosyncratic economic rules and distinctions for profitability. If you don't understand those economic rules and distinctions, you'd have a better chance picking stocks because they rhyme with orange.

I picked stocks because they had fallen a long way and I figured they would bounce back. At the time I didn't know the difference between an undervalued stock and a falling knife. I have cuts now to remind me of the difference. I created double jeopardy for myself by picking a falling stock in an industry I knew nothing about. All this stock-picking genius was, of course, aided by the wonderful research tools of the Internet at my disposal. We now have access to enough information to actually make us think we know what we are doing. Don't ever forget the difference between information and wisdom.

I told myself I was a good stock picker because my portfolio was up. This was probably the most subtle deception of all—and one that many individuals will avoid investigating for fear that they too are in denial of their own speculative prowess. After the correction, I went through my portfolio to see how many of my stocks were up versus down. I had three that were up and nine that were down since I had bought them. Of the three that were up, two were up considerably and accounted for the 20 percent profit I was showing. I had gone fishing, landed two big fish, lost all my good lures in the process, and came to shore feeling like a good fisherman. My reality check showed that I was not a good fisherman; I was just lucky to be in a stocked pond.

Facing up to the truth about my own portfolio and abilities has tempered my desire to go out there shopping for a deal. Many people will sooner or later realize that they are not as smart as they think they are. There are professionals out there who spend 12 hours a day studying this stuff and many of them feel lucky to get a 7 percent annual return on average. Humility will go a long way regarding your personal wealth. This may be an indicator of how the meek eventually inherit the earth.

Investor Error 2: Too Much Focus on Past Returns

"Past performance cannot guarantee future results." These words on the little caveat you read on the bottom of every prospectus are the truest words you'll read in the prospectus. Many people who chase hot stocks and funds have the same experience as a dog that chases parked cars. Just because a fund returned 68 percent last year promises nothing for the next year, but that doesn't stop thousands of people from moving their money from fund to fund on a year-to-year basis. This activity goes on so much that all companies now have penalties for transferring money before a reasonable period of time. Some people are now treating mutual funds like a day trader treats stocks.

Studies show that the funds that beat the market one year most often trail the industry average the next year. The exceptions to that rule have more to do with who is managing the fund and how consistent the philosophy of that fund is. Many funds switch their basic investing philosophy and even their managers without investors being aware of the changes. These changes ultimately affect your personal wealth. It's important to decide on your own philosophy of investing and invest in funds that mirror that philosophy.

You can learn a lot by looking backward, but there is also a lot that can fool you by looking backward as well. If, in looking backward, you see a company that has for years increased its earnings and dividends, you are seeing good indicators—all other factors being equal. But if you simply look at how a stock price has appreciated and trust that it will continue to do so, you may be in for an unpleasant surprise. The fact that Cisco Systems went up 10,000 percent in nine years is no guarantee that it will go up even 10 percent in the next five years—or, for that matter, lose 50 percent in the next five years.

Investor Error 3: Hanging Out with Losers

Many investors suffer from what behavioral finance experts call *regret syndrome.* The aversion we all have to emotions of regret is what causes us to hang out with losers in our portfolio. We have taken the axiom "You don't lose money until you sell" to irrational lengths. The question we need to ask ourselves is how much more are we going to lose by not putting that money in an investment with better prospects? Meir Statman, professor of finance at Santa Clara University, explains that it is a rare individual who can own up to a bad investment. "They avoid regret by holding on to a loser."

It's not easy to admit a mistake, especially a mistake with our money. It may make us feel stupid and ashamed and often angry with ourselves to let hard-earned wages slip away because of greed. Ari Kiev, author of *Trading to Win: The Psychology of Mastering the Markets,* states: "It's a denial of reality. We don't want to admit that we were wrong and take a loss. The hope is that the stock will turn around." If you buy a car that is a lemon, how long do you continue to pump money into it? Some stocks are lemons and the first few signs of trouble are simply signs of more trouble to come. As my friend Gary DeMoss, a veteran of the financial services industry, put it, "After watching a few stocks I bought go down to zero, I decided I would let somebody else do the research on what stocks to buy." Gary has the bulk of his investments in mutual funds now. The best cure for a mistake is to admit it and learn from it not to wrap ourselves in the illusion of better days ahead. Take the loss, mark it in the ledger under "tuition paid," and move on with your investment life.

Investor Error 4: Believing You Have an Information Advantage

"With a million dollars and a hot tip you can go broke in a year."
                                                              —*Warren Buffett*

One of the fallacies of the information age is that you can profit easily from the plethora of information available on the Internet. "Information is easily accessible, so you can know what the pros know and make more money than ever before" is the theme of so many do-it-yourself financial services ads these days. One thing these ads neglect to tell you, however, is that once information becomes readily available and widely circulated, it no longer has any value. How can you claim an information edge when everyone else knows what you do? Even more ludicrous is buying a stock or fund touted in a financial magazine or newspaper. If there were any value to be bought, it was bought by the people who knew about it while the magazine was going to press. The smart money has already taken the profit while the masses are naively following the pundit's latest column or article.

James J. Cramer, cofounder of The Street.com, knows how much unreliable information is out there and has been duped into bad trades himself by such information. He warns that the Internet has served to expedite the flow of false and misleading information. He writes:

> Take these examples. A television hotshot speaks from the floor of some exchange somewhere telling me that National Gift Wrap and Box Co. is set to open a buck or two higher. Real news? Nah, that commentator got a call from someone long on National Gift who wants out before some bad news hits.
>
> A message on a chat board talks about National Gift losing a key retail order to its competitor. Scoop? Hardly. That's just someone trying to smash down National Gift in order to cover a short profitably.
>
> An analyst pushes National Gift, talking about massive undervaluation. Buying opportunity? Oh, please, that's just the more powerful investment banking arm pressuring the nonrevenue-producing analyst into saying something positive about National Gift, a potential client. Too cynical? I don't think so. Every day I hear and see things that I am supposed to hear and see, communicated to me by someone who wants me to take action . . . mil-

lions of others get fooled out of their pensions and their hard-earned savings every day of the week through manipulative stories masked as New Financial Journalism.

Investor Error 5: Not Paying Yourself First

"A couple of years ago when my father died, he left my siblings and me a very nice inheritance. All of us, except one, invested the monies toward our own retirement. With any luck at all, we'll be there in five to ten years. My sister who didn't invest took her money and gave the bulk of it to her daughters. One daughter bought a house and the other bought furniture, clothes, a vehicle, and so on. Within a year the sister who gave her inheritance away was in dire straits because her husband became ill. Suddenly faced with the loss of income and potential for losing a spouse, she realized the foolishness of her generosity. Do you think her daughters were there to help her financially when she was struggling? Forget about it—they're too consumed with their own lives."

—Jane, 56

"I almost feel a sense of guilt saying it, but in some ways I feel that we did too much for our kids. We had it hammered in our heads that we had to provide all the money for their college expenses and we did for three kids. Two of those kids are now making more money than we will ever see and spending it as fast as they make it. We are getting to an age where we would like to slow down and do some things for ourselves, but we won't have enough money for many years. I'm happy we were able to help our children as much as we did, but it seems somewhat inequitable that they have it so good and we are so far from our own dream. I see now that there were other ways we could have helped them through school, and even if they had gotten loans, they could have paid them off with little stress."

—Jack, 58

This building block for financial well-being is built on the premise that people can borrow for college but they cannot borrow for retirement. This applies to those individuals who have marginal savings for their own emancipation and are breaking their own financial backs by giving their wealth to their children. According to financial writer Cort Smith, "There is a fundamental notion growing these days that parents don't *owe* their children a college education." This notion is gaining broader acceptance as more and more baby boomers realize that the life they have always dreamed of may be out of reach until it's too late if they put too much of their savings toward their children's education. In many cases, it's not a dream life that is being sacrificed. For some it means working longer and harder than they want to at later ages and, consequently, having levels of stress at a time when they could have been enjoying free time and the fruits of their labors.

> *"Who says the parent is obligated to provide a full ride for college for their kids? Is it pride? People don't realize how important it is to hold on to their retirement savings. I tell clients their priority is them-selves. Kids have many years to work off tuition debt; parents don't."*
> *—Nancy Bryant, financial advisor*

Even if you can afford to hand your children their future on a silver platter, it may not be wise to do so. Each year, U.S. Trust, which manages the passed-on riches of wealthy people, conducts a survey of its clients to gauge their concerns. In one survey they found that 64 percent of these clients are afraid that their children won't know the value of money, and 45 percent are afraid that their children won't take financial responsibility for themselves. According to the PNC Financial Services Group study, almost half (49 percent) of respondents with children at home worry that their kids will grow up feeling "entitled," and nearly as many, 44 percent, believe their children are spoiled. While nine out of ten respondents with children agree that it is important for children to learn the value of money through hard work, half of these respondents say they do not believe kids today know the true value of a dollar. However, less than one-third (29 percent) of respondents encourage their children to take after-school jobs. There are certainly moral and behavioral pitfalls waiting for those who get too much too easily, but many wealthy parents have found that having money needn't interfere with raising responsible children.

In a recent *Forbes* article entitled "Who's Spoiled?" author Brigid McMenamin noted that many children with wealthy parents end up being fiscally responsible and quite industrious if they were raised with proper values and a hands-on parental approach. Children whose parents left the bulk of parenting chores to hired help were far less successful. An example of proper values and motivation is Matthew Zell, son of Chicago billionaire Sam Zell. The younger Zell says, "It was always expected of me that I would work. My father wanted me to give my best effort." Matthew Zell, after attending the University of Illinois, went to work at a computer service firm. After a while he decided to start his own company and used $5,000 he had saved on his own as seed capital.

Successful parents agree that you need to teach your kids self-sufficiency, even though the teaching methods are not always met with glee. Edwin Locke, author of *The Prime Movers: Traits of the Great Wealth Creators,* comments that regardless of how rich you are, your kids need to know that they can earn their own keep. "If you subordinate that to other things, then you don't love your child." Strong words to the wise echo back to the old saying about teaching someone to fish rather than giving the person a fish. All children, no matter how wealthy their parents, need to learn financial independence.

Tips from wealthy parents, whose children are responsible, hardworking citizens, included what I call the Ten Commandments of Leaving a Financial Legacy:

1. Let them experience reality, which means not bailing them out when they screw up.
2. Show them what you value. Demonstrate with your life what matters most. Point out your heroes and mentors.
3. Encourage them to think. Ask their opinions and nurture their independent thinking skills.
4. Express delight when they do something well. This helps to build a sense that they *can* do things.
5. Give them opportunities to earn money. If they don't earn it, it doesn't have any value.
6. Let them enjoy the fruits of their labor. If you don't, it will dampen their initiative.
7. Let your children handle money. This is how they learn budgeting and restraint.
8. Make your children pay for the big things they want, such as college, cars, travel, and the like.
9. Once they finish school, let them support themselves.

10. Tell them not to expect an inheritance until they are old and gray. Why sow the seeds of lethargy?

In my own home we came up with a good compromise regarding the children's college costs. I'm sure this plan was greatly influenced by my experience and that of my wife. We had both paid our own way through school and had to work through school and during the summers. We also had loans to pay off after we graduated. We think that the hard work helped us to take our educational opportunity more seriously.

Here is the compromise we came up with: We told our children that we would match whatever amount of money that they saved for college. If they save $1, they receive $1. If they save $5,000 each year, they will receive $5,000 each year from us. We are leaving it up to their own initiative and work ethic. My oldest son responded by deciding to attend a less expensive junior college before transferring to the four-year school that has the major he wants. Another financial technique we have used with this son as he grew up was paying for half of his car insurance if he made the B honor roll in school. Otherwise, he would have to pay all the insurance himself. (He spent only one miserable semester off the honor roll during high school.) My second son, although only 13, has already saved over $1,000 toward his college fund, which he invests in the stock market. He accumulates money through odd jobs and gift money.

Think about yourself. What good are you to your family and the world if you are miserable? This is not encouragement for selfishness but rather for common sense and self-preservation. Why would anyone want to potentially surrender the best years of their life and make life too easy for their children in the same process? The children need to learn the same lessons you learned and in the same fashion you learned them. In the end, it will be your children's character, not their credentials, that will give you the greatest pleasure.

Women especially need to spend more time thinking about their financial well-being in later years. According to a report by Prudential, although women planning for retirement have many of the same concerns as men, women face certain issues that may make it more difficult for them to save for retirement:

- Women, on average, earn only 76 percent of what men earn (U.S. Department of Labor)

- Women live, on average, seven years longer than men (Census Bureau)
- Elderly women are three times as likely to be widowed as men (Census Bureau)
- The national median concerns are staying at home to raise a family, divorce, dependence on spouse's income, etc.

According to the 401(k) helpcenter.com, women lag behind on several other financial issues:

- Women report contributing a median of 6 percent of their pay to their company-sponsored retirement account, compared to 7 percent for men.
- Women report spending just five hours per year monitoring and managing their retirement accounts, compared to ten hours for men.
- Women report lower current retirement savings ($71,800 for female workers versus $122,700 for male workers).
- Women report not knowing as much as they should about retirement investing (80 percent for female workers versus 67 percent for male workers).
- Despite having increasingly longer life expectancies, women estimate that they will need to save an average of just $639,000 to meet their retirement goals—one-third lower than men, who estimated they would need an average of $941,000.

"Women statistically live longer than men, are more likely to take time off from their careers or work part-time, and often earn less," said Collinson. "These circumstances create added challenges for women when it comes to saving, planning for retirement, and budgeting for postretirement expenses."

Another way we need to think about ourselves is to occasionally take time out from our saving and retirement savings obsession to do something fun and frivolous for ourselves. Karen Ramsay, author of *Everything You Know about Money Is Wrong,* sometimes encourages clients who are having no fun that it is OK to take time out from their retirement contributions for a short period to have some fun while they're young enough to enjoy it. Ramsay asked one couple what their dreams were, and they defeatedly announced, "to go back to Europe for a vacation, but that will never happen." Ramsay's advice startled them. She told them to *not* maximize their contribution to their 401(k) and IRA for one year and go on that vacation to help reinvigorate their life. They did it, had the time of their lives, and never regretted it. There is more to life than saving for the future. Don't forget to reward yourself; it helps to fuel your initiative for the future.

Reality: Your Money Matures Faster When You Do

Any good thing taken beyond the bounds of balance is no longer a good thing. Life is full of illustrations, as seen in the following, about stepping over the invisible lines of imbalance:

- Physical rest becomes laziness.
- Quietness becomes noncommunication.
- The enjoyment of life becomes intemperance.
- Physical pleasure becomes licentiousness.
- Enjoyment of food becomes gluttony.
- Self-care becomes selfishness.
- Self-respect becomes conceit.
- Cautiousness becomes anxiety.
- Being positive becomes insensitive.
- Loving-kindness becomes overprotection.
- Judgment becomes criticism.
- Conscientiousness becomes perfectionism.
- Interest in possessions of others becomes covetousness.
- Ability to profit becomes avarice and greed.
- Generosity becomes wastefulness.

There is an invisible line that we come to and can cross in all areas of life that marks the difference between balance and imbalance, discipline and mastery, chaos and control. We must constantly address and regulate all these compartments to keep areas of our life from spinning out of control. Once we identify where the lines are that we should not cross and develop emotional and logical thought patterns that keep us from crossing those lines, we have achieved what is commonly called maturity.

Money maturity. Money maturity comes by becoming aware of where we are—both intellectually and emotionally—with money issues.

It comes by honestly examining our money behaviors and getting assistance where we are weak. It comes by acknowledging the places where money controls us instead of our controlling the money. Money maturity is a difficult issue for many. I have met hundreds of people who will not go to a financial professional for fear of what that person will see in their spending and saving habits. They are afraid of being embarrassed and feeling ashamed at their level of progress. They are afraid of feeling stupid. This fear exacerbates the problem and impedes the solution, which will begin with a humble acknowledgment that they don't know everything they need to know and that they have made mistakes. Anyone who has ever had money has made mistakes about it; it is an inherent fact of the human condition.

Money maturity is achieved when we are willing to go below the surface of our money behavior to ask ourselves why we feel the way we do about money. Our behavior is rooted in beliefs and values we learned. These beliefs and values have helped to form a personal identity with money, as seen in the following diverse comments:

- "I'm a saver."
- "I'm a spender."
- "I'll never have enough money."
- "I can't get enough money."
- "Riches will ruin you."
- "I'll never get ahead."
- "There will always be money."
- "I'd better enjoy it now because I may not be here tomorrow."

Our attitudes and beliefs about money have their genesis in messages we have received during our lifetime. The beliefs we have settled on are also premised on observations of our family and others' financial behaviors. Look back at your family life to see what values you have picked up:

- In your home was there an atmosphere of scarcity, plenty, or moderation?
- How did your parents and their parents handle money?
- Was money a source of conflict within your home?
- Was money a taboo topic or dealt with in family discussions?
- Did your parents try to teach you specific lessons regarding money management? What were those lessons?

As we grew up, we observed people other than family members and began to form habits and patterns of our own. Our financial behavior is rooted in our beliefs regarding money and life. Those who spend constantly believe that there will always be money available and also believe that they should live for the moment. Those who never spend and hoard their money believe that the earning spout can dry up at any time and that you must sacrifice the present to have hope for the future. These driving and controlling beliefs are based on observations people have made in their lifetime. Look back at the formation of your own beliefs:

- Did you work when you were young?
- How old were you when you had to take financial responsibility for yourself?
- What was your first experience with debt? How did you handle that situation?
- What was the financial status of your closest friends growing up?
- How did you feel about people who had a lot of money?
- When did you start saving money? Why did you start saving?
- Have you ever felt rejection or inferiority because of your financial status?
- Has money been a comfortable or stressful topic in your intimate relationships?
- Have you used money as a means to control others or have you had others try to control you with money?
- How does money contribute to your happiness?
- How does money cause you tension and stress?

When you take a more introspective look at your own patterns and behaviors regarding money, you will see certain attitudes and beliefs surfacing. Some of these attitudes and beliefs are in balance and some are not. You may have to face the fact that your behavior or attitude is causing stress in other people's lives. You may discover that you have a hard time talking about money matters and need to ask yourself why. Money is a deeply personal issue. Our attitudes and behaviors regarding money are windows to our soul. I know that many people fail to get help for financial matters because they don't wish to open up this window.

Developing personal wealth or money maturity hinges on your ability to examine why you do as you do and then get the assistance you need to develop the *habits of prosperity*. When we become cognitively aware of our own level of maturity on the financial learning curve, we are well positioned for growth, both financially and as human beings. The values and beliefs that affect our financial well-being include understanding our risk tolerance, our patterns of saving and spending, and the beliefs that undergird our money habits. We need to assess where we are on the financial planning learning curve and decide how we will improve both our understanding and habits. Raising your financial well-being is, on one hand, a learning issue and, on the other hand, a self-examination issue. To increase your financial well-being requires honesty and a degree of humility. We need to be honest about what we don't know and start asking for answers from someone who can explain. We need to be honest about our levels of stress, tension, and insecurity regarding money and savings, and ask ourselves how we can improve our emotional approach to money matters. The end result of intellectual pursuit and applied emotional intelligence is greater financial well-being. The New Retirementality recognizes that once your awareness is raised, it is just a matter of time before your personal portfolio follows.

The New Retirementality Is . . .	• Not overestimating your own financial savvy. • Refusing to hang on to investments for the wrong reasons. • Understanding the difference between financial information and financial wisdom. • Teaching your children how to earn and respect money, not just how to spend it. • Making sure your financial house is built *first*. • Facing the emotional and behavioral issues that are robbing you of wealth.

The New Retirementality Challenge

Learn the habits of financial prosperity.

Think about it: Am I committed to any losing strategies? Am I afraid to implement any test strategies? Is there a decision maker in my life with whom I do not agree?

Research it: Review how those around and/or important to me are doing with their money. Locate a good resource for financial information. What is the role of debt in my current financial picture?

Decide and take action:

- Decide on the principles you will use to guide your financial decisions.
- Decide on your use of debt and make changes to bring reality in line with your principles.

CHAPTER 20

Finding the Right Wealth-Building Partner

> *"The best interest of the patient is the only interest that matters."*
> —*Dr. William Mayo*
> *(said back in 1905)*

Think of yourself as a person who will surely possess wealth. What do people with wealth do? They hire someone to help them manage and protect that wealth. Why haven't *you* made that move yet? When I ask that question, answers run the gamut from distrust to embarrassment and many emotions in between. Let's examine some of the major objections people have to getting help and how this resistance may be impeding their personal wealth-building process.

"I'm doing just fine on my own." Many people manage their own stock and/or mutual fund portfolios and get good returns. Some of these people are truly savvy investors, and others are fortunate beneficiaries of a great bull market and good timing. The more your portfolio grows, the more you feel the need to get some help in managing your personal wealth. Many people seem quite content to remain alone while *growing* their assets, but that mind-set is subject to change when the issue shifts to *protecting* those assets.

Ask yourself these two questions:

1. Do I know everything I need to know about asset allocation and protection, tax-reduction strategies, and estate management?
2. Do I want to invest the time and effort to learn these issues? Do I want to continue to invest the time it takes to keep up with the markets and remain competent as an investor?

If you answered yes to these questions and have the time and interest in devoting yourself to building and protecting your assets, then you can go it alone. One caveat: don't assume you can possibly know all there is to know. Even if you want to do it on your own, it would be wise to pay for a consultation and get some direction from a professional money manager who knows his or her way around the brambles of managing wealth. Some professionals consult for an hourly fee or for a one-time fee.

"I don't want to have to pay for services that I can get for a fraction of the cost." Why would any individuals pay $200 for a stock trade that they could execute on their own for $10 or less? That is the question that has led to the boom in online trading accounts and autonomous money management. As a response, most brokerages, banks, and the like have been forced to lower their trading fees. Most firms now offer fee-only type accounts in which you pay about 1 percent of your assets for their management services.

If you know exactly what you want to own (stocks, bonds, mutual funds, etc.) and know how to go about buying them at the best price, then you are a candidate to do it on your own. This assumes that you are well informed and can keep up on those holdings for any changes that could threaten the security of your investments.

I have an online trading account but don't hold the bulk of my assets in that account. I have enough there to occasionally make trades and take advantage of opportunities that I see in the marketplace, although I have been wrong as often as I have been right. This account is more or less there to satisfy my need to take advantage of ideas at a low cost. It is a cross between a hobby and entrepreneurialism. I have placed the bulk of my assets with direction from my accountant, who has an established track record. I had specific criteria in selecting this individual, and he has earned my trust over the years.

One fact of economic life that people often fail to equate to their investments is that, most of the time, you get what you pay for. That I can buy a stock for only $8 doesn't mean I'm going to profit from that purchase. In fact, because it is so easy and inexpensive to buy in and out of that stock increases the odds that I will act on impulse and trade in and out at the wrong times. *More important than the cost of making an investment is the quality of that investment.* If you refuse to pay a 5 percent load for a mutual fund that has produced 30 percent in returns the last five years, are you better off with a no-load fund that has returned 10 percent in the last five years? Of course not. In some cases you do get what you pay for.

The questions we need answered are simple: Is the service, expertise, and quality of investment worth the fee I'm paying? Is it giving me peace of mind? What am I willing to pay for that?

"I don't have enough money to talk to a professional." Many people have the idea that if they don't have $100,000, no professional will talk to them. Although some advisors have minimum amounts they will work with, the majority will help individuals start their wealth-building process with whatever they have. I have heard many people express embarrassment at bringing the small amount of money they possessed to a professional. My answer to these people is that any professionals worth their weight in salt will respect them where they are and help them to build from there. You have to start somewhere, and your money is not going to grow by worrying that it's not enough. Don't let embarrassment convince you that your worth as an individual is measured by your fiscal net worth. Work with someone who will respect where you are—and build from there.

"I don't think I can trust anyone to manage my money." Maybe you have heard or read stories or have had a bad experience yourself with a self-serving broker or advisor. "Once burned, their fault; twice burned, my fault," you tell yourself. There are some bad apples (read selfish) as there are some good apples out there. Unless you want to do all the research, selection, planning, execution, and review work on your own, you need to establish a clear profile of the type of person you want to work with and start interviewing until you find a match that feels right to you. Finding a match is as much about personal chemistry as it is financial philosophy.

If you have a bad experience with a doctor, do you neglect medical care? Think of your wealth as fiscal health. There are some highly competent and personable professionals out there who have built their reputation by helping others reach their goals and putting their clients' interests first. Remember, the online brokerage ads and the do-it-yourself proponents want you to believe that nobody is to be trusted and that you should do this all on your own. Call me stupid, but when I'm looking to blame someone for making the wrong financial moves, I find myself at the top of the list. I have made more than my share of mistakes—many of which would have been avoided with professional consultation. The opposite also holds true. There have been instances when my instincts were right and I allowed a professional to talk me out of a decision. But on the whole, I would rather find someone worthy of my trust and not have all the stress myself. In my case, I work with someone who advises me *and* consults with me when I think I have an idea. The bottom line is that we need someone worthy of our trust.

Because of the nature of my work, I have met literally thousands of brokers, advisors, planners, bankers, and accountants. All of these professionals are clamoring for your business. Some of these professionals I would trust my financial life to because of their integrity and competence. Others I wouldn't give a wooden nickel to because of their self-centeredness and lack of competence. Some of them are so busy selling that they don't really keep up with the products they are supposed to be expert in. They just keep telling the same story and selling the same products to everyone. Others I have met listen with great curiosity to each of their clients to figure out a strategy that is best for the clients, and then work hard to earn the clients' trust and loyalty.

After observing this wide range of integrity/competence, I have developed the following criteria for interviewing a financial professional to help you manage your wealth. Use this assessment after talking to a professional, and you will greatly increase your odds of finding the wealth-building partner you need.

Finding a Wealth-Building Partner

1. *What was your first impression of the individual?* Was she personable and respectful, or officious and/or arrogant?

   The individual's personality is a good indicator of the kind of service and attention you can expect to receive down the road should problems or concerns arise.

2. *What kind of questions did the financial professional ask you?* Did he ask more about your money or more about your life, values, and goals?

   The best people in the business know they cannot do right by you if they do not have a clear understanding of where you've been, who you are, and where you want to go. Those who only inquire about your assets are only interested in your assets.

3. *Did the financial professional demonstrate good listening skills?* Did she carefully summarize your concerns, goals, and level of risk tolerance?

   If you get the feeling you are not dealing with a good listener, move on. If the individual is paying close attention now, you know that is what you can expect later. If the individual pretends to listen but just charges ahead with an agenda that seems to miss the point of what you told her, move on. If the professional dominates the conversation, get out as fast as you can!

4. *Did the financial professional explain matters in a language you could understand or did he use jargon and talk over your head?*

   Those who talk over your head probably want to keep you in the dark or simply aren't smart enough to make matters understandable. Anyone who makes you feel stupid is not worthy of your business. A sure sign of competence is the ability to make complex matters seem simple and understandable. A good advisor will also be a good teacher and will help you improve your financial well-being.

5. *Is the financial professional willing to disclose her own personal holdings?*

   You would be amazed at the number of financial professionals whose personal financial lives are a mess. There are also many who are not buying what they are selling. If financial professionals are trying to sell something they don't own, I want to know why. If you find an advisor who does for her clients what she does for herself, you have a greater potential for trust.

6. *Does the financial professional have a track record that can be documented?*

   Unless you want to be somebody's guinea pig, you should ask to see the professional's performance record. Check to see that the individual has done well in down markets as well as in up markets. Ask for references and talk to those who have been clients for a long period (beware of shills when asking for references).

7. *Does the financial professional articulate a clear philosophy regarding investments and wealth building?*

   If the professional doesn't have a clear philosophical compass that has been fine-tuned through experience, he is more likely to be one of those people who just follows the crowd. The dime-a-dozen advisor who sells whatever he is told to sell is not the person you are looking for. I like to see advisors who are comfortable talking about their mistakes as well as their victories—a good investment philosophy borrows from the lessons of both failure and success.

8. *Ask the financial professional why she got into this business.*

   Here you will hear answers ranging from seemingly being on a mission to help other people to seemingly only pretending to be on a mission to help other people but really on a mission to help themselves. I read between the lines on this answer. I want to get the sense that the financial professional is fascinated about money matters, curious about people, and motivated by her work.

If you walk out of an interview satisfied that these bases have been covered, you have a great chance of partnering with a trustworthy individual. Cunning individuals may have the ability to fake these integral characteristics but they cannot fake them for long. You want a concerned and competent professional who is in the profession for the right reasons. You want to find out what the person's motives are. After taking him or her through the preceding questions, you will have a pretty good indication.

A Personal Safety Net

When I was building an addition onto my home for our new baby boy, I decided I wanted to do some of the work myself to save money. I had had a little experience doing electrical wiring and decided to tackle it with a little consultation. The builder agreed to inspect my work before the official inspector came in. When I was done with the wiring, the builder came to check my work. When he came to the last connection I had made, he showed me how I had erred and informed me that it could have easily started a fire. Then and there I decided some projects are far too important to try to tackle alone with a limited degree of experience. I believe that retirement or emancipation planning is one of those projects.

When I travel to a faraway place, I like to get the advice of a trusted travel agent who has actually been there. I have found that faraway places don't always look and feel as pleasant as in the pictures in the brochures. Sure, I pay more by not doing it on my own, but my travel agent provides me with two intangibles that I value: experience and confidence. I want the peace of mind that comes from knowing I will not have unpleasant surprises when I arrive. I think of a good financial professional as a tour guide in a fiscal maze.

Guides of every description can be found today: advisors who charge a one-time fee to design an investment plan; advisors who charge consultation fees by the hour; advisors who charge a small percentage of assets under management (they make more money when you make more money). You can find a person and an arrangement you will be comfortable with in today's financial marketplace. Good financial professionals are worth their weight in gold.

Consider the following example from financial columnist Roger Thomas:

> On December 26, 1972, and October 26, 1982, the Dow Jones Industrial Average (DIJA) closed at exactly the same level—1,006.
>
> If you had invested $100,000 in 1972, what do you think it would have been worth in 1982? The answer to that question may surprise you. Some think that their $100,000 would still be worth $100,000 because the market didn't rise—but they would be mistaken.
>
> If you had invested $100,000 in the 30 stocks that make up the DJIA, your money would have grown to $169,000 because of dividend reinvestment.
>
> If you had invested your money in a professionally managed mutual fund, your $100,000 would have grown to $221,000. The expertise of these professionals pays off.

But if you had invested with a trusted financial advisor who suggested a diversified portfolio of three time-tested mutual funds, your account would have grown to $240,000.

What difference can a good advisor make? In this ten-year period, the answer is about $69,000!

And, we may be in for another ten years like 1972–1982. The investment marketplace is changing for the better. Financial firms have received the wake-up call that it takes people skills, integrity, and competence to win the trust of today's more savvy client. The advisor of the future will take a more holistic approach and will work to establish relationships that last a lifetime. Janet Briaud, a financial planner from Texas, articulates what planning will look like in the future: "I try to help people from the human capital side, the psychological capital side, and financial capital side. Until I can get my arms around those issues, I won't do a plan." What Briaud is saying is that she takes an interest in her clients as human beings, not just as a bundle of assets. Professionals who operate with this ethic will prosper in the future because today's clients will not settle for anything less—and their antennae are alerted for counterfeits.

You have a greater chance of reaching your emancipation goals with teaching, training, and coaching. A good advisor will provide you with all of these. It simply comes down to finding someone you can trust—someone who wants the satisfaction of helping you reach your goals. The New Retirementality recognizes both the freedoms and perils of the new financial marketplace. The New Retirementality recognizes the need for wisdom and experience, not just information and the lowest fee. The New Retirementality recognizes that if people want to, they can do the work and go it alone; but it also recognizes the value of the time and stress that can be saved by joining up with the right wealth-building partner.

The New Retirementality Is . . .	<ul><li>Understanding that you will have to invest both time and money to build your personal wealth.</li><li>Working with a financial professional who will respect your individuality and help you articulate and reach your goals.</li><li>Spreading your risk in a wise financial approach that ensures growth even in turbulent market periods.</li></ul>

CHAPTER 21

Giving Your
Life Away

> *"Owning things is an obsession in our culture. If we own it, we feel we can control it; if we can control it, we feel it will give us more pleasure. The idea is an illusion."*
>
> —*Richard Foster, author*

> *"The only things you keep in this world are the things you give away."*
>
> —*Anonymous*

A revitalized offering of human energy could be the greatest windfall of all for our society to come out of the New Retirementality.

Sir John Templeton of Templeton Fund fame and a great wealth builder believes that seeking spiritual wealth is the next great challenge for the 21st century. He stated:

> For more than 45 years, I worked diligently to help people obtain higher profits. This seemed to bring happiness to the investors, but only temporarily. It never gave them—or me—true happiness. Also, my diligence did not seem to help make the world a better place than I found it. During all that time I kept searching for ways my brief life on this planet could produce permanent benefits for everyone. So I sold all my moneymaking activities to a competitor in order to devote my life to a vastly

more important purpose. I wanted to give 100% of my time and resources toward helping the world build spiritual wealth.

Templeton used his money to start the John Templeton Foundation in 1987. Each year his foundation donates over $20 million to encourage entrepreneurs who are trying various methods to increase our base of spiritual information. Because of his efforts, 65 medical graduate schools teach courses in spirituality. The foundation sponsors courses at over 400 universities to find out what has been, or might be, discovered through scientific research to enlarge human concepts of divinity.

Templeton has done this because he believes we need to address larger questions in life such as these: "Are there realities humans cannot comprehend that are vastly more awesome than the things we can see or touch?" "Is there an intellect more vast than humanity can imagine?" "Why do people who devote their lives to a noble purpose usually become happy?" Sir John Templeton became a happier man because he has found a way to give his life away.

By planning and saving for our own emancipation, we can liberate our own life to the point of giving it away to people and causes that we feel great passion about helping. This sort of noble goal has provided the needed boost of intrinsic motivation that many people have needed to establish the discipline and lifestyle necessary to arrive at a place of both emancipation and benevolence.

The kind of benevolence we are witnessing today goes beyond pushing a cart around a hospital. As Dave, my barber, informs me, volunteering is not the great answer to many people's retirement discomfort. He said, "I've watched a lot of guys go through the retirement cycle. They retire thinking they'll just take it easy. After a few months of nothing to do, they are bored with themselves. Then they decide to volunteer in some cause to get reinvigorated, but that is no magic move either. I've heard many people say that they were still unsatisfied even after volunteering. The key seems to be putting your life into something you are passionate about."

As Figure 21.1 shows, there are some well-defined intangibles that any volunteer needs to take from the experience to make it worthwhile. As this figure illustrates, making a difference does not always translate into a sense of satisfaction. But it is a sense of satisfaction more than any other factor that makes the experience worthwhile for the volunteer. This is especially true for the younger retirees that our nation is

FIGURE 21.1 | Motives for Volunteering

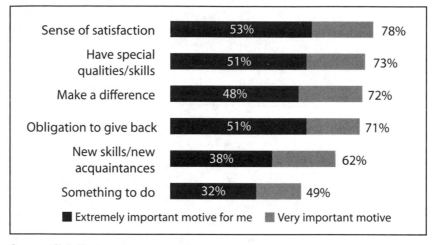

Source: Civic Ventures.

seeing more and more of. Older retirees may volunteer simply to have something to do or to make new acquaintances, but these motives are unlikely for younger retirees, who feel they have many options for how to best spend their time and energy.

According to a study by Michael Callow, the concept of volunteering is often defined in altruistic terms, but the perceived motives for volunteering are often more egoistic. "In all cases, volunteering was viewed primarily as a choice endeavor that benefited not only others but also themselves. If they did not feel that they benefited personally from the experience, then there was little point in continuing to volunteer. The perceived motives for volunteering included: the feel-good factor, the need for socialization, a search for structure, and a search for purpose. Subjects identified two additional yet unexpected benefits that arose once they began to volunteer: a sense of control and reimbursements."

Creative Benevolence

One important asset that any emancipated individual has to offer—and that society desperately needs—is experience. The experience you gained in achieving your own freedom can be the gift you give to charitable organizations. I'm not speaking of just sitting on a board but of actually donating the professional skills you've acquired to help take these organizations to a higher level of expertise. I'm inspired by the number of people who have told me that their ultimate goal is to give their expertise to causes they deeply believe in.

Chuck Palmer is one such example. Palmer is a CPA by training and has had a very successful career. He sold his practice but retained a few of his favorite accounts to keep himself connected to the business. Because he had retired early, he still felt he had a lot of energy and valuable time to give. When taking a close look at the organizations whose causes he admired, Palmer decided that the best gift he could give was not money but professional skill. Many of these organizations were in dire need of accounting and budgetary advice and management, which they couldn't afford. Palmer saw an opportunity for some creative benevolence. He now runs an accounting practice that helps a few select causes at absolutely no charge to the charitable organization. This sort of pro bono effort is catching on with many other professionals who have been blessed with both skill and financial prosperity. More than just giving away money, they want to give away their life, their wisdom, and their passion. This desire to give is not just obligatory but is fueled more by gratitude than anything else.

I have met the marketing professional who wants to help worthy nonprofits learn to be better at promoting their cause. There is the Internet engineer who wants to help charities learn to fully utilize the Internet for communicating with their constituents. There is the doctor who takes six trips a year to Third World countries to give free medical care. There is the chiropractor who takes trips to eastern Europe to treat people with long-standing industrial injuries for free. There is the business lawyer who helps nonprofits get their legal affairs in order. There is the former sales professional who now raises funds for her favorite charity. There is the former professor who now gives his life to helping illiterate adults. There is the entrepreneur who now helps his favorite causes to develop a business plan and acts as mentor and encourager to burned-out, nonprofit directors. There is the former executive who now teaches part-time at a community college. There is the former manager who is now a corporate coach. My personal accountant, Mark Eldridge of Financial Freedom, Inc., generously donates his services to nonprofit concerns.

Some of these people are giving their life away without material compensation because they have enough to sustain themselves. Still others are doing so but being compensated in the process. All of them feel they are optimizing their benevolent potential by utilizing their abilities and experience in a way that brings tangible change in other people's lives. They all attest that such benevolent expression, whether daily or periodic, has added a rich perspective to their sense of fulfillment and purpose.

Volunteering Payoffs

"University students today are literally bombarded by organizations saying, 'Come work with us.' I don't find that in the take out interviews for those who are retiring . . . there is so much potential activity out there that is not being tapped or utilized."
—Freeman Bradley, author

The model for giving your life away is changing. According to a study by Peter D. Hart Research Associates entitled "The New Face of Retirement," one approach that appeals to the traditionally retired crowd today is a program that would offer retirees selected benefits for their volunteer efforts. Such benefits would include weekly stipends, education credits, or reduced costs for prescription drugs in exchange for 15 hours a week of community service. Sixty-one percent of retired Americans over the age of 50 express interest in this type of program and 69 percent of nonretired people in this age group would like to see this sort of approach.

A 2005 study by MetLife Foundation and Civic Ventures revealed that retirees are looking for work that merges with volunteering initiatives. Half of adults 50–70 say they are interested in taking jobs now or in the future to help improve the quality of life in their communities; 78 percent of these want to help the poor, elderly, and others in need; 56 percent are interested in dealing with health issues; 55 percent are interested in teaching or other educational positions; and 45 percent want to work with youth in a program.

A compromise approach to contributing our time and efforts may well become a reality for several reasons. One is that many people who would like to donate their efforts to causes they believe in can use assistance. Many lower-income retirees said they would be highly motivated by a prescription drug incentive. Many retirees feel they are trading wealth for health with the large amounts of money they spend on prescription drugs and would gladly give of their time for such a trade-off.

Something to Give

The bottom line is that most people feel that they have something to give, but not all people feel they can afford to give. The traits that people offer as their most important potential contributions include:

- Experience (36 percent)
- Wisdom and perspective (30 percent)
- Patience and freedom from other distractions (16 percent)
- Time (13 percent)
- Determination and resolve (8 percent)

One of the travesties of recent American culture is how little the premium is that we have placed on these traits and, in fact, dismiss them on the basis of a person's age. This cultural bias is changing because of the millions of baby boomers now entering later stages of life. Three in four Americans report being involved in some sort of community service during the past year. About 50 percent, however, admit that their involvement has been limited to one-time or sporadic involvement. A 2004 study on volunteering in the United States by the U.S. Bureau of Labor Statistics revealed that the volunteer ratio for those over 65 was only 25 percent, although the time commitment for this age group was higher than other groups. There seems to be plenty of upside for volunteering for the new retirees. Overwhelmingly, the greatest intrinsic motivation for those who are already retired is the need to feel important and engaged.

According to a Princeton survey, "The New Face of Work," fully half of all adults ages 50–75 say they are interested in taking jobs now or in the future to help improve the quality of life in their communities.

The coming generation of mature Americans will not allow itself to be labeled secondary citizens relegated to retirement communities as past generations have been and will continue to be engaged in the communities where they live—even if it means living in two communities. Current involvement in raising money for charities, helping the elderly, working with children and youth, and involvement in local community issues point to a higher sense of civic engagement for future retirees. These individuals are not going to give their time and effort to just anybody. Instead, they will focus on the causes and people who recognize the unique contribution of wisdom, experience, and energy they bring. Their efforts will go to causes that help them feel important.

New Rules of Engagement

> *"I think we need a new word to replace 'retirement.' Retirement in the generation preceding mine meant that you worked until age 65 and at that point you ceased working, took a well-deserved rest. If you had the means, you went to Florida and played golf, because you had very little time remaining. Now one retires at 55 or 65 with a number of years left. With much more energy and certainly far better health, one has time to be used more constructively than awaiting death."*
> —Dick Shore, retired administrator, 69

One of the heroes of the highly engaged retiree has been former President Jimmy Carter. More than 43 percent of today's retirees said Carter was a great example of the ideals they are seeking in retirement. Carter, since leaving the presidency over 20 years ago, has worked tirelessly for Habitat for Humanity and as an informal diplomatic ambassador. Other famous retirees who get the nod of approval include Colin Powell, John Glenn, and Jerry Lewis—all of whom ignored the old rules and definitions of retirement.

According to the Hart study, well-defined new rules for retirement taking hold in our society are the following:

- *Assertiveness*—Instead of shrinking from old age and retirement, Americans of this generation are embracing later life and asserting themselves as valuable members of the community with special and unique traits to offer. Increasingly, seniors see their maturity as an asset rather than a frailty, and, as a result, they are eager to stay engaged in, rather than withdrawn from, their environment.
- *Meaningful involvement*—Americans' attitudes toward volunteering and community service reflect their general approach to retirement and later life. Although these adults express a strong desire

to be involved in volunteer activities, they are seeking meaningful activities that take advantage of their special traits rather than activities that merely fill time.

- *A benevolence boom*—Even though a majority of mature Americans express a promising interest in incorporating volunteer and community service activities into their retirement plans, those who have not yet retired express immeasurably more interest. In fact, the findings suggest that this generation of older adults may flood our nation's civic institutions early in this century in the same way in which they overwhelmed the institutions of higher education in the 1950s and 1960s.

Philanthropy with an Attitude

The same kind of radical baby boomer thinking and involvement that has brought dynamic change to the rules of business and society is working its way into charitable causes and civic engagement. Take, for example, the new wave of philanthropists called "cybersaints," who are bringing an entrepreneurial twist to the world of charity. The average high-tech millionaire is not some Gen-X techie. The average millionaire is a person who has worked 23 years in the field and comes from a modest economic background.

In venture philanthropy, people are throwing more than just money at causes. They are integrating the elements that make other sectors of the economy successful and bringing them to the philanthropic sector, such as long-range business goals, projections of need, accountability, and a plan for self-sufficiency. Cate Muther, a former Cisco executive who left to found a charitable fund, calls the new type of giving "philanthropy with an attitude."

In coming years we will witness a tidal wave of creative solutions and energetic efforts toward remedying social injustices and long-standing problems. This benevolence boom will be fueled by the boomers' continuing spiritual quest to find real meaning in this world. Many have found that material success has left them wanting. Many have come to believe that the vacuous void in their soul they have experienced as a result of a life of accumulating can be filled by a life of giving. There are millions who are looking for the right opportunity to apply the things they have learned into something they can believe in.

What Do You Believe In? What Do You Have to Give?

There are a million ways to give your life away. Each method is as unique as the experience of the individual doing the giving. What valuable skills and insights have you gained in your journey? What causes could greatly benefit from the wisdom and insight you possess? What societal ills and injustices are you passionate about fixing? Could your time and expertise do more toward fixing these problems than just writing out a check? Would having the goal of giving your life away act as a powerful motivator to help you reach financial independence so you could apply your time as freely as you wish?

In my own life, such a goal has been the most potent motivator for an aggressive and disciplined savings program. My wife and I have been much more disciplined than what comes naturally because we want the freedom to pursue efforts that we think can make the most impact in the world. Even this book has become a part of that effort. The royalties from this book have been designated to the ONE LIFE charity, which aids suicide prevention work around the globe. My company has been involved for years in writing life skills curricula for schools, and one of those curricula was on the topic of suicide prevention. A book I wrote on the topic was translated into Spanish, Polish, and Slavic, and I started receiving invitations to countries to help them find ways of addressing suicide prevention with their young people. What I found in many of these countries were people eager to help their young but lacking the resources or training to do so. They simply could not afford such "luxuries."

Together with other concerned parties, we started ONE LIFE for the purpose of providing suicide prevention education and life skills training for teens anywhere in the world at no charge to the recipients. One thing you quickly learn by spending time in Third World countries is that they all look to the United States for answers. We have the most advanced answers for what ails the world. We also have the kinds of resources that most of these people could never dream of having. In ONE LIFE I found a way to connect American resources and resourcefulness to a tragic need in other nations without burdening those who want to help with impossible expenses. This is a model of benevolence that I believe we will see more of in coming years. We will utilize our entrepreneurial spirit and resourcefulness to help other people of the world solve their physical, social, and practical problems. We in America have so much that we can give ideas and resources to help the many unmet needs in our world. Consider the following facts.

If we could shrink the earth's nearly 6 billion people to a village of 100 people, the profile of that village would look like this:

- 57 Asians, 21 Europeans, 14 North and South Americans, and 8 Africans
- 50 suffering from malnutrition
- 70 unable to read
- 80 living in substandard housing
- Only 1 with a college education
- 50 percent of the world's wealth in the hands of 6 people

And 6 of these people would be citizens of the United States.

More to Life

At last count there were 7.2 million millionaires in America, and that number is growing each day. To qualify, people have to possess $1 million or more in investable assets, meaning the value of their home doesn't count. There are now over 600,000 pentamillionaires—those with investable assets of over $5 million. That is up from 400,000 pentamillionaires in 1995; by 2010 the number could possibly reach one million.

How much accumulation is enough? At what point do we say, "I've got what I need to live a comfortable life; now how can I put some of this wealth to work in helping others?" And I don't believe you have to possess a million dollars to make a difference in the world. What this world needs more than anything is energy and creative approaches to perennial problems. Many people of this generation are catching the vision of giving their life away as a route to true fulfillment. Consider that at least one-half of the men and women entering seminaries today to become priests, ministers, or rabbis are over the age of 35! Many of these people are sacrificing successful careers and prosperous lifestyles but are content in their transition.

The people making this transition to service have come to their decision after wrestling with the idea that there must be more to life. Those who have pursued religious studies later in life share two essential traits: (1) they were willing to risk, and (2) they were willing to search.

This new breed of midlife clergy, after asking themselves, "What am I living for?" seem to be motivated by three common things: a sense of dissatisfaction, a desire to serve, and a sense of calling. The dissatisfaction came with the realization that material achievements were not satisfying their spiritual appetites. The sense of service came when taking a personal inventory of their strengths and weaknesses and the decision that the best use they could make of those abilities was in the service of others. The sense of calling was expressed as an "inner leading" that God was calling them to a life of giving.

Ted Schmitt, a senior executive at a major movie studio who made a transition to a life of religious service, articulated his decision this way: "When problems hit and family members died, it made me evaluate what life is. Is it corporate quarterly profits or something more? I didn't think I had the ability *not* to be selfish, not to worry about money and things, but those things aren't important. Now I have no aspirations to do anything but be a good priest."

It does not require religious service to give your life away. The means and methods by which people are doing so are incredibly diverse. Some do so by giving money to causes they want promoted, which lends an extra layer of meaning to the everyday work they do to gain that money. Still others do it by lending their expertise and skill to causes and organizations that are making a difference in people's lives. They are doing it at different levels of commitment. Some give a day or two a month, and others give a part or all of every day. The important thing for all these people is that they feel they've translated their abilities and assets from self-serving to the realm of benevolence.

I have come to believe that the great and ultimate end of the New Retirementality is to emancipate our lives financially so that we can follow the lead of our working soul. This means doing work that gives our hands, our head, and our heart satisfaction. I'm working on the assumption that I don't get a second shot at this earthly existence. I certainly don't want to give away my life to frustrating work and empty pursuits. My hope is that many reading this book will not only pursue and achieve financial emancipation, but that this emancipation will lead to more involvement in the service of some aspect of human injustice, suffering, or other noble pursuits serving your fellow man.

With emancipation, the great reward to both ourselves and the world we live in will be that we are now free to give our life away. As long as we owe others and must burn the candle at both ends to pay those we owe, we are not free. As long as we are handcuffed or chained to work that takes more from us than it gives us, we are not free. As long as we are driven to get results to such extremes that all our meaningful relationships suffer, we are not free.

Freedom is the goal. Freedom to give is the ultimate goal.

The New Retirementality Is...	• Finding personal and creative ways of demonstrating benevolence. • Giving your talents and experience as well as your substance. • Realizing that wealth brings a responsibility to help solve societal injustices and needs.

For more information about the New Retirementality workshops, training courses, audios, or videos, contact http://www.mitchanthony.com.

Bibliography

AARP. *AARP Annual Report 2003*, June 2004. http://assets.aarp.org/www .aarp.org_/articles/aboutaarp/AARP2004AnnualReport.pdf.

———. "The Numerous Benefits of Walking." http://www.aarp.org/health/ fitness/walking/a2004-06-17-walking-numerousbenefits.html.

Abramson, Alexis, and Merril Silverstein. *Images of Aging in America 2004: A Summary of Selected Findings*. November 2004. http://assets.aarp.org/ rgcenter/general/images_aging.pdf.

Adams, Raymond. "Strength Training: A natural prescription for staying healthy and fit." *GRC News*, 2003. http://www.sfu.ca/grc/grcn_pdfs/vol22no1.pdf.

Administration on Aging. *A Profile of Older Americans*. 2004. http://www .aoa.gov/prof/Statistics/profile/2004/profiles2004.asp.

Ajilon Finance. "Trouble Finding the Perfect Gift for Your Boss—How About a Little Respect?" 14 October 2003. http://www.ajilonfinance.com/articles/ af_bossday_101403.asp.

Alderman, Lesley. "Did Someone Say Roll Over." *Barron's*, 27 March 2000, R16.

Anderson, Neil. *The Bondage Breaker.* Harvest House Books, 1993.

Arias, Elizabeth, and Betty L. Smith. "Deaths: Preliminary Data for 2001." *National Vital Statistics Reports* 51, no. 5 (2003). http://www.cdc.gov/nchs/ data/nvsr/nvsr51/nvsr51_05.pdf.

Arndorfer, James B. "More planners using both couch and calculator." *Investment News*, 7 February 2000.

Australian Prudential Regulation Authority. "APRA releases latest edition of Superannuation Trends." Press release, 2 August 2004. http://www.apra .gov.au/media-releases/04_26.cfm.

Balfour, Brad. "Who is the Smoothest of Them All?" *Sky*, April 2000, 38.

Bass, Carla. "Job applicants should consider workplace health." *The Dallas Morning News*, as quoted in the *Post-Bulletin*, "Give your employer a fitness test," 27 May 2000, 1c.

Bodie, Zvi. "Pensions as Retirement Income Insurance." *Journal of Economic Literature* 28, March 1990, 28–49.

Bolles, Richard N. *The Three Boxes of Life: And How to Get out of Them.* Ten Speed Press, 1981.

Bradley, Susan K. "Sudden Retirement." *Journal of Financial Planning,* April 2000, 38–40.

"Brain Drain." *BusinessWeek,* 20 Sept. 1999, 113–24.

Brauer, David, and the Congressional Budget Office. "CBO's Projections of the Labor Force." September 2004. http://www.cbo.gov/showdo.cfm?index =5803&sequence=0#t10.

Bronfenbrenner Life Course Center. "Cornell Employment and Family Careers Institute." *Issue Brief* 1:1 (Fall 1998).

———. "Tapping the Talents of America's 'Seasoned' Citizens." *Issue Brief* 2:1 (Spring 1997).

Bronte, Lydia. *The Longevity Factor.* HarperCollins, 1993.

Brown, S. Kathi. *Staying Ahead of the Curve 2003: The AARP Working in Retirement Study, Executive Summary.* 2003. http://assets.aarp.org/rgcenter/ econ/multiwork_2003_1.pdf.

Burtless, Gary, and Joseph F. Quinn. "Retirement Trends and Policies to Encourage Work among Older Americans." Prepared for the annual conference of the National Academy of Social Insurance, Washington, D.C., 26–27 January 2000, 1–23.

Callow, Michael. "Identifying Promotional Appeals for Targeting Potential Volunteers: An Exploratory Study on Volunteering Motives Among Retirees." *International Journal of Nonprofit and Voluntary Sector Marketing* 9, no. 3 (24 May 2004): 261–74. http://www.charityfundraising.org/Callow %20-%20Volunteering%20motives.pdf.

Capgemini and Merrill Lynch. *World Wealth Report.* 2004. http://www.ml.com/ media/18252.pdf.

Careerbuilder.com. "More Than One-Third of Career Moms Would Take Less Pay in Exchange for More Time with Family, According to CareerBuilder .com's Annual Mother's Day Survey." 2 May 2005. http://www.prnewswire .com/cgi-bin/stories.pl?ACCT=109&STORY=/www/story/05-02-2005/0003536447&EDATE=.

Carter, Jimmy. *The Virtues of Aging.* Ballantine, 1998.

Chapman, Elwood N., and Marion E. Haynes. *Comfort Zones: Planning Your Future.* Crisp, 1997.

CivicVentures. "Fact Sheet on Older Americans." 2005. http://www.civicventures .org/261.html.

"Cognitive Function Improves with Exercise." *Clinician Review.* November 2004. http://www.findarticles.com/p/articles/mi_m0BUY/is_11_14/ai_ n7586301.

"Community Colleges' Role in Teacher Preparation." 2003. http://www
.communitycollegepolicy.org/html/Issues/Issue.asp?issueID=2&catID=2&
absLevel=1.

Congressional Budget Office. "Updated Long-Term Projections for Social Security." January 2005. http://www.cbo.gov/ftpdocs/60xx/doc6064/03-03-
LongTermProjections.pdf.

Covey, Stephen. *The Seven Habits of Highly Effective People.* Fireside Books,
Simon & Schuster, 1989.

Cramer, James J. "Tales from the duped side." *Forbes ASAP,* 2 October 2000,
77–78.

Cruz, Humberto. "Looking toward the golden years." *Chicago Tribune,* 24
March 2000, D6, classified 3.

"DALBAR Study Shows Market Timers Lose Their Money." Press release, 1
April 2004. http://www.dalbar.com/content/showpage.asp?page=2004040101.

Deacle, Scott. "Banking for the well-to-do." 2000. http://www.virginiabusiness
.com/magazine/yr2000/sep00/bank.html.

Del Webb. *Baby Boomer Report, Annual Opinion Survey: 2003 Survey Results
Summary.* 2003. http://www.pulte.com/PressRoom/BabyBoomer2003
Summary.pdf.

Deloitte Touche Tohmatsu. "Top Five Benefit Priorities for 2000." Conducted
by the International Society of Certified Employee Benefit Specialists and
Deloitte & Touche, 2000.

Dierdorff, Jack. "It Ain't Over When It's Over." *BusinessWeek,* 20 September
1999, 126.

Dortch, Shannon. "How to sell savings." *American Demographics,* Ithaca,
Feb. 1998.

Ellis, David. "Retirement blunder: Raiding the 401(k)." *CNN/Money,* 25 July
2005. http://money.cnn.com/2005/07/25/retirement/401k_survey/.

Epstein, Gene. "Retire! Hell, No!" *Barron's,* 27 March 2000, R22, 24.

ExecuNet. *Silver Linings: Experienced Executives Gaining the Edge.* 2005.
http://www.execunet.com/promo/pdf/AgeDiscrimination.pdf.

Farrell, Chris. "Managing Your Freelance Income." *Right on the Money.*
http://www.rightonthemoney.org/shows/208-freelance/show-208html.

Field, Anne. "A living or a life?" *Fast Company,* January–February 2000,
256–64.

"Focus on Financial Planning." *Employee Benefit Plan Review,* April 1999,
30–31.

Fox, Susannah. "Older Americans and the Internet." 28 March 2003. http://www.pewinternet.org/PPF/r/117/report_display.asp.

Fraynor, Jean B. "Total Life Planning: A New Frontier in Work-Life Benefits." *Employee Benefits Journal,* December 1999, 29–32.

"Friends Are the Key." *Unconventional Wisdom,* Fall 1999, 1.

Gandel, Stephen, Michael Sivy, and Tara Kalwarski. "Follow the wealth." *CNN/ Money,* 25 March 2005. http://money.cnn.com/2005/03/25/pf/boomers3 _0504/.

Gist, John, Ke Bin Wu, and Satyendra Verma. "The Distribution of Financial Wealth Among Boomers." AARP Public Policy Institute, July 2004. http://assets.aarp.org/rgcenter/econ/dd99_distribution.pdf.

Goleman, Daniel. *Emotional Intelligence.* Bloomsbury Publishing, 1995.

Goozner, Merrill, and Michael Tackett. "Bush to propose changing Social Security accounts." *Chicago Tribune,* 14 May 2000, 12A.

Guttman, Monika. "CyberSaints." *USA Weekend,* 15-17 Sept. 2000, 6–8.

Harris Interactive. "Pulte Homes—Baby Boomer Study." May 2005. http://onlinepressroom.net/pulte/babyboomer/.

Herman, Tracy. "Detecting Demand." *Registered Representative*/http://www.Rrmag.com, April 2000, 61–70.

HSBC. "The future of retirement in a world of rising life expectancies." 10 May 2005. http://www.hsbcusa.com/ourcompany/pdf/future_of_retirement _fact_sheets_en_us.pdf.

Interim Services Inc. "The Emerging Workforce Study." *1999 Emerging Workforce Study,* 1–3.

"Investing for the Future." *Unconventional Wisdom,* Summer 1999, 3.

Jahnke, William. "Wealth Navigation." *Investment Advisor,* June 2000, 66–68, 70.

Jamieson, Dan. "More than Money." *Special Retirement Planning,* originally appeared in the January 1996 issue of *Registered Representative* magazine.

Kantrowitz, Barbara. "Special Report: The New Middle Age." *Newsweek,* 3 April 2000, 57–59.

Laing, Jonathan R. "No Fear." *Barron's,* 27 March 2000, R4–6.

Lewis, Allyson. *The Million Dollar Car and $250,000 Pizza.* Dearborn Trade, 2000.

Luce, Maria. "Less Than Meets the Eye." *Barron's,* 27 March 2000, R18–20.

McClellan, Judi L., and Richard Holden. "The New Workforce: Age and Ethnic Changes." http://www.calmis.ca.gov/specialreports/Aging-Workforce .pdf.

McMenamin, Brigid. "Who's Spoiled?" *Forbes,* 12 June 2000, 266–76.

Meeks, Fleming. "A Nation of Millionaires." *Barron's,* 27 March 2000, R26.

Mellan, Olivia. "Karma Chameleon." *Investment Advisor,* August 2000, 111–12.

Merrill Lynch and Ken Dychtwald. *The Merrill Lynch New Retirement Survey.* 2005.

MetLife and Civic Ventures. *New Face of Work Survey.* June 2005. http://www.civicventures.org/survey.html.

Mishel, Walter, and Phillip K. Peake. "Predicting Adolescent Cognitive and Self-Regulatory Competencies from Pre-school Delay of Gratification." *Developmental Psychology* 26, no. 6 (1990), 978–86.

Moen, Phyllis. "Recasting Careers: Changing Reference Groups, Risks, and Realities." *Generations,* Spring 1998, 40–45.

———. Cornell Retirement and Well-Being Study. Quoted in "Increase Well-Being," *Unconventional Wisdom,* Spring 1999, 1.

Movelier, Steve. "The Business of Advice." *Investment Advisor,* February 2000, 107–9.

Nathans-Spiro, Leah, and Michael Schroeder. "Can you trust?" *BusinessWeek,* 20 February 1995, 70–76.

Neuwirth Research Inc. "Investors and the Internet: The Impact on the Advisor-Client Relationship." *Forum for Investor Advice,* Spring 2000, 1–30.

Norton, Leslie P. "The Wealth Revolution." *Barron's,* 18 September 2000, 33–38.

"Obstacles to Financial Freedom. *2000 Unconventional Wisdom,* 2–4.

Opiela, Nancy. "Retirement Mind Games." *Journal of Financial Planning,* April 2000, 60–68.

Opsata, Margaret. "Class Act." *Investment Advisor,* April 2000, 65–66.

———. "Right as Rain." *Investment Advisor,* June 2000, 44–50.

PaineWebber. "Retirement Revisited: An Index of Optimism Special Report." *The PaineWebber Poll of Investor Attitudes* (1998), 1–12.

Peter D. Hart Research Associates, Inc. "The New Face of Retirement: Older Americans, Civic Engagement, and the Longevity Revolution." A survey conducted for Civic Ventures, September 1999.

Phoenix Home Life Mutual Insurance Company. "1999 Phoenix Fiscal Survey of Adults." http://www.phl.comMutualnews/Fiscal/ff-highlights.htm.

PNC Financial Services Group. "Many Wealthy Americans Have Done Nothing to Protect Assets and are Worried about Financial Security, Family Values, According to the Largest Study of its Kind Released Today." Press release, 10 January 2005. http://www.pncadvisors.com/print/pdf/1,1218,,00

.html?PDF=L2ZpbGVzL3NlY3Rpb24vcGRmL1dlYWx0aGFuZFZZhb
HVlU3VydmV5XzE2MzQucGRm.

Pollan, Stephen M., and Mark Levine. "The Rise and Fall of Retirement."
Worth, December/January 1995, 64–74.

Princeton Survey Research Associates. "Discontent Beneath the Boom." *Newsweek,* 3 April 2000, 1–37.

Prudential Retirement. "Americans Closest to Retirement are Ill-Prepared to
Generate a Retirement 'Paycheck'." Press release, 23 February 2005. http://
www2.prudential.com/cit/pressrel.nsf/0/56c2a50f12ac0da985256fb10049e
db2/$FILE/02-23-05_Workplace_rept_newsrelease.pdf.

Pullen, Courtney. "Listening to Retirement." *Journal of Financial Planning,*
April 2000, 50–51.

Quinn, Jacqueline M. "Mainstreaming Financial Education as an Employee
Benefit." *Journal of Financial Planning,* May 2000, 71–79.

Quinn, Jane Bryant. "Planning: The Next Stage." *Newsweek,* 3 April 2000.

Ramsay, Karen. *Everything You Know about Money Is Wrong.* Regan Books,
1999.

Rix, Sara E. *Update on the Older Worker: 2004.* April 2005. http://assets.aarp
.org/rgcenter/econ/dd114_worker.pdf.

Roizen, Michael F. *Real Age: Are You as Young as You Can Be?* HarperCollins,
1999.

Roper ASW. "Baby Boomers Envision Retirement II: Survey of Baby Boomers Expectations for Retirement." A survey conducted for the AARP, May
2004. http://assets.aarp.org/rgcenter/econ/boomers_envision.pdf.

Roper Starch Worldwide. Commissioned by the AARP. "Baby Boomers Look
Toward Retirement." 2 June 1998, 1–5. Press release.

Rowe, John W., and Robert L. Kahn. *Successful Aging.* DTP Trade Paperbacks, 1998, 132–33, 167–80.

Samuelson, Robert J. "Darling, It'll All Be Yours—Soon." *Newsweek,* 3 April
2000, 66–68.

Schuchardt, Jane. "The Power of Partnerships." *Newsletter: Association for Financial Counseling and Planning Education* 18, no. 3 (July 2000), 1–8.

Shagrin, Steve. "Retirement Planning Motivates Employees and Produces Results for Employers." *Employee Benefit Plan Review,* April 1999, 10–12.

Shell, Adam. "Tech stock lovers refuse to give up." *USA Today,* 19 May 2000,
3B.

"SHRM Shows Organizations Slowly Preparing for Worker Shortage in 2010."
22 June 2003. http://www.shrm.org/press_published/CMS_004818.asp.

Smith, Cort. "Hoop Dreams." *Investment Advisor,* August 2000, 48–54.

"Special Report: By the Numbers: A Boomer's Life." *Newsweek,* 3 April 2000, 60.

Stein, Michael K. *The Prosperous Retirement: Guide to the New Reality.* EMSTCO, 1998.

Stoneman, Bill. "High Finance, Hard Sell." *American Demographics,* February 1998, 43–47.

"Successful Aging." *Unconventional Wisdom,* Winter 2000, 3.

Templeton, Sir John. "The New Jerusalem." *Forbes ASAP,* 2 October 2000, 84.

"Top Five Reasons People Stay in Their Jobs." *The CPA Journal Online.* June 2004. http://www.nysscpa.org/cpajournal/2004/604/perspectives/p16a.htm.

Udell, Byron. "Preparing for Retirement? Here's Your Planning Guide for the Future." 2004. http://www.newlifestyles.com/resources/articles/PreparingForRetirement.aspx.

U.S. Census Bureau. "America's Families and Living Arrangements: 2004." 29 June 2005. http://www.census.gov/population/www/socdemo/hh-fam/cps2004.html.

———. "National Population Estimates for the 2000s: 1/1/2005 to 3/1/2005." 8 June 2005. http://www.census.gov/popest/national/asrh/2004_nat_civ.html.

———. "Population Projections of the United States by Age, Sex, Race, Hispanic Origin, and Nativity: 1999 to 2100." February 2000. http://www.census.gov/population/projections/nation/summary/np-t3-f.pdf.

———. "Table 4b." *Current Population Survey (CPS),* May 2005. http://www.census.gov/population/www/socdemo/voting.html.

———. "U.S. Interim Projections by Age, Sex, Race, and Hispanic Origin." 18 May 2004. http://www.census.gov/ipc/www/usinterimproj/natprojtab02b.pdf.

U.S. Department of Commerce. *A Nation Online: How Americans are Expanding Their Use of the Internet.* February 2002. http://www.ntia.doc.gov/ntiahome/dn/anationonline2.pdf.

U.S. Department of Labor Bureau of Labor Statistics. "Civilian labor force 16 and older by sex, age, race, and Hispanic origin." 11 February 2004. http://www.bls.gov/emp/emplab2002-01.htm.

———. "Consumer Expenditures in 2003." June 2005. http://stats.bls.gov/cex/csxann03.pdf.

———. "Number of Jobs Held, Labor Market Activity, and Earnings Growth Among Younger Baby Boomers: Recent Results from a Longitudinal Survey." 25 August 2004. http://www.bls.gov/news.release/pdf/nlsoy.pdf.

————. "Volunteering in the United States, 2004." Press release, 16 December 2004. http://www.bls.gov/news.release/volun.nr0.htm.

Vásquez, Ian. "Testimony of Ian Vásquez, Director of the Project on Global Economic Liberty at the Cato Institute before the Committee on Ways and Means Subcommittee on Social Security." 16 June 2005. http://www.socialsecurity.org/pubs/testimony/ct-iv061605.html.

Wagner, Richard B. "Enough and Beyond: Getting Past 'More.'" *Journal of Financial Planning,* May, 2000, 51–54.

Wallwork-Winik, Lyric. "When the Call Comes Later in Life." *Parade Magazine,* 17 October 1999, 4–6.

————. "There must be more to life." *Parade Magazine,* 17 October 1999.

Watson Wyatt. "Managing the Workforce of the Future." *Demographics & Destiny* (1999), 1–6.

————. "Phased Retirement: Reshaping the End of Work." *1999 Survey Report,* 1–12.

Welch, William M. "Earnings penalty repeal assured." *USA Today,* 23 March 2000, 4A.

"What Are Your Retirement Plans?" *BusinessWeek Online,* 20 Sept. 1999.

"What Is Successful Aging?" *Unconventional Wisdom,* Winter 1999, 1.

"Workers' Retirement Preparations: Savers vs. Nonsavers." *2000 Retirement Confidence Survey.*

WorkZ Staff. "Job Satisfaction and Retention Survey." 23 September 2004. http://www.workz.com/content/view_content.html?section_id=506&content_id=6632.

Index

O–P

R

S